GI Rights
AND
Army Justice

YOU HAVE A CONSTITUTIONAL
RIGHT TO POSSESS THIS BOOK

To deprive you of a critical guide, such as this one, to military life and law would violate your constitutional rights. There exists no valid military purpose in prohibiting its possession or use.

—Chapter Five
The Soldier's First Amendment Rights

GI Rights
AND
Army Justice

The Draftee's Guide
to
Military Life and Law

by
Robert S. Rivkin

Grove Press, Inc. - New York

Permission is gratefully acknowledged to quote from the following:

"next to of course god," copyright, 1926, by Horace Liveright; renewed, 1954, by E. E. Cummings. Reprinted from his volume, *Poems 1923–1954,* by permission of Harcourt, Brace and World, Inc.

"i sing of Olaf glad and big," copyright, 1931, 1959, by E. E. Cummings. Reprinted from his volume, *Poems 1923–1954,* by permission of Harcourt, Brace and World, Inc.

"Oh! What a Lovely War," by Theatre Workshop, Charles Chilton and the members of the original cast; Methuen & Co., Ltd.

"I Am Waiting," by Lawrence Ferlinghetti, from *A Coney Island of the Mind.* Copyright © 1958 by Lawrence Ferlinghetti. Reprinted by permission of New Directions Publishing Corporation.

ACKNOWLEDGMENTS

A project like this one could not be completed in a vacuum or solely in a library stack. A great many people, inside and outside the Army, helped me collect the material for this book and made contributions to the manuscript. I am especially grateful to Carl Rogers, Edwin Oppenheimer, Curry First, Andy Stapp, Mike Wittels, Rowland Watts, Jeffrey M. Kassover, and Larry Pesavento.

I also want to thank Luther Charles West, Melvin L. Wulf, Edward F. Sherman, and Marvin M. Karpatkin for their very useful suggestions and comments on the manuscript.

Any errors are my own responsibility. Because human rights for American soldiers are not likely to be won without persistence over a long period of time, corrections or suggestions from readers for future editions are welcome.

—R. S. R.

Contents

Introduction   xvii

1   *Induction and Reception Stations*   3

    INDUCTION

    HAVE YOU BEEN KIDNAPED?

    HURRY UP AND WAIT

    ASSHOLES AND ELBOWS

    CONTRABAND

    KEEP A DIARY

    YOUR ARMY HAIRCUT MAY BE ILLEGAL

    TAKING YOUR CLOTHING IS ILLEGAL

    KP DURING PROCESSING IS ILLEGAL

    TESTING AND THE PERSONNEL
       INTERVIEW

    SMILE AT THE REENLISTMENT
       COUNSELOR

2 *Basic and Advanced Individual Training:
The Military Mind Minus Its Couth*   17

    ORGANIZED TERROR
    GRASS DRILL
    PSYCHOLOGICAL BRUTALITY
      "You're All Fakers"
      Degrading Names
      The Dying Cockroach
      Grunting and Growling: "Kill, Kill,
        Kill!"
      Looting and Pillaging
      Contempt for Trainees' Safety
    PHYSICAL BRUTALITY
      The Blanket Party
      How To Prevent a Blanket Party
    YOUR MEDICAL RIGHTS
      The Threat of "Recycling"
      The Duffel Bag Ploy
      Documenting Your Injuries
      Medical Discharges
      Treatment You Don't Want
    CHAPLAINS WHO WORSHIP THE ARMY
    LAWYERS WHO DON'T WORSHIP THE
      ARMY
    ADVANCED INDIVIDUAL TRAINING
    SPECIAL TRAINING COMPANIES
    POCKETS OF SANITY

3 *Life as Permanent Party: Person or
Personnel?*   45

    WELCOME "HOME"
    YOU HAVE TWO "BOSSES"

YOUR MILITARY OCCUPATIONAL
    SPECIALTY
KP AND OTHER KRAZY PASTIMES
"ALWAYS VOLUNTEER"
NURSE YOUR PAPER WORK
DOUBLE-CHECK ALL ADVICE
YOU TOO CAN BE PROMOTED
DELAYING OVERSEAS SHIPMENT
    Inadequate Training
    Change of Status
    Hardship to Family
    Miscellaneous Deferments
    Vietnam Deferments
    Applying for CO Discharge
    Applying for Compassionate
        Reassignment or Hardship Discharge
GETTING OUT EARLY

The Military Mind   67

THE AUTHORITARIAN PERSONALITY
HUMILIATION $+$ FEAR $=$ OBEDIENCE
COVER YOUR ASS AND THE ELUSIVE
    NIRVANA
CRITICISM IS ALWAYS SUSPECT
"MICKEY MOUSE": THE
    GLORIFICATION OF TRIVIA
THE GLORIFICATION OF KILLING
THE TRAGEDY OF THE BLACK CAREER
    SOLDIER
IS THE ARMY A "COMMUNIST
    CONSPIRACY"?

5 *The Soldier's First Amendment Rights:*
Freedom of Expression 90

THE MILITARY MIND AND DISSENTERS
BACKGROUND OF FREE SPEECH IN THE
MILITARY
THE IMPORTANCE OF FREE SPEECH
Vehicle for Democracy
Human Dignity
Skepticism Toward Absolute Truth
MILITARY MURK IN THE MIDDLE OF
A MUDDLE
A MINI-FREEDOM: THE RIGHT TO
GRIPE
The Threat To Pursue One's Rights
Unauthorized Complaining
Restrictions on Nonpolitical
Speech
THREATS, INSULTS, AND
DISRESPECTFUL REMARKS
CRITICISM OF AMERICAN SOCIETY,
THE MILITARY SYSTEM, AND THE WAR
COUNSELING, ADVOCATING, OR
INCITING OTHERS TO BREAK THE LAW
SPEECH BEARING ON NATIONAL
SECURITY
TECHNICAL CRIMES AND FREE SPEECH
PORNOGRAPHY AND OBSCENITY
PROTEST DEMONSTRATIONS
"POLITICAL" ACTIVITIES
THE RIGHT TO FREE ASSOCIATION:
CIVILIANS
FREE ASSOCIATION IN THE MILITARY
THE SECURITY PROGRAM

6 *The Soldier's Right to Privacy* 146

    PRIVACY IN MILITARY QUARTERS
    ROUTINE AND "SHAKEDOWN"
       INSPECTIONS
    "INSPECTION" AS EXCUSE FOR
       ILLEGAL SEARCH
    Civilian Searches
    Military Searches
    LEGAL SEARCHES THAT BECOME
       ILLEGAL
    WHO MAY CONDUCT A SEARCH
    SEARCHES BY "CONSENT"
    "SEARCHES" THAT VIOLATE THE
       FIFTH AMENDMENT OR ARTICLE 31
    SEARCHES IN FOREIGN LANDS
    SEARCH AND SEIZURE OF MAIL
    LEAVES, PASSES, DRINKING, AND
       DRUGS
    MARRIAGE AND SEXUAL
       RELATIONSHIPS
    FAMILY LIFE AND OBLIGATIONS
    AUTOMOBILES
    THE SOLDIER AS CONSUMER AND
       DEBTOR
    EMPLOYMENT AND EXPLOITATION
    RELIGIOUS PRACTICES

7 *How To File a Complaint or Bring Charges* 180

    THE CHAIN OF COMMAND: A
       STALLING TACTIC
    THE DRAFTEE'S HIDDEN WEAPON:
       ARTICLE 138
    THE INSPECTOR GENERAL

WRITING YOUR CONGRESSMAN
RACIAL DISCRIMINATION
  Public Facilities, Schools, and
  Events
  Off-Post Housing
YOU CAN "SUE" YOUR SERGEANT:
  ARTICLE 139
CIVIL ACTIONS IN LOCAL COURTS

8   *Orders To Commit War Crimes and Other*
    Illegalities   200

ORDERS TO COMMIT WAR CRIMES
ORDERS AS PUNISHMENT
ORDERS FOR THE PURPOSE OF
  INCREASING PUNISHMENT
ORDERS BASED ON ILLEGAL
  ADMINISTRATIVE ACTION
ORDERS TO OBSERVE NONPENAL
  REGULATIONS
ORDERS TO REFRAIN FROM DOING
  THINGS THAT ARE BEYOND ONE'S
  CONTROL

9   *The Framework of Military Law*   213

SOURCES OF MILITARY LAW
  The Constitution
  Uniform Code of Military Justice
  Army Regulations and DOD
    Directives
  Manual for Courts-Martial
  Standing Operating Procedures

Court Cases and Published
   Opinions
ARTICLE 15: NONJUDICIAL
   PUNISHMENT
THE COURTS
   Summary Courts-Martial
   Special Courts-Martial
   General Courts-Martial
   Courts of Military Review
   U.S. Court of Military Appeals
      (COMA)
THE JUDGE ADVOCATE GENERAL
FEDERAL COURTS AND HABEAS
   CORPUS

*Courts-Martial in Action: The Military
Mind in Wonderland*   241

THE MILITARY MIND VS. THE
   LAWYERS
SOLIDARITY: THE MILITARY MIND IN
   COURT
ENLISTED MEN ON COURTS: A
   REFORM TURNED SHAM
SELECTIVE ENFORCEMENT OF
   MILITARY LAW
THE CONVENING AUTHORITY PICKS
   THE PLAYERS
THE "LAWLESS ROLE" OF THE STAFF
   JUDGE ADVOCATE
SPECIAL PROBLEMS OF THE ARMY
   DEFENSE COUNSEL
AN ARMY DEFENDERS CORPS

MILITARY "BAIL"
THE LAW OF THE STOCKADE

11   *Military Interrogations and Self-
     Incrimination*   280

ARTICLE 31 AND THE FIFTH
    AMENDMENT
WHEN ARE THE WARNINGS
    REQUIRED?
THE RIGHT TO CONSULT A LAWYER
TRICKS OF GOVERNMENT AGENTS
    The Undercover Agent
    Preliminary Gratuitous Advice
    Bluff on a Split Pair
    The Promise of Immunity
    The Mutt-and-Jeff Routine
DON'T WAIVE YOUR RIGHTS

12   *Conscientious Objectors in the Army*   294

THE CCCO AND THE AFSC
WHICH COS ARE ELIGIBLE FOR
    DISCHARGE
PREPARING THE APPLICATION
STATUS AFTER APPLICATION IS
    SUBMITTED
INTERVIEWS
FILING AFTER RECEIVING OVERSEAS
    ORDERS
HABEAS CORPUS AND INJUNCTIONS
NONCOMBATANT STATUS
ONE MAN'S STRUGGLE: CONSCIENCE
    VS. THE SYSTEM

13   *Administrative Discharges: Getting Out
     for Good*   311

          GROUNDS FOR GETTING OUT
               Unfitness and Unsuitability
               Misconduct: Fraudulent Entry,
                    Civilian Crimes, AWOL, or
                    Desertion
               Homosexuality
               Dependency or Hardship
               Medical Reasons
               National Security
               Minority
               Miscellaneous Reasons
          FIGHTING A DISCHARGE: BOARDS,
          HEARINGS, AND PROCEDURAL
          RIGHTS
               Board for Correction of Military
                    Records
               Discharge Review Board
               Federal District Courts and the
                    United States Court of Claims

14   *An Army of the People*   333

          THE MYTH THAT DISCIPLINE WILL
               CRUMBLE IN COMBAT IN THE
               ABSENCE OF TERROR IN TRAINING
          THE MYTH THAT THE
               GLORIFICATION OF TRIVIA
               INCREASES COMBAT PROFICIENCY
          THE MYTH THAT THE THOUGHTFUL
               SOLDIER IS A DETRIMENT IN
               COMBAT

THE MYTH THAT ENLISTED MEN
SUPPORT THE ARMY'S CASTE
SYSTEM
THE MYTH THAT MILITARY JUSTICE
IS FAIR AND IMPARTIAL
THE MYTH THAT THE EXISTING
SYSTEM WORKS
THE MYTH THAT OUR ARMY IS
AMERICAN

Appendix A: *Resolutions of the National
Conference on GI Rights*   355

Appendix B: *GI Newspapers and Coffeehouses, Counseling Organiza-
tions and Lawyer Referral
Services*   357

Index   371

Introduction

America's voice abroad has begun to resemble that of a muttering lunatic on a crowded city street. In both cases, people no longer listen. Exactly why this has happened to the land of the free and the home of the brave may become the greatest political question of our generation, and the dispute over the answer could either generate our worst crisis or ease our nation's rebirth. One explanation is advanced in this book. It is that, in some ways, we have become the enemy.

To explain "the law" without reference to its context is to distort. And to speak of military law without examining who dispenses it and who receives it is to fabricate. To a certain extent this is a book about the time-honored values of Duty, Honor, Country, as well as the law. Its thesis is that the military have a duty to honor our country's Constitution or we shall not have preserved those values for which, as a nation, we came into being. Thus it is written for the GI, the potential or prospective GI, the military commander, the concerned layman, the national policy maker, the radical, the conservative, and the cop-out.

A draftee's guide is necessary because of an arrangement developed over the years between Congress and the generals to put certain laws designed to protect the soldier on the books and then to forget they exist. I do not mean to say that this is a great conspiracy to augment the military power. Rather, it is descriptive of what has happened: abdication by Congress—because of misplaced trust—of its responsibility to see that the GI, who is chosen for perhaps the ultimate sacrifice, isn't getting unnecessarily shafted in the process.

As is apparent to any legally trained noncareer person with exposure to "military justice," a gargantuan gap has developed between what Congress has told the military to do and what it has required them to do. Until very recently it has mattered little to anybody but its victims that "military justice" is a misnomer, a disgrace to the institution that fosters it and to the legislature that tolerates it. Congress has cared little, for instance, to correct a "court" structure that amounts to a legally sanctioned system of stacked juries. It has, until recently, tolerated inept, untrained nonlawyers provided soldiers at special courts-martial. It still tolerates the existence of the kangaroo summary court. To that extent Congress has partaken of the lawlessness that characterizes military discipline.

The draftee or reluctant enlistee is not to be envied. First, if drafted before 1970, he was selected for induction by his draft board, a "little group of neighbors," through a process, the Selective Service System, which is so capricious and unfair and irrational that it would have been declared unconstitutional had its subject matter been anything but the national defense. If he was drafted thereafter, he was further victimized by plain bad luck. Second, he is compensated at a rate so low that the free labor he provides the government amounts to an extra tax, what economists have called an "implicit tax," which no taxpayer in the country but the enlisted serviceman has to pay. Not only has he been called upon to take extraordinary risks for questionable ends, he is forced to finance his country's misadventures for a wage that amounts to less than one-third of what he would receive in the "real world" for labor he would not have voluntarily performed for three times his civilian earnings. Third, he may have been asked to

provide the flesh needed to keep the ante up at prolonged peace talks, while his country is slowly, inevitably, and painfully withdrawing from its most stupid
war. Fourth, he is treated, especially in training, as
though he deserves to be punished for something. More
than just compulsory cooperation—the system demands
the submission of his individuality to the collective
consciousness of a crazy machine that concurrently
values brutality and blandness.

It's this last aspect of the GI's "sentence" that this
book deals with. In documenting the Army way of life,
I have relied when possible on firsthand sources and
personal experience. I have also avoided using names in
relating certain outrageous abuses, since what is needed
is not more retribution but massive reform of a national
institution.

Reform is urgent because of what every GI learns,
sooner or later, about the military: The system's laws
and rules are twisted to put him in his "place"; there is
no such thing in the Army as equal enforcement of the
law. Those endowed with power over his actions would,
if they could, exercise absolute power; any restrictions
on the kinds of things that may legally be done *to* him
are sources of annoyance, frustration, and contempt to
the authorities, who regard these restrictions as placed
there to create only the appearance of justice. Armed
with this guide, the GI will have a chance to fight back
effectively, sometimes by merely forcing the Army to
follow its own rules.

Our most conscientious scholars are engaged in a
desperate search for ways to "control the military," but
their efforts have been directed at control from the
pinnacle of the military-industrial complex. This manual
seeks to help the GI and the conscientious civilian
exercise a measure of control from the bottom.

Although I have written mostly about the Army, *the
reader should be aware that military law—essentially
the Uniform Code of Military Justice—is the same in
all the armed forces, and that most of what is observed*

about life and law in the Army applies as well to the Navy, the Marines, and the Air Force. And although Army Regulations do not govern the other services, their own regulations are usually very similar to the Army's. However, the new GI should heed these warnings:

1) Regard this guidebook not as a complete road map but merely as a basic introduction into the bureaucratic military labyrinth.

2) At various times parts of this book will become out of date. This will be corrected if new editions or supplements are published. However, since regulations are being rewritten all the time, there is no way to be absolutely certain that the one in hand is current. This is not to alarm the reader into inaction, but merely to suggest that every effort should be made to double-check when a matter is important. Also, the law is changing with great rapidity, particularly in the area of constitutional rights. The soldier can feel fairly confident that any movement will be toward the expansion—not the reduction—of his rights. So if he errs on the side of caution where it is recommended in this book, he should be safe.

3) No attempt has been made to replace or duplicate the services of a lawyer, either at an Army Legal Assistance Office or at trial. Rather, the book attempts to help the citizen-soldier understand his reactions to the insanity that suddenly surrounds him, so that he may, with courage, breathe some life into the law by which the military purports to be governed. The elements of each military crime are not discussed, nor is there any treatment of some of the procedural rights available at a court-martial trial. Most military lawyers are familiar with these. The emphasis here is on life in the Army before the GI has occasion to come into contact with a lawyer, as well as on those areas with which some military and civilian lawyers may be unfamiliar. To assist them, some chapters are heavily footnoted. Of course, the GI may sometimes need to refer someone in authority to a cited regulation or law case upon which he has

taken a particular stand, if he expects to be taken seriously.

A word about the organization of the book. The general reader who has no prospect of becoming a soldier may wish to skip the chapters on How To File a Complaint or Bring Charges, The Framework of Military Law, Conscientious Objectors, and Administrative Discharges. The potential draftee, however, should familiarize himself with their contents before his induction. Although somewhat technical, they describe procedures of self-protection which the citizen-soldier should know about.

One additional caution deserves to be underscored. The fact that the GI knows his rights doesn't mean he gets them. And even when he does get them, this doesn't mean that in certain situations he will not suffer. Therefore, an attempt has been made here to portray the realities of power as well as the law. Although it is evident that GIs, *especially collectively,* can wield a great deal more power than the Army has led them to believe, this does not mean that individuals struggling against oppression cannot get hurt. Even with the assistance of the Constitution, the civilian courts, civilian lawyers, counseling groups, and a sometimes sympathetic public press, there remain certain powers that the Army will always be able to use against the "troublemaker." The punitive transfer to an undesirable or dangerous duty station is one frequently used weapon. As Melvin Wulf, Legal Director of the American Civil Liberties Union, has pointed out, "At worst, they can deliberately get him killed; at best, they can transfer him north of the Arctic Circle where he will have only penguins for companionship for two years." At the same time, *any* low-ranking soldier who asserts a right against authority can be deemed a "troublemaker," and to that extent this is a book about how to become exactly that. For each decision, a soldier may be called upon to explore the depth of his values and weigh the strength of his personal resources against the risks that must be taken.

On Induction Day the draftee may take That Step Forward as the least painful of all his alternatives. This guide is designed to assist him within the law to endure his chosen alternative. By using it judiciously he might just force his country to keep some of its promises and help to make it once more the kind of place young men flock toward, not from, in search of freedom.

If the administration has found that it cannot form an army without conscription, it will find, if it venture on these experiments, that it cannot enforce conscription without an army.

—DANIEL WEBSTER, Address to Congress,
December 1814

Obedience to the Law Is Freedom.

—Sign formerly over main
portal of Fort Dix Stockade

America has come alive deep down in its raw guts, and vast contending forces of revolutionary momentum are squaring off in this land for decisive showdowns from which no one can purchase sanctuary. .

—ELDRIDGE CLEAVER, *Soul on Ice*

GI Rights
AND
Army Justice

1

Induction
and Reception Stations

At first astonished, then embittered, and finally in-
different, we recognized that what matters is not the
mind but the boot and brush, not intelligence but the
system, not freedom but drill. We became soldiers with
eagerness and enthusiasm, but they have done everything to knock that out of us. After three weeks it was
no longer incomprehensible to us that a braided post-
man should have more authority over us than had
formerly our parents, our teachers, and the whole
gamut of culture from Plato to Goethe. With our
young, awakened eyes we saw that the classical con-
ception of the Fatherland held by our teachers resolved itself here into a renunciation of personality
such as one would not ask of the meanest servant . . .
— ERICH MARIA REMARQUE,
All Quiet on the Western Front

INDUCTION

It is somber. In the beginning nobody says much, not
much at all. A few moments ago, in an otherwise pleas-
ant fluorescent-lighted room, you may well have taken
That Step Forward. You were surprised that the lieutenant's pep talk wasn't as gung ho as you thought it

would be. He may have told you an old joke he saves
for all his induction speeches to cheer himself up:
"You're in the Army now, so face reality. If you don't
you're neurotic. A neurotic is someone who builds
castles in the sky, a psychotic lives in them, and the
psychiatrist collects the rent." Polite laughter.

Later, there was a man in the waiting room wearing a
yellowed shirt and a gaunt, lined face. He presented
each and every one of you with a free toiletry kit, a
New Testament, and a very faraway look in his eyes.
All courtesy of the Salvation Army. He made a short
talk, finishing with, "Make sure you pray too, fellows—
we'll be pulling for you, but you can't rely on us alone."
This statement brought to mind again the graffito on the
wall of the induction station john, "This has been my
last civilian shit," which you'd been trying to forget.

Because the plane never arrived, our first night in the
Army early in 1967 was spent in the musty wing of the
Statler-Hilton Hotel at Kennedy Airport in New York
City. It was right there and exactly at midnight that
Lenny from the Village slit his wrists and walked across
the hall to the opposite room, to make certain that
somebody called the cops. The next morning, before
dawn, the Statler-Hilton served an Army-style breakfast
and people made jokes about Lenny, who had been
removed to St. Albans Naval Hospital.

A cop who felt he shouldn't have been drafted because of his health announced at the breakfast table,
"Did you hear about last night? Lenny cut himself
shaving." As soon as breakfast was over, the cop pushed
back his chair and proclaimed with funereal dignity, "I
think I'll retire to my room and wallow in self-pity." But
he was shipped, along with the rest of us, to the Fort
Jackson reception station.

HAVE YOU BEEN KIDNAPED?

That's no joke. Draft refusers have been kidnaped
many times. They have been told to "wait here" or "go

there" and imagined they were being processed for arrest. Actually their wishes were being ignored and they were shipped out to the reception station along with those who had accepted induction. If this happened to you—two days or six months or two years ago—find a civilian lawyer immediately and have him file a petition for a writ of habeas corpus in your behalf in the nearest federal district court. If you have a good case, one of the groups listed in Appendix B should be able to find a lawyer willing to help you. Although most of the habeas corpus petitions presented to federal courts by military personnel are turned down because the petitioner has failed to "exhaust his administrative remedies," in the situation where the claim is that *there was in fact no induction* the military should not be able to raise this argument successfully.[1]

A typical case is that of John Walter Phifer, who refused induction at the Fort Hamilton, Brooklyn, induction station. He was taken into a room where the captain tried to talk him into accepting induction. He refused, but was put on a bus and taken to Kennedy Airport for shipment to Fort Jackson, South Carolina. He didn't like it very much at the airport, so he went home and stayed there for eight months. When the military finally picked him up, they brought him to the Fort Dix Stockade and planned to charge him with desertion. The Army's morning report said he'd gone AWOL from Fort Jackson, South Carolina. Phifer had actually never been to Fort Jackson. His lawyer, Rowland Watts, of the Workers Defense League, filed a petition for a writ of habeas corpus in a federal district court in New Jersey.[2] A hearing was held and the judge decided that Phifer was not in the Army and should be released. The Army then had to let him go. Of course, he was still open to prosecution in a federal court for refusing induction, but at least he was out of the military's clutches. Which for him was fortunate, because he wouldn't have liked basic training one bit.

The longer you stay in the Army without claiming

that you refused induction, the less likely it is that a court will believe you. Some courts have held that the step forward is not essential to create military jurisdiction, especially when it appears that the individual acquiesced in his new status as a soldier by accepting pay and going through training.[3]

HURRY UP AND WAIT

One of the first principles of his new life style that the recruit becomes accustomed to is Hurry Up and Wait. Recruits and trainees never walk where they're going. They run or "double-time." Even if the drill sergeants know there is plenty of time to get the troops from one processing point to another, they force them to react as though the reception station were undergoing a constant mortar barrage. The reason given to justify rapid assembly of troops only to have them wait, sometimes for hours, to be processed is that the habit of instant obedience is transferable to combat. But there is another, unstated reason. It is to underscore the individual's loss of worth.

If what is done with the soldier's time is of no consequence to the Army, if time is treated as having no value at all, then the person whose time is taken from him is not worth very much either. This is not worked out on a rational level while it is happening, but many draftees realize much later that this aspect of their dehumanization has had its intended effect. And they recall that writing a letter, or reading a book, or even having a bull session *meant* less because those activities could be interrupted at any time, so that the recruits could immediately assemble to do nothing together.

ASSHOLES AND ELBOWS

One of the first things the recruits will do together is stretch at arm's length across the entire expanse of the company area in a single line and wonder what's going on. They find out soon enough. This is the first "police call" formation, and it is introduced by a sergeant who's been waiting for the moment: "All right, pick up everything that don't grow. All I want to see is assholes and elbows." And, languorously, the line moves forward, and everything that doesn't grow is picked up by the new recruits. Five times a day, for nine weeks.

CONTRABAND

The Army is not very understanding about drugs, so leave your cubes and bennies, your joints and juice at home. Also, any knife with a blade of three inches or more will be confiscated, as well as any "obscenity." You should be able to keep a pocketknife. Unless what you have brought along as reading material is hard-core pornography, you have a right not to give up your literature. The inspecting corporal's notion of what is obscene is not controlling on you.

But if you should refuse, expect a lot of harassment before you are allowed to keep any book. Be prepared for a scene of major proportions. The corporal is not used to having raw recruits say no to anything, and he won't know in this case that he's wrong. In fact, don't expect a military court-martial, whose members won't be very well read on recent Supreme Court decisions narrowing the definition of obscenity, to be any more understanding. If you make a stand in this area be prepared for a fight. But first read Chapter Five, The Soldier's First Amendment Rights.

KEEP A DIARY

You might want to publish your memoirs. More importantly, if you keep a diary you will be in a better position to assert your rights under the Constitution, military law, and Army Regulations. You will be better able to document any abuses you discover or become the victim of. Record all significant incidents, including names, dates, places, times, dialogues when possible, and witnesses. If, when you decide the time is ripe, you make your complaints to the persons and in the ways described in this book, you will more easily be able to back up what you say. (And that's one secret to blowing the minds of the sergeants who think they've got you where they want you.)

YOUR ARMY HAIRCUT
MAY BE ILLEGAL

It is the Army's theory that the quicker you are made the victim of a series of personal outrages, the quicker you'll become a soldier. Probably no outrage is more effective to instill a sense of powerlessness than the traditional basic training haircut, which is actually a shave with electric clippers. Although they know that you consider it an outrage to have all your hair shaved off, the lifers value a shaven head as a sign of masculinity, patriotism, and good grooming, while regarding long hair, beards, and Afros as badges of femininity or subversion.

Defending the haircut-shave on the grounds of uniformity and hygiene falls short of conviction, since both requirements could be easily satisfied without making freaks out of recruits. Why, then, is it still used? Simply because it is known to be an outrage. It heightens your anxiety and makes you feel helpless. It is part of the program carefully planned in the Pentagon to remake you into a Thing. It is no wonder, then, that a psychiatrist's study of basic training has actually uncovered the same pattern of symptoms found among inmates of concentration camps.[4] Your stress level begins to approach that of a schizophrenic.[5] In all likelihood you have never suffered a disaster like this before, in which you are made to feel they can do anything they like with you.[6]

Let's admit that the haircut in itself, apart from its

symbolic value, is a pretty insignificant deprivation. But it is important because it represents your first glimpse of the fraud of military law. In contrast to actual practice, the Army Regulation on appearance states:

> (1) It is the responsibility of commanders to see that military personnel present a neat and soldierly appearance. Commanders will establish policies and standards in the area of personal appearance to insure that the members of their command appear neat and soldierly. *Degrading or depersonalizing actions, such as the practice of requiring heads of soldiers to be shaved, are forbidden.* However, a soldier may voluntarily have his head shaved. [Italics added.]
>
> (2) The hair, including sideburns, will be well-groomed, cut short or medium length, and neatly trimmed at all times. The face will be clean shaven, with the exception that wearing of a neatly trimmed mustache is permitted.[7]

There would seem to be no reason why this regulation should not apply to recruits as well as to permanent party personnel. If you consider the haircut your fellow recruits are getting to be degrading and depersonalizing (notice that shaving of heads is *merely one illustration* of a degrading act), you may refuse to submit to it. However, a court-martial is almost sure to follow, and there is no certainty that the reviewing authorities will agree that the basic training haircut is illegal.

Another approach is to protest but submit to the haircut, indicating that you are going to file a complaint immediately afterward. (The procedures for filing a complaint are spelled out in Chapter Seven, How To File a Complaint or Bring Charges.) *However, remember this throughout your Army career: Whenever you feel your rights have been or are about to be trampled upon, be polite and respectful in asserting them. The "authorities" will try to provoke you into insulting them or perhaps threatening them;* they have ways of doing this. If they succeed, you've lost the case, no matter how right you were in refusing to follow an unlawful order. *If they threaten or unreasonably harass or strike you, there are remedies which you can pursue.*

TAKING YOUR CLOTHING
IS ILLEGAL

One of the first procedures you will be herded through is clothing issue. In a huge barnlike building, where the only thing that counts to the Army is speed, you will be moved in confusion from one counter to another, and the clothing will come flying. You might as well catch it. Alterations will be completed before you're out of the building and sometimes the uniforms will fit. More likely you will have to get part of your uniform altered at your own expense during basic training to pass the inspections. One feature of these clothing issue mills is that the civilians who work there are, in mind and heart, sergeants. You don't have to take their abuse. Since it's not an offense to be disrespectful to a civilian, you can tell them what you please; just make sure you're talking to a civilian.

Once you're the World's Best-Dressed Soldier, you will almost certainly be ordered to send home or throw away the civilian clothing you wore into the Army; you will be told that you are not authorized to have it in basic training. *Don't believe it.* The clothing regulation states:

> Disposition of civilian clothing. Receptees will be informed that they may keep their civilian clothes. However, if they want to send their civilian clothes home, they may make arrangements with the local transportation officer to have them shipped at government expense. The mode of shipping civilian clothing at government expense is at the option of the local transportation officer.[8]

The order to ship your clothing home is illegal. An order to ship it by commercial means at your expense is illegal. (Some reception station sergeants were thought

to have received kickbacks from certain delivery company employees for directing the recruits to their company offices rather than to the U.S. Post Office. That
may have had something to do with the recent change
in the Army Regulation authorizing shipment at government expense.) Once you get to basic training,
however, your company commander can require that all
civilian clothing be stored somewhere besides your personal lockers.

KP DURING PROCESSING
IS ILLEGAL

During processing it is not uncommon to be selected
in the evenings or mornings for kitchen police duty. As
chow is announced over the public address system, the
anticipated warning booms forth: "Last ten out of the
mess hall are on KP." There's almost a riot to get into
the mess hall. There is a rush to get on line, a rush to
eat, and a rush to get out. The tableau of dozens of
shoving recruits on the dirty-tray line near the exit
gobbling their food standing up would be incomprehensible to an outsider—unless he knew how much it
means to you to avoid KP. *If this is happening to your
group, it is illegal.* The regulation makes this perfectly
clear:

> Kitchen police duties. a. The reception station
> commanders are authorized to retain nonprior
> service receptees for 1 day to perform kitchen
> police duties, provided such duty will not delay
> receptees' entry into training. Scheduling of re-
> ceptees for such duty during processing will be
> avoided. Kitchen police duties may be performed
> on nonprocessing days, or upon completion of
> processing.[9]

As a matter of fact, just about everything you go
through at any Army reception station violates official
Army policy. That's good in a way, because if you

understand it early you will realize that the only way to "receive" your rights in the Army is to fight for them, carefully but firmly. And, when necessary, you might even remind the training cadre of the Pentagon's nice guideline for processing:

> Processing will be conducted in such a manner that the receptee will be impressed with the efficiency of the Army and the attention given to the receptee's welfare.[10]

TESTING AND THE PERSONNEL INTERVIEW

The most important part of the endless paper work and processing at the reception station is your personnel interview. You actually get an opportunity to sit down and talk with someone, face to face, and tell him about your background, your educational, vocational, and professional qualifications, and your preferences for an Army job. All Army jobs are coded and everyone is given one. This is your first, and in all likelihood your last, chance to choose a military occupational specialty (MOS). *Certainly it's the most important chance, since an unpopular MOS is difficult to get rid of.* As you talk with the interviewer he will fill in the information you give him on your DA Form 20, which will comprise the most significant part of your Army personnel records, your 201 File. In theory you are supposed to be selected for the area in which you both are qualified and *wish to continue working.* In practice, the interview takes a couple of minutes and you are generally recommended for an MOS the interviewer believes best fits your experience. Your choice is entered in one box and his choice *for* you is entered in another.

There's no practical way of verifying the kinds of jobs and educational background the interviewer puts down on your form. The information goes to Washington and through a computer, which then decides what school assignment for advanced individual training (AIT) or automatic MOS you will get. Since very few people volunteer to be "awarded" an infantry MOS, the majority of those who get stuck with an assignment to advanced infantry training aren't volunteers. The best way to prevent this from happening is to have a specialty, something to make you stand out. If you're a college graduate with a degree in sociology the computer will have no trouble in selecting you to be an infantryman. But if you're a commercial artist, musician, nuclear physicist, or court reporter your chances of getting a decent school or direct MOS right out of basic training are better. There is space on the Form 20 for your "rare and unusual" qualifications to be entered. Try to get the clerk to print the letters RAU in the appropriate box. Army Regulation 600–200 contains a list of some rare and unusual qualifications. Examples are having a hobby of making rocket engines, being a licensed amateur radio operator or a commercial artist, or any other background which justifies the entry. A special DA Form 1294 should be filled out by the clerk and sent to Washington later.[11] In addition, letters and documents attesting to your special qualifications are supposed to be considered by the interviewer. If you are a college graduate, bring a copy of your transcript or degree to prove it.

A good portion of your processing will be devoted to taking a battery of tests to determine where your primary aptitudes lie. There is no one single test for infantry, so you should try to do as well on the verbal and arithmetic tests as you can, since they comprise your General-Technical (GT) or Army IQ.

There are some additional tests that can be extremely important. If you are an enlistee, and your GT score is 100 or higher, you *must* be allowed to take the Army Language Aptitude Test (ALAT). This one will determine your eligibility to apply for or be assigned to the Defense Language Institute at the Presidio of Monterey,

California, something you might like to do. The Institute has unusual prestige in academic circles and is one of the more worthwhile places to serve your time. The processing sergeants might give the test to you as a draftee upon request at the testing center, or they might make you submit a disposition form (DF) requesting permission to take the test. (Virtually all personnel requests are submitted on the DF.) The problem with this is that, as a draftee, you stand practically no chance of being assigned to the Institute unless you reenlist for a year to do so.

If you claim proficiency in a language and they have the test there on tape—and they probably do—they *must* administer it to you. The same rule applies if you claim skill in typing and/or shorthand. All you need to do is claim the skills. If you don't, the chances are good that they'll never be mentioned.

If you're a college graduate, or received a GT of 110 or more, you will be given tests to determine whether you qualify to become an officer; the first is the Officers Candidate Test (OCT) and the second, if you pass the first, is the Officer Leadership Inventory (OLI). I would recommend taking and passing them. During basic training you'll be given a few chances to go to lectures and pep talks instead of training, while you're "deciding" whether to go to Officers Candidate School (OCS). You used to be able to go to OCS and then drop out without increasing your term of service. This has been changed recently, and if you sign up to go to OCS and drop out you're in for three years, brother! And OCS means months of harassment worse than in basic.

Depending on how you want to score on these tests, you can come off as a killer or a fag. Although Army psychologists have worked for many years at perfecting them, there's nothing easier than psyching out the Army psychology tests. The questions give you choices between things like whether you'd prefer to lead a platoon into battle or teach ballet to junior high school girls.

SMILE AT THE REENLISTMENT COUNSELOR

A required interview at the reception station is with the reenlistment people. The assumption is that, since you love what you've seen of the Army so far (two or three days' worth), you should be given an early opportunity to re-up for another year or two. These fatherly charlatans used to tell you that if you remained a draftee going to Vietnam was a "certainty," which was a lie. They used to tell you that if you went Regular Army and gave them another year, you'd not only get an Army school of your choice but your chances of going to Vietnam were greatly diminished, which was a lie.

Don't sign. Take your chances. There are options later on.

Notes

1. *U.S. v. Hall,* 17 USCMA 88, 37 CMR 352 (1967). See AR 635–200, ch. 5, sec. III, para. 5–5 (rev. 25 April 1969), which provides an administrative procedure for release by "Special Order" where an induction was due to "error" or denial of a "procedural right" by a draft board; however, if there was no induction at all, there is no reason for requiring the illegally detained individual to go through the Army's procedures.
2. *Phifer v. Collins* (D.C.N.J. Aug. 1968), record on file at Workers Defense League, New York. See also *Corrigan v. Secretary of the Army,* 211 F.2d 293 (9th Cir., 1954).
3. *Brown v. Resor,* 407 F.2d 281 (5th Cir., 1969).
4. Dr. Peter G. Bourne, "Some Observations on the Psychosocial Phenomena Seen in Basic Training," *Psychiatry: Journal for the Study of Interpersonal Processes,* May 1967, vol. 30, no. 2, p. 192.
5. *Ibid.,* p. 189.

6. *Ibid.,* p. 191:

> Particularly meaningful for the late adolescent are the loss of personal clothing and the shaving of his head; the latter factor reaffirms in his mind the Army's right to do with him what it wishes even in terms of such intimate areas as one's physical appearance.

7. AR 600–20, para. 31 (rev. 18 Dec. 1969).
8. AR 612–10, Processing Procedures at U.S. Army Reception Stations, para. 2–8 (rev. 20 May 1969).
9. AR 612–10, para. 2–12.
10. AR 612–10, para. 2–2(b).
11. AR 600–200, para. 2–15 (rev. 22 April 1969) and Appendix II (rev. 12 Sept. 1969); AR 612–10, Appendix A and Appendix B (rev. 24 Nov. 1969).

2

Basic and Advanced
Individual Training:
The Military Mind Minus Its Couth

. . . but—though all kinds of officers
(a yearning nation's blueeyed pride)
their passive prey did kick and curse
until for wear their clarion
voices and boots were much the worse,
and egged the firstclassprivates on
his rectum wickedly to tease
by means of skilfully applied
bayonets roasted hot with heat—
Olaf (upon what were once knees)
does almost ceaselessly repeat
"there is some s. I will not eat"
      —e.e. cummings, "i sing of Olaf glad and big"

ORGANIZED TERROR

After being cajoled, kicked, and pulled off the trucks
that take you from the reception station to your basic
training unit, you run like hell toward the first formation with a sixty-six-pound duffel bag on your back. If
one of the drill sergeants should trip you on the way
and you should happen to crumple in a heap, cushion-

ing the duffel bag in its descent, you will have completed your first exercise of basic combat training: Being Tripped by Training Cadre on Way to First Formation. It's a good introduction.

Watch the cadre out of the corner of your eye. Some of them will be swarming, screaming, swooping, and spraying spittle on selected recruits whose duffel bags have fallen from their assigned upright positions in the formation whose symmetry has been so thoughtfully planned in the Pentagon. My first formation included this scene:

> "Get over here, little girl, before I bust your fuckin' head open!"
>
> "Y . . . y . . . y . . . y . . . yes, sir."
>
> "Sir! Sir! Did you call me 'sir'? I'm a goddam sergeant—I *work* for a living!"
>
> "Y . . . y . . . y . . . yes, sir, Sergeant."
>
> "Not 'sir,' you dumb dipshit!" his hands at the recruit's throat in mock strangulation. "You're not too bright, are you?"
>
> "N . . . n . . . n . . . no, Sergeant."
>
> "You're fat, though, aren't you?"
>
> "Yes, Sergeant."
>
> "You're a fat sack of shit, aren't you?"
>
> "Yes, Sergeant, I'm a fat sack of shit."
>
> The sergeant softened. "And we're going to knock some of that shit out of you, aren't we?"
>
> "Yes, Sergeant."[1]

Other sergeants will be amused by this kind of thing. But some will be merely bored. Don't forget who they are, for they could be the sane ones who have slipped into your training company, and you may need their help later on.

GRASS DRILL

Next comes platoon formation and Grass Drill, which, unlike the duffel bag festivity, is probably legal and can be justified as physical conditioning to the rigors of basic training. It consists of standing outside the barracks in platoon formation and reacting within the first thirty seconds to the following sequential orders:

> Fall on your stomachs! On your feet! On your stomachs! On your backs! On your feet! On your stomachs! On your knees! On your backs! On your stomachs! On your feet!

You will be bawled out the next day for having a filthy set of fatigues on, or, if you have changed them already, for *not* having a filthy set of fatigues on. *The System has arranged it so that you cannot possibly do anything right in the first few weeks of basic training.* (This is called "military psychology" and is described in Chapter Four, The Military Mind.)

After the initial grass drill you'll be invited into the barracks, your home for the next eight weeks, and, by way of instruction from a drill sergeant, you will gain your first insight into the Army's ardent preoccupation with daily hygiene for the floor you're sitting on. You'll also be asked to fill out an information form for the Public Information Office (PIO). This information will provide the basis for an Army press release to your local newspaper (which might be the kind to announce your "graduation" from basic training). You do not have to fill it out, or you can write across it, "Not for Release."

PSYCHOLOGICAL BRUTALITY

Anything can and will be done to you that the training cadre believe (1) is necessary to break you down, (2) will "make a man out of you," and (3) they can get away with. Let them know from the beginning that they will be held accountable for any actions which deprive you of your rights, and the chances are that you'll have an easier time of basic training. Your not being afraid upsets their mental apple cart, because you are not responding as a typical trainee. Keep in mind the Army

Regulation which says that "degrading or depersonalizing actions . . . are forbidden."[2] Threats to "kick
your ass" or to "go behind the barracks" (fight out your
differences) are illegal and could subject the cadre
involved to court-martial for wrongful communication
of a threat.[3] The first time you are threatened or degraded by a member of the cadre, you might say
something like this: "Sergeant, Army Regulations forbid
degrading and depersonalizing actions against trainees. I
deem what you have just done to be degrading, and I
respectfully request that you stop this practice. If you
don't, I will be forced to file a complaint against you."
Try to have some friendly witnesses around when you
say it, since their presence should discourage any out-
burst. The sergeant might even go away, muttering to
himself in simple astonishment.

Many of the threats communicated to trainees might
not be considered by a military commander to be
prohibited by the regulation, but you should record
them in your diary anyway. If something happens to
you or a fellow trainee later on, you will be able to
document the atmosphere of the company and show
that those cloaked with authority broke the spirit if not
the letter of the rules by which they are supposed to be
bound. In general, your treatment will depend very
much on the kind of commanding officer you have and
the extent to which his Mind has been Militarized. If he
is a dull youth who feels his manhood has been enhanced by virtue of having endured in Officers Candidate School the same silly harassment that he's about to
dish out to you, there will be trouble. (Officer candidates sometimes have to scrub floors with toothbrushes
to demonstrate their capacity for leadership in the
Army.) In such cases the crazier drill sergeants take
over and run the company. If, on the other hand, he is
intelligent and humane (which does happen), your
basic combat training may be very different from the
kind most recruits experience.

Many who have served in the Army think you should have to learn to "take it," as they did, to become a man. They've got it backwards. You don't have to take it, and to the extent that you don't you're more of a man than the drafted civilian in the docile generation that preceded you, and more of a man than the average lifer. A psychiatrist who did a study of men in basic training tells of the trainee's discovery of the Army's false promise to make him a "man" overnight:

> For a large number of men entering Basic Training, the process is viewed as a form of masculine initiation rite, with the implied message from the Army, "Allow yourself to be subjected to this process with its indignities and discomforts and at the end if you can take it you will have achieved manly status." Many recruits find at the end of Basic Training that they do not feel very different from the way they felt at the start, and they feel that in some way the Army has broken faith with them.[4]

Is it any wonder, when the whole system, from the lying recruiter to the inane re-up talk on your discharge date, is based on deception?

Some examples of what to expect are related here. (I have not used the myriads of hearsay accounts, since the Army has been known to respond, "It ain't so." The incidents described in this section and the next two took place in my basic training company. The stories are typical, and every soldier could provide his own.)

"You're All Fakers"

Included in the catchall term "harassment" is the psychological brutality that lubricates the gears of the Military Mind in basic training. It takes as many forms as the Creative Brute can create. One of the most common is that, when it comes to claims of sickness, disability, or simple exhaustion, "you're all fakers."

One day the company was double-timing to the

dental clinic. After freezing weather it had suddenly become hot, and one of the trainees fell by the side of the road, apparently from the heat. Since this happened with some frequency to one or another of us, no one thought anything of it at first. Only this time was different. The man's mouth frothed white foam. His entire body was shaking and he was obviously unconscious. Everyone gaped helplessly until a sergeant came running up: "GET THAT LITTLE MOTHER-FUCKIN' FAKER UP!"[5] Dumfounded, we stared at the sergeant. In turn, he stared at the frothing, vibrating body beneath him for a long time, just to make sure, and then walked away. The stricken soldier never showed up for training again. The sergeant did, unshaken.

Degrading Names

In basic training you double-time everywhere. There's always someone with sore feet, a sprained ankle, shin splints, or an upset stomach who falls out and walks behind, catching up with the company a few minutes later. Everything is done to keep you in formation, the fallacious assumption being that if you are permitted to fall out in training for a sprained ankle you'll want to do it in combat too. You are called a lot of things designed by the Military Mind to make you want to fall back in:

"Dipshit!"
"Pussy!"
"Dud!"
"Little girl!"

The same methods are used to force someone to finish the low crawl, or do the parallel bars with open blisters on his hands, or jump over the pit on the Run, Dodge, and Jump. You have your remedies, listed in Chapter Seven, How To File a Complaint or Bring Charges. Remember: "Degrading or depersonalizing actions . . . are forbidden."

The Dying Cockroach

One of the lower-level hazing methods, harmless enough, is the Dying Cockroach. The men in the platoon are required to lie down on their backs, thrust their arms and legs in the air, wiggle them around, and make squealing sounds. Perhaps this is what West Point professors of psychology mean when they speak in scholarly journals of basic combat training as a scientific method for inculcating in you "those characteristics necessary for social cohesion and teamwork."[6]

Grunting and Growling: "Kill, Kill, Kill!"

One day all the lawyers from the Fort Polk Legal Assistance Office set up shop in the lobby of a movie theater at the fort's Vietnam-oriented advanced infantry brigade for the purpose of writing en masse (and on orders) the wills of the trainees. They were first to receive a talk on their legal affairs from one of the JAG lawyers. The lawyers were waiting for the trainees to arrive when suddenly they burst into the theater from all sides screaming, "Kill, kill!" When their sergeants permitted the screaming to subside, they sat down to hear a lecture on why they should make out their wills.

Surely the memoirs of some two-thousand-year-old Carthaginian general still control our Army's concept of the soldier as an animalistic killer. The American draftee wonders why a fuss is made about his growling all the time and his screaming "Kill, kill, kill!" wherever he goes in basic or advanced infantry training. He thinks it is pretty stupid, and he knows it does not work. With very few exceptions, he shouts when his sergeant wants him to shout because that way the sergeant will leave him alone. As a matter of fact, sergeants increasingly resort to petty bribes to get their trainees to growl. Just as a child will sing for a piece of candy, so will the trainee shout "Kill, kill, kill!" nice and loud so the sergeant will let him take a five-minute break for a smoke.

Looting and Pillaging

Looting and Pillaging is a special block of instruction that you won't find in the lesson plan, but sometimes it's squeezed in. After bayonet training it is required that all bayonets be turned in at the supply room, for obvious reasons. One day the first sergeant may announce at a company formation that "a bayonet is missing." He will then announce that whoever has it had better turn it in at once. (He doesn't say, "I'm taking off for a half-hour and when I return it had better be here," which he could do if he were really interested in getting the bayonet back.) Since naturally no one comes forward, it is announced that a "shakedown" will take place immediately. A shakedown is a search of the barracks or of individuals, designed not to get evidence of a crime but to protect the "health, safety, morals, or efficiency" of the unit. It is still considered legal by military courts and is justified on the grounds of "military necessity."[7]

When shakedown day arrived at my basic training unit the drill instructors (DIs) storm-trooped into the barracks and ordered the men to open their wall and foot lockers and stand nearby while they proceeded to rampage as they had done moments before in the other barracks. They ripped everything out of the lockers and threw clothing on the floor, stripped the bunks, over-turned mattresses, and even threw towels hanging on the bunks to the ground—as though a bayonet might be hanging in a towel. They also confiscated any food they found in the lockers and ate as they looted, bringing to a swift and military conclusion their lesson on looting and pillaging.[8]

The bayonet wasn't found, and it was announced that we were to replace everything in our lockers and expect another shakedown in thirty minutes. It never came. The next day, first thing in the morning, Character

Guidance was scheduled, and the chaplain talked on "A Sense of Duty." His message was that a sense of duty comes from belief in God and the Dignity of Man as it was embodied in our Constitution by the Founding Fathers.[9] We learned a few days later that the company had a habit of "losing" a bayonet at least once each cycle.

Looting and pillaging is an offense against Article 103 of the Uniform Code of Military Justice (UCMJ), *but only when it is conducted against the enemy; apparently those who drafted the law never imagined that American soldiers would be victimized in this way by American soldiers.* It is likely, however, that the acts described were "disorders to the prejudice of good order and discipline in the service," a crime under Article 134 of the UCMJ, since they tended to undermine the faith of the troops in the legitimacy of the noncommissioned officers' authority. It was certainly "conduct of a nature to bring discredit upon the armed forces," also an Article 134 offense. This article is rarely invoked against the Gestapo tactics of the cadre, but is frequently used to punish some minor impropriety of the trainee. You can avail yourself of it, however, whenever anything as unpleasant as looting and pillaging is done to you. How to handle this problem is discussed in detail in Chapter Seven.

Contempt for Trainees' Safety

Another form of psychological brutality is treating recruits as if their personal safety were a matter of no importance. Perhaps, as the cadre see it, this is a deliberate attempt to prepare the soldier for his role in combat. Nevertheless, it is forbidden by several of the Army's own regulations.

One vivid example of this contempt took place on bivouac. On orders from the field first sergeant, the men wore their helmet liners to the evening formation and left their "softcaps" (baseball caps) in their tents some miles distant. The sergeant believed he had given an order to wear softcaps for evening formation and accused fully seven-eighths of the company of deliberate disobedience. Before the men could eat they had to go back to get their softcaps. Seventy-seven trainees were pushed into the back of an open truck with shaky, removable wooden slats for sides and driven to the tent area. Another sergeant got into the cab of the truck and made the driver, a trainee, hurtle around corners at high speed, throwing the seventy-seven people against one side of the truck or the other, each time cracking the wooden slats a little more. Grateful for having arrived at the tent area without a disaster, the men informed the sergeant of the dangerous situation. He responded with swift military firmness:

> Don't you be leanin' against the sides of my fuckin' truck![10]

True, it's not an abuse of the same magnitude as lining people up in a row and machine-gunning them, but it requires the same quality of mind and temperament. Whether this is the kind of soldier we should seek to create is a question the whole country faces. Whether it pays for you to make a "federal case" out of such an incident depends on the severity of the offense, the witnesses available, timing, the attitude of your CO, your temperament, and the risks you are willing to take.

PHYSICAL BRUTALITY

Psychological brutality inexorably prepares you to accept physical brutality. Every Army trainee knows that the drill instructors aren't supposed to beat you. This contrasts with the Marines, where recruits are brainwashed to believe that the DIs are *supposed* to beat them, and where beating is an everyday experience for most recruits, despite an official ban.[11] Since premeditated physical beating is relatively rare in the Army, many draftees are uncertain about exactly what the cadre can and cannot do.

Be assured that except in self-defense, or to preserve order, or for good reason related to training (such as demonstrating how to hold the rifle), no member of the cadre has a right to touch you.

Article 128 of the UCMJ makes it a crime to commit an assault or battery on anyone. An assault is defined as the attempt or offer to do bodily harm, whether or not the attempt or offer is consummated. Examples of assaults found in the *Manual for Courts-Martial* are:

> . . . raising a stick over another's head as if to strike him and causing him to apprehend that he will be struck, striking at another with a cane or fist, assuming a threatening attitude and hurrying toward another so as to cause him to apprehend bodily harm . . .[12]

A battery, as well as an assault, is committed against you if there is a physical touching. The practice of Kick Ass, in which squad leaders and platoon guides (trainees acting as cadre) are encouraged to kick anyone who is not enthusiastic enough in training, is a violation of Article 128, and you can and should press charges against anyone who insists on doing this to you after you have warned him you would not appreciate it. *Simple assaults are so commonly inflicted upon trainees that the stockades would be overflowing with sergeants if the Army ever attempted to prosecute all of them at once.* It won't. But it has prosecuted some, and it may prosecute the one who assaulted you.

An example of the kind of assault that should be reported, and would probably be punished, occurred at the physical combat proficiency test (PCPT) site where the trainees in my company had just completed their tests and were calling their scores to the field first sergeant, who was recording them. Since everyone was milling around and talking it was difficult to hear the scores, and the sergeant unsuccessfully asked for quiet a few times. To help him get it, another sergeant picked up a hunk of coal, took aim, and hurled it at one of the trainees. It hit him squarely in the neck and he fell to the ground, choking. The commanding officer, who was standing nearby, turned his head away and began to talk to someone else, while other trainees assisted the fallen recruit.[13] The sergeant went over to him, apologized, and it was forgotten. Except for the fact that he had committed an assault, a battery, oppression, and maltreatment, and had engaged in "conduct of a nature to bring discredit upon the armed forces," it was an insignificant incident.

Normally one trainee will not be heard to complain about what is done to another, but in such a situation you would be perfectly correct to report the incident and insist that an investigation be made. It would be best to assure yourself beforehand that fellow trainees would be prepared to back up your complaint, so that you would not be where the Army wants you, isolated and alone.

The Blanket Party

When the cadre really want to see someone worked over they are rarely dumb enough to do it themselves. Instead they let it be known they will not especially stand in the way of a trainee Blanket Party, in which a blanket is thrown over the head of the victim and the celebrants proceed to party by pounding him.

A variation of the blanket party occurred during my basic training. One night an emotionally disturbed black youth beat up another trainee. The next day a number of the platoon guides and squad leaders began to round up support to throw a little blanket party for the assailant. In the meantime the cadre made him sleep outside the orderly room in a pup tent (which was illegal) while they decided what to do with him. One afternoon, as the black recruit was trying to set up his pup tent by knocking the metal tent pegs into the ground, a member of the cadre—just for fun—kept knocking the tent down. When the recruit finally obliged him by angrily gesturing with the tent peg, the others were ready. With a baseball bat, one of the platoon guides broke the recruit's raised forearm in four places. Rumors began to circulate soon thereafter that people were going to get the ones who got the recruit, and at that point the field first sergeant held a formation and told the company to "stop the nonsense."[14] The recruit insisted to hospital authorities that he "fell," and his friends could not persuade him to do otherwise. He was too afraid of what else the system might do to him.

How To Prevent a Blanket Party

If you think you are about to become the victim of a blanket party, (1) write home immediately, telling your family all about your feelings and the reasons for having them; (2) let someone outside the company know what you are worried about, whether it's a friend, a lawyer at the Legal Assistance Office, or some other person on the post; (3) demand to see your commanding officer immediately, and if the sergeants are screening him from you tell them that if you don't see him people outside the company will be taking action to investigate the company—you don't have to be specific; and (4) *tell the CO why you are worried and that you have forewarned your family and people on the installation about your fears.*

He will see to it that nothing happens to you, if only to Cover His Ass.[15]

YOUR MEDICAL RIGHTS

When a young Puerto Rican trainee in my platoon had a double tooth extraction he returned from the dentist with his mouth still bleeding. He wanted to lie down and miss training that afternoon but was afraid to ask the first sergeant, partly because his English was uncertain. I told the first sergeant about the situation and his response was, "Let me tie a pistol belt around his neck. That'll stop the bleeding."[16]

On a windy, bitterly cold day several trainees on their way to sick call were refused permission to wait indoors and stood outside the supply room for a half-hour. When a protest was raised the cadre member replied, "Let them freeze. If someone dies I'll make them carry him."[17]

So it went. And so it still goes. Each year trainees in the American Army die from neglect because their drill instructors discourage or prevent them from going on sick call.[18] Frequently the death-dealing disease is meningitis, an inflammation of the membranes of the brain or spinal cord. You should know its symptoms: headache, chills, nausea, stiff neck, sore muscles, and a rash on the chest. Of course these are symptoms of several less serious illnesses as well, but the only way to be sure what you have is to get competent medical advice.

The Threat of "Recycling"

When you consider the components of the Military Mind, it's amazing more soldiers don't become seriously ill during basic (and advanced infantry) training. Every conceivable pressure and threat is used to prevent you from going on sick call. One of the most powerful threats is that if you miss training you might be "recycled," meaning you might not "graduate" from basic training and could be put into the next cycle, increasing your misery for weeks. However, the governing regulation prohibits arbitrary recycling:

> a. (2) Trainees who cannot continue BCT because of illness or injury of a temporary nature which requires one week or less for treatment, will be retained at the training activity until their physical condition permits them to resume training.
>
> (3) In cases where the temporary illness or injury will preclude return to participation in BCT for a period of more than one week, the local commander may advance the trainee to AIT if, in the commander's judgment, the individual is suf-

ficiently qualified and physically able to participate in such training, and provided the AIT installation has the necessary facilities to complete the individual's POR [overseas shipment] qualifications, if not completed in BCT . . .[19]

Two things become obvious: (1) *You cannot legally be kept from graduating from basic training just because you've gone on sick call once—or a dozen times —so long as you complete all your tests, which almost everyone does, and so long as you have not had an illness that has kept you out of training for more than a week.* Even if you spend a week in the hospital, you are supposed to resume training with the same unit. (2) *If you've missed more than a week's training, your CO can decide to let you graduate and move on to advanced training.*

In practice, commanding officers sometimes use recycling as a means of punishment. Your CO may claim that the reason for recycling you is your failure to march in cadence, or a "defective attitude." In such a case, see Chapter Seven.

The Duffel Bag Ploy

Beware the Duffel Bag Ploy, by which you are not permitted to go on sick call unless you first pack all your belongings (emptying your foot and wall lockers) and, having stuffed them into the duffel bag, carry it to the supply room for "storage." We do not know how many of those who have died from diseases as serious as meningitis could have been saved if they had not been discouraged from going on sick call by ridicule and humiliation of this sort. There is no way to gauge how many thousands of complaints have been made to congressmen without result except occasional indignation and a soothing letter from the Chief of Staff stating that the regulations encouraging good health are uniformly followed in his command and that a particular soldier "never asked" to go on sick call. On these matters the Army keeps no statistics.

The Army has detailed rules and regulations which emphasize that you have a right to preserve your health.[20] The fact that these are almost always ignored should not prevent you from reminding the cadre that they exist. For example, one Department of the Army circular on cold injury prevention warns that:

> Cold injury may occur wherever the temperature falls below 50 degrees F. . . . Proper first aid treatment for cold injury can prevent serious complications that arise from improper handling.[21]

Heat injury can be even more dangerous, but as another circular points out:

> Heat injuries are preventable except under the most extreme conditions . . . Personnel who appear to be ill or who complain of illness should be provided with immediate medical care.[22]

There are things you can be certain of: (1) *You should not be discouraged from going on sick call at any time for any reason that you consider important.* (2) *When you get there, you have a right to see the doctor each and every time, so long as he is there.* That is, you do not have to be seen by the corpsman and be satisfied with that. When you talk to the medical corpsman (who may be a cartoon character or a genius), *insist on seeing the doctor.* If you don't, the first six times on sick call you are likely to be sent away with Cepacol, Micrin, and aspirin. Keep repeating to yourself over and over: *"It's the only body I've got."*

Documenting Your Injuries

If you develop any disabilities while in the Army— and this applies to your entire tour of duty—get them down on your medical records. Make sure the doctor records your past and present complaints. Make certain the results of all laboratory tests are in your file. Otherwise, if your condition should linger or get worse, you will never be assured of receiving disability compensation from the Veterans Administration. No one else is going to care whether all the *i*'s are dotted and all the *t*'s crossed in your Army records. Everyone else has too many other customers to worry about. Although the Military Mind is constantly devising ways of making you think less about "self-satisfaction" and "self-actualization," this is the time in your life when it's most justified. Don't feel bad about it; for one thing, you will be emulating the lifers. Draftees serving in Vietnam have expressed honest amazement at how many of the career noncommissioned officers at the front lines—in combat and off the gravy train for the first time in their lives—exercise every trick the Army has taught them to get back where it's safe.

Medical Discharges

Discharges can be obtained more easily during basic training than later. If you're not going to make it, and you can convince the Army of that fact, they'll give you generous helpings of grief in the process, but they'll let you go. But you've got to have a reason, and you cannot be the only one who thinks you're not fit. Check AR 40–501 and see what the medical requirements are for discharge for your particular affliction. If you can convince a board of Army doctors that you come within one of the definitions in the AR, then a medical discharge is possible. (The medical discharge is discussed at greater length in Chapter Thirteen, Administrative Discharges.)

For this proceeding, as for many others you may have to face, a civilian lawyer would be a worthwhile investment. A sympathetic civilian doctor would also be very helpful. And don't ever forget that, the way the Army presently functions, you come last in their eyes. You had better come first in yours.

Treatment You Don't Want

Sometimes a soldier does not want to submit himself to treatment or inoculations. The military services take the official position that the soldier has no choice in the matter, even if his objections to treatment are grounded in religious scruples.

> . . . Medical personnel are expected to use only that amount of force necessary to administer the immunization. The commonly used expression "refusal to take shots" erroneously suggests that the individual concerned has an option between being immunized or being punished for his refusal. This is incorrect. A soldier scheduled for immunization will routinely be inoculated at his turn, unless he defies superior authority in which event the inoculation will be specially accomplished.[23]

Unofficially, some doctors and medics will respect the desire of a religiously motivated person not to be inoculated.

With respect to surgery to be performed on a soldier's body for the purpose of restoring him to duty, the Army takes the same position as with inoculations. However, when someone objects to an operation on religious grounds, a board will be appointed, and a chaplain will be required to sit on it. What his role is supposed to be is unclear, since religious objection is no defense to refusal to submit to an operation which the soldier is ordered to undergo.

As a practical matter, the soldier will not usually be forced to undergo the operation but will instead be court-martialed for refusal to obey a direct order. The law on the matter is unclear, since cases of refusal are so rare, and civilian counsel should be consulted in this kind of situation.

CHAPLAINS WHO WORSHIP THE ARMY

The great majority of Army chaplains are career officers, while only a small proportion of lawyers at the Legal Assistance Office (or for that matter in any other section of the Staff Judge Advocate's Office) want anything but to complete their tours and get out forever.

That alone should determine where you go for most kinds of advice and guidance.

It goes without saying that the lawyer is neither trained nor equipped to handle your spiritual needs, except in unusual circumstances. *By the same token, the chaplain should not be expected to think as your advocate when you come to him with a military justice or disciplinary problem. After all, he too is a lifer, and his fitness report gets written by his commander, who is usually a line officer.* As one deeply religious conscientious objector puts it, the chaplain's primary MOS is Army and his secondary MOS is God. Most draftees are shocked to discover how true this is.

One former draftee tells the story of the time he went to see the chaplain about a problem but ended up listening to the chaplain's problem. The chaplain, much too old to be still a captain, lamented that he had been thus rewarded for his refusal to "fink on the men." At weekly meetings in the officers' club his fellow chaplains would tell the other officers about the details of their consultations with the troops. Like line officers, they would say, "When I become colonel . . ."

The chaplain is expected to support the Army way as creatively as he can.[24] At Fort Polk's Vietnam-oriented training brigade, called "Tigerland," one chaplain outdid himself in this cause. Visitors gazed in astonishment at the two billboards in front of his chapel. One was a cartoon of a harelipped tiger with a long white beard and the wings of an angel, smiling at the halo hovering over his head. The caption painted on the border read:

SMILE, GOD LOVES YOU

On the other side of the walk was another tiger, casting a lascivious eye at the Good Book, upon which shone a ray of light from Heaven Itself. The caption:

KEEP THE FAITH

There was, by implication, a place in Heaven for tigers too. Meanwhile, in Vietnam, regimental chaplains pray for the "wisdom to find the bastards and the strength to pile on."[25]

What is the key, then, to getting constructive help from Army chaplains? Appreciate their limitations beforehand. Since they too are in the Army, their promotions depend on pleasing their superiors. They are expected to go to bat on occasion for men with serious personal problems but are not appreciated for anything that might make the Army look bad, and are particularly frowned on for actions that expose official wrongdoing too often.

At least one consultation with your chaplain is recommended, if only to find out what kind of fellow he is and how far he is willing to go to prevent an injustice. Generally speaking, chaplains are better than most officers in helping to work out personal or family problems unrelated to the military. But they are of little use in problems of "adjustment" to or acceptance of military brainwashing or discipline. *They will support or avoid criticism of the use of humiliation, fear, or psychological brutality in training situations. For hard advice from people who are trained to inquire into the limits of authority, you should go to Legal Assistance as often as may reasonably be required.*

LAWYERS WHO DON'T WORSHIP THE ARMY

At the Legal Assistance offices I worked in, about a third of the trainees who came in for help, with problems ranging from reducing car payments under the Soldiers and Sailors Civil Relief Act to getting out of the Army for bed-wetting, arrived announcing their "appointment." That is, their first sergeants, after two or three weeks of constant supplications by the trainees, had finally gotten around to calling the office that morning to make the "appointment." Appointments and nonappointments were always handled the same way:

first come, first served. *Don't let your company stall you off for more than a day or two. Legal Assistance offices simply do not and cannot operate on an appointment-only basis.*

The legal advisers are always qualified lawyers. In the Army, as in civilian life, it is improper to allow a layman to give legal advice. Sometimes enlisted men are on the Legal Assistance staff. They are draftees who chose two years of living like you over four years as a captain in the Judge Advocate General's Corps.

Anything you tell any lawyer in the JAG Office or anything a clerk—civilian or military—learns through the performance of his or her work for a military lawyer cannot, over your objections, be used in any manner against you in a future legal proceeding. What a client tells his lawyer, civilian or military, is a privileged communication, and no sergeant, CO, or commanding general has any right to know its content if the client wishes to exercise his privilege. (This is also true with respect to chaplains, but doctors are excluded from the privilege.) The lawyer is consequently prohibited by professional ethics from divulging information without the client's consent. As a practical matter, your CO will be more helpful if you give him a general idea of the problem, but he cannot legally order you to discuss it with him.

There is an exception to the rule of confidentiality. A statement of intention to commit a crime or offense *in the future* is not privileged and your lawyer is not bound to keep that information to himself. But as for acts and events that occurred in the past, you can discuss them and seek legal advice without fear of incriminating yourself. This is a necessary part of the right to keep silent. It is embodied in the Constitution and controls the Army's interrogation methods as well as those of civilian agencies. To anticipate briefly the discussion in Chapter Eleven, Military Interrogations and Self-Incrimination, do not forget that in dealings with the military police or any representative of Army authority you should *never discuss anything with them (aside from your identity) if there is the slightest chance that you may end up a defendant in a court-martial, unless you have first requested and received a lawyer's advice.*

ADVANCED INDIVIDUAL TRAINING

Toward the end of basic training, excitement and anxiety increase considerably as the time draws near when everyone will receive an Advanced Individual Training assignment. Some will luck out and be sent to a personnel course to become clerks; others will draw infantry assignments. If you fear a bad assignment (and who doesn't?), try to use your ingenuity to get some time away from the company during basic and visit the offices on post where you may have some special talent to offer. (See also Chapter Three, Life as Permanent Party.)

Basic training cadre will tell you that you have no control over your assignment to AIT because the Department of the Army makes the assignments by computer. That's only half true. If a local unit wants you badly enough, it can arrange for orders to assign you to it for on-the-job training (OJT). In that way *it is possible to bypass AIT completely, which is emphatically recommended,* since it is largely a continuation of basic (restrictive pass policies, physical training tests, ceaseless inspections, marching, and harassment). Even after you arrive at your AIT station, it is possible to correct a mistake if you don't belong there. For example, if you already have the qualifications that you're expected to get from an AIT school you should be awarded the MOS immediately and be placed in OJT.[26]

Everybody in the Army is entitled to thirty days' leave each year. *You do not have to take leave,* even if it is granted by your permanent change of station (PCS) orders at the end of basic. If you refuse to take your leave at that time because you want to save it for later, they may require you to sign a waiver. In this waiver you'll give up your right to take leave at the end of AIT as well (unless you're put on orders for Vietnam).[27] Just remember, that is *your* choice to make.

AIT is so similar to basic training that most of what we've said about the latter applies to the former. The main difference is that most of your duty hours will be spent in a classroom getting droned at in a military manner by an Army instructor. (You sleep a lot, but try not to get caught.) Grades in the endless stream of examinations could be important in getting good assignments after AIT. For example, the highest-scoring students in Finance AIT will find it easier to get assigned to the comptroller's office, where the work is more interesting than at the finance office.

If you flunk exams during AIT you can be recycled. You are limited to one academic recycling of two weeks for a course of less than eight weeks' duration and two recyclings of two weeks each for each course longer than eight weeks.[28] If, after recycling, you flunk out of an AIT class you may be assigned to one more attuned to your "talents"—like infantry or cooks' school. It is possible to fail every AIT class but infantry. That the System won't "let" you do, except at great cost in discomfort and pain. Your test results may be falsified if necessary to get you to pass. Even more likely, you'll be shipped off to "special training" to bring you up to the level of the others.

SPECIAL TRAINING COMPANIES

Life in an Army special training company is even less fun than basic training. Trainees, basic and AIT, are sent there when their performance, usually on physical training tests, is so far below the Army's minimum standards that there is a serious question whether they will be able to contribute anything to the Army's mission. The true purpose of special training is to make life so unbearable for the boys sent there that they will do anything to get out—even go back to basic training and try to get through it this time around. They get less sleep, more details, even more training than in basic, a great deal more harassment and psychological brutality, and no personal freedom whatsoever. If, after the Army has tried everything, you still can't pass the required tests of basic training, you are supposed to be considered for an "unfitness" discharge.[29] If no one is very obliging, you can get the ball rolling yourself by applying for a discharge on those or other grounds. (See Chapter Thirteen, Administrative Discharges.)

POCKETS OF SANITY

To save your sanity from the onslaught of silliness which basic training and AIT happen to be, it's nice to have a place to hide. This doesn't mean the kind of hiding for which you can be subjected to discipline, but finding a place where you can nurture your dwindling self-respect, rekindle your civilian values, and wonder for the first time, perhaps, about what a democratic country will do to its youth in the name of self-preservation.

That place could be the unit or post library, or the gym, or the GI coffeehouse downtown, or a local college campus, or an off-post movie. If you are attracted to the coffeehouse, either out of curiosity or because you want to find out how you can organize politically from inside the Army, you cannot be prevented from going there, and it cannot legally be put off limits by your local commander. However, special Armed Forces Disciplinary Boards do have the power to place establishments off limits, and there are indications that they are moving against the coffeehouses.[30]

These acts of political desperation follow a series of incidents in which government agents are known to have planted illegal drugs in at least one coffeehouse in an attempt to create a reason for declaring it off limits.

The people who run these havens are exceedingly cautious about preventing drugs from being brought onto the premises, since they are kept continuously aware of their unpopularity in the local communities.[31] Don't think you can go there to smoke grass or pop pills. If you try it, they'll accuse you of being a government agent and throw you the hell out.

As long as passes are made available to the company in general, yours cannot be withheld because you went to the coffeehouse the past weekend and your CO found out about it. If you can prove that his motive for denying you a pass on a subsequent weekend was his distaste for this activity, there are grounds for a complaint under Article 138 of the UCMJ (see Chapter Seven, How To File a Complaint or Bring Charges) or even a restraining order from a federal district court. *But since this is a frontier area in the law, expect harassment if you want to exercise your right to free association while in training—and for that matter, later on too.*

For those spare moments when there is no prospect of getting a pass, the library provides the least military atmosphere you'll find on post. No one there will *order* you to read. You may sit and stare vacantly into space in complete disbelief that the Army provides a place like that. Actually, you should spend your time leafing through the index to the Army Regulations (AR 310–1) and reading any ARs that are of interest to you. In all likelihood this will be your world for the next two or three years and you may as well try to learn as much as you can about it.

The best escape of all is provided by the music room, with which most Army libraries are equipped; at large installations they are surprisingly well-stocked with good music. Simply hope that when you arrive nobody will be playing Sousa marches. And make sure you wake up in time to report for duty, or you might find yourself, like Clevinger in *Catch-22,* actually being court-martialed for listening to classical music.

Notes

1. Company E, 3rd Battalion, 1st Training Brigade, Fort Jackson, South Carolina, Jan. 26, 1967.

2. AR 600–20, para. 31 (rev. 4 Nov. 1969).

3. This is a violation of Article 134, the general article that serves as a catchall for antisocial behavior.

4. Dr. Peter G. Bourne, "Some Observations on the Psychosocial Phenomena Seen in Basic Training," *Psychiatry: Journal for the Study of Interpersonal Processes,* May 1967, vol. 30, no. 2, p. 194.

5. Co. E, 3rd Bn., 1st Tng. Bde., Ft. Jackson, S.C., Feb. 15, 1967.

6. Col. Samuel H. Hays (ex-Director of Military Leadership and Psychology at the U.S. Military Academy), "Military Training in the U.S. Today," *Current History,* July 1968, p. 51.

7. See discussion of shakedown inspections in Chapter Six, The Soldier's Right to Privacy.

8. Co. E, 3rd Bn., 1st Tng. Bde., Ft. Jackson, S.C., Feb. 20, 1967.

9. Co. E, 3rd Bn., 1st Tng. Bde., Ft. Jackson, S.C., Feb. 21, 1967.

10. Co. E, 3rd Bn., 1st Tng. Bde., Ft. Jackson, S.C., March 14, 1967.

11. "Recruit Maltreatment Persisting in Marines Despite Official Ban," *New York Times,* Oct. 13, 1969, p. 1; "Psychologist Charges Brutality is 'Normal' in Marine Training," *New York Times,* April 1, 1969, p. 28.

12. *Manual for Courts-Martial,* 1969, para. 207, pp. 28–61.

13. Co. E, 3rd Bn., 1st Tng. Bde., Ft. Jackson, S.C., Feb. 1967.

14. Co. E, 3rd Bn., 1st Tng. Bde., Ft. Jackson, S.C., March 4, 1967.

15. Covering Your Ass is a special preoccupation of the Military Mind. See discussion in Chapter Four, The Military Mind.

16. Co. E, 3rd Bn., 1st Tng. Bde., Ft. Jackson, S.C., Feb. 7, 1967.

17. Co. E, 3rd Bn., 1st Tng. Bde., Ft. Jackson, S.C., Feb. 8, 1967.

18. "Army Is Called Negligent in Fatal Illness of G.I.," *New York Times,* March 29, 1969, p. 11. See also March 18, 1969, p. 49; March 21, 1969, p. 28; March 27, 1969, p. 3.
19. AR 612–200, para. 2–7 (rev. 16 Feb. 1970).
20. AR 40–5, para. 1–3 (rev. 13 March 1969):

> Particular attention will be devoted to (1) assurance that all eligible personnel, military and civilian, are physically, mentally, and psychologically suited to their tasks and that their physical and mental health are maintained during service or employment . . . and (8) minimization of the harmful effects of unavoidable excessive fatigue and adverse climatologic factors.

21. DA Circular 40–64, Prevention of Cold Injury, paras. 2 and 7 (15 Dec. 1969). The circular continues:

> . . . Moisture is another important factor in producing cold injury. Every effort must be made to keep clothing dry . . . The most vulnerable areas of the body, i.e., the feet, hands, and face, warrant special attention. Wet socks, boots, and mittens must be changed in cold climates at the earliest opportunity. Cold injury may occur even when the temperature is higher than 50 degrees F., when body tissues are in contact with wet clothing.

22. DA Circular 40–58, Prevention of Heat Injury, paras. 3 and 7 (28 March 1969). The circular continues:

> 8(a) Formations, parades, and reviews should be held to a minimum during hot periods and scheduled so as to avoid exposure to direct rays of the sun during the warmer hours of the day. (b) Field lectures and rest periods should be carried out in open shade rather than in the direct heat of the sun or in enclosed spaces lacking adequate ventilation.

23. AR 600–20, para. 48(c)2(b) (rev. 30 June 1969).
24. AR 165–20, para. 2 (rev. 18 May 1966):

> The status of the Chaplain in the Army is that of a religious leader and a staff officer. His duties are those which normally pertain to his profession as a clergyman and those which are prescribed by law, *modified by the mission and distinctive conditions and circumstances of the Department of the Army.* [Italics added.]

25. Dr. Gordon S. Livingston, "Letter from a Vietnam Veteran," *Saturday Review,* Sept. 20, 1969.

26. AR 612–200, Processing Procedures at Training Activities, para. 3–2(b)1(b) (rev. 24 July 1969).

27. AR 612–200, para. 2–11 (rev. 24 May 1968).

28. AR 612–200, para. 3–2(d) (rev. 24 July 1969).

29. AR 612–200, para. 3–6(a)4 (rev. 24 July 1969).

30. Probably the Army's first move was against the Shelter Half coffeehouse, in Tacoma, Washington, when, in January 1970, an Armed Forces Disciplinary Control Board attempted to place the coffeehouse off limits for permitting "dissident counseling and literature" on its premises. When the coffeehouse's lawyers indicated they would put up a fight, the Board indefinitely postponed the hearing.

31. Local residents attempted to evict the proprietors of the coffeehouse near Fort Knox, Kentucky: "Antiwar Coffeehouse Vexes Town near Fort Knox," *New York Times,* Nov. 8, 1969, p. 13. And local authorities in Columbia, S.C., closed down the UFO, the country's first GI coffeehouse, and forced it into "exile" on the campus of the University of South Carolina.

3

Life as Permanent Party: Person or Personnel?

A good soldier has his heart and soul in it. When he receives an order, he gets a hard on, and when he sends his lance into the enemy's guts, he comes . . . He lets himself be torn to pieces for his superior officer, and as he lies dying he takes note that his corporal is nodding approval. That's reward enough for him. That's all he wants.
— BERTOLT BRECHT, *The Caucasian Chalk Circle*

WELCOME "HOME"

With a "whitewall" haircut there's no way of hiding the fact that you just got out of basic training or AIT. Don't try. Make use of it instead. First, *don't be in a hurry to process into the company where you've been assigned as permanent party*. If a good position should open up on the post for which you would have to be assigned to another company, it will be easier to disengage from one you haven't fully processed into and

45

from which you can emerge unknown and, even better, unscathed. On the other hand, if you end up staying in that company, the longer it takes you to get settled, the longer it'll take them to put you on the duty roster. If your name fails to appear on it for a few weeks, don't ask why it's not there. You might miss a few KPs and a field march or two, which would be thoroughly to your credit. So in the beginning, lay low.

Much of your time these first few weeks, especially the first couple of days, should be spent checking around the post for a situation that might be better than the one you've been given. *Contrary to popular myth, you can switch jobs in the Army with relative ease and frequency—if you do it with finesse.* Even before you unpack, go to the service club and get the post newspaper, a map, and information on any special activities for which you may qualify. Perhaps, for instance, the post band just lost its xylophonist, or the chaplain his assistant, or the education director his interviewer. Even if you tried and failed in the reception station and again in AIT, don't give up now. If an office indicates that it has an opening, and you haven't yet processed through post personnel, have the office that wants you call up the clerk there and ask him to have your orders changed. Then you might not even have to deal with the company you were assigned to out of AIT.

Before actually completing any prospective change, talk with the people in the unit you are thinking of switching into and see if there are reasons why that company might be undesirable. In other words, gather all the information you can to make a rational choice whether it's worth the trouble you're going to ask for by switching companies. Avoid asking the NCOs what they think, because their first reaction will be what a hell of a nerve you've got to ask about a new job. You're not supposed to have that much gall so soon.

Special Services (*not* Special Forces) is probably the best deal in the Army for a draftee. It operates the service clubs, pools, golf courses, craft shops, gymnasium, and the entertainment activities that originate on or travel to the post. The theater workshop is part of the Special Services program and is likely to harbor the installation's most un-Army types. If you think you qualify, let them know you're interested. Since Special Services positions are coveted, there isn't likely to be an opening for a stranger, but get to know the people who work in the unit and perhaps something will open up.

YOU HAVE TWO "BOSSES"

You live in a company and work either there or at a "section." As soon as you can after signing into the company, find out who the local powers are. Do this by talking to the friendlier of your future barracks mates. Find out who the important personalities in the orderly room are and remember their names, taking notes if necessary. Find out who's helpful and who's not, who's reliable and who's uninformed. In the company your commanding officer is the nominal boss (for most decisions, the first sergeant is the real boss), and at work it's the section head. The company commander is usually a lieutenant or a captain and the section head a major or a colonel. However, the one with the most power over your life is your company commander. It is he who is responsible for your welfare, equipment, training, and discipline. If you do something wrong at work, the matter will be referred to your company commander for disciplinary action. Your work section can also "fire" you and return you to the company for disposition as your CO sees fit, which usually means reassignment to a bad job. The section head, however, being of higher rank than your company commander, can, if he chooses, be helpful to you—either by relieving you of unpleasant company duties or, if you should happen to get into some minor trouble, by "suggesting" it be forgotten.

YOUR MILITARY OCCUPATIONAL SPECIALTY

The Army has always excelled in securing the right man for the wrong job.[1] If you are assigned to a job that has nothing to do with the one you've been trained for, it may be best to stick it out for a while, particularly if you're new at the company. But if you have lost hope of securing anyone's help in changing to a job you are trained for, file an Article 138 or an Inspector General complaint, in case the ARs are being violated to your detriment. Let's assume you've been school-trained as a personnel specialist and you're being used as a supply clerk. The governing AR authorizes the use of personnel outside their primary or secondary MOSs only when the assignment (1) is under actual combat conditions, (2) is to meet an urgent military requirement, or (3) is for the sole purpose of qualifying the individual for award of a shortage MOS, commensurate with his pay grade. The shortage cannot be merely a local one but must be included on an official Army list of critical MOSs.[2]

Of course, the language is broad enough to permit your commander to find an "urgent military requirement" for a supply clerk at this time. But if you file or threaten to file a complaint he may make efforts to switch you, if only to get rid of a troublemaker.

Your MOS can be withdrawn locally only for certain specific reasons, although the Department of the Army can do it at any time. The post personnel office cannot properly withdraw your MOS and give you another one unless it's on the Army list of critical ones, referred to above, or unless one of the following things has happened: (1) erroneous award of MOS; (2) medical inability to perform required duties; (3) disciplinary action that adversely affects the person's ability to perform duty in that particular MOS (e.g., military police); (4) loss of qualification through disuse after testing; (5) lack of security clearance, if required for the job; (6) inefficient performance in certain situations.[3] Again, the language of the AR is vague.

KP AND OTHER KRAZY PASTIMES

As a device for reminding the Army private or corporal that he is in fact an Army private or corporal, KP is still prized by the Army lifer. (Sadly for those who enlisted in the Army only to be on KP, it is fading away. At some installations, such as the finance center at Fort Harrison in Indianapolis, and in most if not all overseas commands, civilians are hired to do the KP duties.) At any rate, an installation where you cannot "sell" your weekend KP to another permanent party soldier is unheard of. American free enterprise is fostered in this area with the greatest of cooperation from the troops.

One of the first things you should do on arrival in the company is find out who likes to take weekend KPs and what the going rates are (usually between fifteen and twenty dollars, barring inflationary pressures). The rates go down as the month progresses and poverty increases, but they tend to be outrageous right after payday. The cooks don't care who takes KP unless the substitute doesn't show up. In such a case, you've got a problem when you return from the weekend, and perhaps a court-martial too. Pick someone reliable.

Unless you can obtain a medical profile like "no prolonged standing because of flat feet," weekday KP will be difficult to get rid of, so it is worth giving some thought ahead of time to the division of labor in KP duty. At the very bottom of the social hierarchy there is (1) Tray Scraper. Then there are (2) Dishwasher, also known as "Side Sink," (3) Pots and Pans, also known as "Rear Sink," and (4) the aristocrat of KP, the Dining Room Orderly (DRO). The early bird takes his pick.

Tray scraping presents very little challenge, but you'll

have to deal directly with the public and sometimes suffer the primeval vengeance of your inconsiderate friends who, lacking any sense of proportion, will jibe, tease, and smirk at you simply because the day before when *they* had KP you did the same to them. Side Sink is better exercise. You stack up the dishes on one end of the dishwasher and unstack them on the other. In the course of fourteen hours of KP this gets a little repetitive. As DRO you get to take orders from and serve beverages to the company commander and executive officer (not to mention the performance of other defense-related activities, such as pouring salt into the sugar shakers and spreading the grease on the tables after each meal so that it is evenly distributed for the next one).

Deciding which KP job is best for you requires a great deal of introspection, and although this must remain a personal decision, it is strongly suggested that Pots and Pans commends itself to the discriminating draftee of the 1970s. It offers the greatest amount of freedom and solitude. You are left to yourself and can work at your own speed. It also has the virtue of variety because sometimes one of its subsidiary chores is raking gravel in the driveway. This gives you a chance to escape from the mess hall on a regular basis, since delivery trucks enter and leave all day long, wreaking havoc with the gravel you've raked and providing a continuing excuse for going outside. From time to time, when the pots and pans get to be a drag, you can always remind the cook, to whom neat gravel is a matter of pride, that the delivery truck just messed up the driveway. "I think I'll go outside and rake a little gravel" is all you say. If you can develop a reputation as an avid raker of gravel and a lousy washer of pots, the cooks will eventually break down, cast aspersions on your manhood, chase you outside, and wash the pots themselves.

Other company duties, such as fire guard, guard duty, and CQ (Charge of Quarters) runner, aren't nearly as arduous as KP. Nevertheless, there is usually an active market in these too, though at more reasonable rates. Guard duty at most low-security installations typically requires that you walk for a couple of hours in the night around the PX or the golf course with an unloaded rifle, which, when you think about what you're guarding, is better than a loaded one. Sitting in your fatigues in a barracks waiting for a fire describes one function of fire guard. The other is stoking the furnace or a smelly coal stove.

CQ runner is a little more complicated, since you have to do the CQ's job at least part of the time. The role of Charge of Quarters is taken pretty seriously by the Army. It must be filled by the NCO, whose responsibilities include answering the telephone, taking messages, ordering the CQ runner to turn on the fire lights at night, ordering the CQ runner to turn off the fire lights in the morning, and preparing the CQ's report, which lists the times at which the CQ runner turned on the fire lights at night and turned off the fire lights in the morning and has the CQ's signature at the bottom verifying exactly when all these things were done.

The other company duties, like police call and formations, are communal events. Morning formation is the rough one, but the more enlightened company commanders are beginning to act less concerned that you get out of bed at reveille, assemble in the darkness, come to attention in the morning mist, and salute a cannon in the distance that's so far away it sounds like a pop, only to go immediately back to bed when the ceremony is over. Some of these lieutenants are pretty sharp, and although they don't go around saying it, they too think this routine is a funny way to build patriotism.

"ALWAYS VOLUNTEER"

Traditional Army wisdom dictates that you should "never volunteer" for anything. If you follow this advice you will be traditional but not very wise. One should always be looking for an opportunity to volunteer for an assignment that will improve his lot. Of course it's usually best to become "indispensable" at your work section if you like it there, and to develop some influence and power in your company. By staying in one place for a period of time you can rapidly build a reservoir of good will and friendships, all of which can come in handy in dozens of situations that only Sergeant Majors of the Army know how to make the most of. But if you're dissatisfied or bored (or dissatisfied *and* bored) with your Army assignment, there are programs for which you may be able to qualify without extending your enlistment, or perhaps by extending it slightly. Of course, any personnel action that you initiate may immediately render you suspect with the cadre of your company, but you might instead receive their assistance, if they are of high caliber.

When you decide on a course of action, the next thing to do is find the post personnel clerk who handles the particular type of paper work you're planning to submit. Ask him for a sample form that's been submitted by someone else and found to be correct. *Let it be your guide. You'll save precious weeks by avoiding its return to you on a technicality.* The form on which you submit your request will, in all likelihood, be the DA Form 2469, the DF. It's a blank sheet of paper, except DF is printed on it, and this is necessary for it to be accepted. (The old 1049 form may still be acceptable at some locations.)

The next step is to talk to the person at your work section who would be most likely to go along with what you want to do. If it is someone in the middle level of authority, such as a sergeant or a warrant officer, and you let him know just how ignorant you are of Army ways and how much you'd appreciate his guidance, that may be enough to produce a swift, smooth approval from the commanding officer of the section. Once the section has approved the personnel action, discuss the matter with your first sergeant and CO, telling them how greatly you desire what you're applying for, emphasizing that the Army will be benefited if you get it. Despite his stiff resistance to your release from the company, and his many groundless objections, your CO will usually recommend approval, since there are few good reasons for keeping a particular soldier in a company. You may encounter no resistance at all, but you should at least be prepared to deal with it. Remember that there's no guarantee that you'll ever get out of the company, so weigh what you say during these difficult hours. You may have a CO who says, as one did, "I didn't get what I asked for—why should you?" But even he recommended "Approval."

Even if your section head and CO should recommend disapproval of your personnel action, they are obligated to forward it to the next highest headquarters, which must forward it to post headquarters. If the program you're applying for, such as the Defense Language Institute, is Army-wide, then the DF must be forwarded to Washington for final action.

NURSE YOUR PAPER WORK

Whatever you do, wherever you may be, nurse your paper work. By that is meant treat it tenderlovingly, trace it, and follow it up at all costs and at all times. No one else will do this for you. *It's the easiest thing in the Army to lose someone's paper work by accident, or, for that matter, accidentally on purpose.* Make sure this does not happen to you a second time on any particular DF without your reporting it to the Inspector General and letting everyone know what you've done. It'll get through the next time.

There is a minor myth that any personnel action submitted by someone in the Army must go through "distribution," the Army's internal message delivery system. This isn't so, and so far as I am aware it never was, except when someone arbitrarily ordered the enlisted man to relinquish his precious DF to the distribution system. It might get through in distribution, but you are much better off hand-carrying your ticket out of there yourself. If you can't do this, telephone the office where you think it is every two days and find out whether it's been logged in and out; if it's been logged out, call the next highest level of command, and keep tracing it for as long as it is in your power to do so.

Your work station may be near a long-distance Army trunk telephone service phone (Autovan). In such a case, use it. You can get the right telephone extension in the Pentagon from your post personnel clerk, if he is willing to part with it. Don't worry about someone in the Pentagon getting angry that you're calling from Fort Sill, Oklahoma, or Fort Lewis, Washington, because he's probably either a civilian or an enlisted man mellowed by the fact that he works at a desk job in Washington instead of at Fort Sill or Fort Lewis. He might just be helpful. It is possible to find the person who has your DF on his desk and to find out the chances of its being approved, whether it's a request to be stationed in Germany, for Warrant Officer Flight Training, for the Defense Language Institute's Swahili course, or for the Army cross-country ski team (there is one). You may also be told that it has to be resubmitted for some picayune reason. You may even have to face the prospect of not having it to resubmit for six weeks, since it has to be sent back down through the command chain it went up on, and in the meantime Army Regulations prohibit you from submitting another DF while the first one is pending. At this point, ask for a three-day pass, or take out your short-timer's calendar and try to think of something soothing.

One reason why the old adage "never volunteer" still has currency is the belief that if a person volunteers for any one location he renders himself automatically liable to transfer to any other place in the world, such as Vietnam in particular. This is not the way it works.[4] The overseas-volunteer DFs go to different desks in the Pentagon, and one clerk does not usually tell another about his business. But if you volunteer for "overseas duty" without further limiting the request, you will have exposed yourself to a real possibility of cheerful compliance with your wish—and be sent to Vietnam. *Your name can always come down on a Vietnam levy (a list of those on overseas assignment) quite independently of your personnel action, but if you suspect there's an improper connection between your DF for somewhere else and the Vietnam assignment, turn to Chapter Seven, How to File a Complaint or Bring Charges.*

DOUBLE-CHECK ALL ADVICE

The Army is full of well-meaning people who have worked in their jobs for short periods of time and who like to give lots of advice. Read ARs yourself. Ask questions. Check and double-check all information and advice against equally or better informed sources, whenever possible, especially if you're going to take some important action on the basis of this information. It's in the nature of the system, with its endless proliferation of regulations, orders, directives, policies, and SOPs, that the lowliest clerk can turn out to be "right" even if, at the time his opinion was rendered, he was ignorant of the relevant facts, confused by the governing regulations, and unaware of the real reasons for his rightness.

YOU TOO CAN BE PROMOTED

Getting promoted is something that draftees are led to believe is completely in the CO's discretion. That's not exactly right. The CO has to have a reason for not promoting you when he promotes someone of the same rank with less time in service and less time in grade. Surely it should not be difficult for him to find a reason. But it frequently is. Instead of telling you he doesn't like your face, he'll cover up by saying "there weren't enough allocations" to promote you. To be able to determine whether he's leveling with you, you need a basic understanding of promotions and how to get them. The Army's promotion system looks like a Chinese puzzle to most draftees, but for the lower levels it works essentially like this: Each Army unit has an organizational chart that lists each job by title, MOS, and maximum authorized grade. These jobs are called "slots." The chart is called either a Table of Distribution (TD) or a Table of Organization and Equipment (TO&E) and is set up by the Department of the Army. No commanding officer may change the TD or TO&E of his unit. For a promotion, there must be a slot and an allocation for an enlisted man.

Allocations are monthly quotas that come down from DA through all levels of command. They are identified by grade and not by MOS. There are also time-in-grade and time-in-service requirements, but the full requirements are waived with great frequency. Assume as an illustration that a Private first class who is ready for promotion to Specialist fourth class (Spec/4) is working in a unit where all the slots are already filled by other Spec/4s or people of higher rank. If the time-in-service and time-in-grade requirements have been fulfilled by the Pfc, and even if there is an *allocation* available for him, he must scout around for an office with an open *slot* that will accept him and get his company commander's permission to make the switch. The personnel specialist, for instance, can frequently work at his own company and receive rapid promotions in the MOS of company clerk. Also, check out promotions into "temporary" MOSs. To be promoted to Spec/5 it is usually necessary to go before a promotion board of sergeants and officers who will interrogate the individual on matters relating to his MOS and the Army in general, but a well-connected Spec/4 can assure his promotion no matter what he tells the promotion board.

Sometimes a unit is allowed to promote a certain number of "exceptional" men without regard to time-in-grade or time-in-service. And occasionally an "over-strength" unit (too many men) can promote without regard to "position vacancies" (slots). Thus men have been known to get promoted to Spec/5 even when they have been in the Army less than a year.

If you happen to be on overseas orders, getting promoted before you leave could be critically important. Unless the orders are for Vietnam, it will take a long time to get promoted at your new overseas station. In the meantime you're losing all that bread. So never believe the quota you've been told is allotted to your company. There may well be other companies in your unit or other units on your post that have not used all their allocations. These are returned to the post personnel office, which returns the unused allocations to the Army Command headquarters.

You can short-circuit the process and retrieve the allocations your company needs to promote everybody by talking to the personnel clerks along the hierarchy and explaining to them the particularly desperate reasons why you need the promotion at this particularly urgent crossroads in your life. When you finally convince your post personnel clerk to make a friendly phone call to your company orderly room and alert the first sergeant that new allocations have just become available for his company, hustle back to the company, meander into the orderly room, and be "informed" of the "news." At this point your CO will have to dream up a new excuse not to promote you, for which he usually lacks the will and imagination. Incidentally, you can also be promoted while in transit.

Your work section can sometimes be of enormous help in getting you promoted. If you're doing a good job there, and especially if you happen to be working in an NCO's slot, your boss can argue with some effectiveness that the "prestige" of the position demands that you be one grade higher. This frequently carries enough weight with the company commander to secure your coveted stripe.

DELAYING OVERSEAS SHIPMENT

When through either your own designs or those of the Pentagon your name appears on an overseas levy, this does not necessarily mean you are going, or, if you *are* going, that it will be when the orders say. If you have volunteered for and received the assignment you wanted, there's still more you can do for yourself. If it is April, for instance, and you are on an August levy, it's up to you to choose when in August you want to leave the country. You do this by going to your post port-call clerk and selecting a date for port call. The chances are he will go along with your wishes. If you want to stay in the States as long as possible and also enjoy a thirty-day leave, you'll request August 31 as your port-call date. That way you will leave your unit around the last week in July, receiving a few days in addition to your authorized leave for "travel time." If you want to go as soon as possible, you can request a port call of August 1 and, still taking a thirty-day leave, depart from your present unit the last week in June. There's room for flexibility.

Inadequate Training

A number of factors can delay or cause cancellation of overseas orders. One is inadequate training. If it is discovered at the overseas replacement station that you have not had the right amount of training for overseas duty in the area to which you have been assigned, they must hold you until the requirements have been fulfilled. The AR sets out certain requirements which are *mandatory,* including qualification and familiarization in arms within a twelve-month period immediately preceding date of overseas movement, the night infiltration course and close combat course, training within the past twelve months to protect against chemical, biological, radiological, and nuclear attack, training lectures and orientations in the Code of Conduct, survival, evasion and escape training, and overseas orientation in such areas as legal rights, community relations, and customs of the country in which you are to be stationed. Many of these requirements may be filled by two-hour lectures.[5]

It is generally known that much of this information is falsified on training records as a matter of course. That's because there's usually too much trivia to be attended to by troop commanders to assure effective training. By the time the men arrive at the overseas replacement station the records are clean, because part of out-processing from the stateside post includes cleaning up your records.

But sometimes the Army gets caught. In the summer of 1968 an activated National Guard unit was readied for shipment to Vietnam, together with tanks, armored personnel carriers, and other heavy equipment. Some of the soldiers at Fort Lewis, Washington, noticed that they were given credit on their records for training in operating the armored personnel carriers, although they had been trained in other MOSs, such as company clerk. They wrote California Congressman Edwin Reinecke that their achievement certificates had been phonied up. The Congressman managed to get the Army to cancel the orders, uncrate the tanks, and train the unit adequately. The falsification of training records was merely a question of "misjudgment," according to official Army sources.[6]

Change of Status

You may have broken a leg or caught mononucleosis while on leave. Any physical disability that would limit your assignment to a particular overseas command (which is usually any disability that would limit your assignment to duty in the States) should prevent your being shipped out until the disability is gone.[7]

Any deficiency in your records that was "predictable" when you left your last station for the overseas replacement station is supposed to be corrected by the commander of the overseas replacement station. If you are missing an inoculation, they'll do it there and ship you out. But:

> If any *unpredictable* change . . . in status occurs, such as a deferment, court action, or disqualifying change in physical condition which cannot be corrected as indicated . . . the individual will be reported to Department of the Army for further instructions . . .[8]

Hardship to Family

A temporary deferment may be obtained when certain hardships would be imposed on the soldier's family as a result of his overseas shipment. A request based solely on family separation "incident to" overseas shipping orders will not be considered. This deferment is limited to situations in which a close relative is not expected to live longer than a year, or in which the soldier's presence would be a "critical factor" in the patient's recovery. Additionally, there is the requirement that the illness must not have existed or been reasonably foreseeable at the time of entry on active duty.[9]

Deferments are also available for soldiers whose wives are expected to have difficult pregnancies or deliveries. There are also some deferments for domestic or financial hardship, but these too are extremely limited.

None of these deferments is supposed to be granted if the soldier will not have enough time left in the Army to ship when the deferment is terminated. How one is supposed to know ahead of time at what point a person who is not expected to live more than a year will die and "terminate" the deferment of the soldier is not explained in the AR.

Miscellaneous Deferments

When a soldier on overseas shipping orders goes AWOL for more than thirty days, he is taken off the overseas replacement station's roster and is reported to the Pentagon as a "deserter." Needless to say, this is not an authorized deferment, and it is of course not recommended. It will result in a temporary cancelation of overseas orders, and almost certainly a court-martial. Soldiers undergoing investigation for possible court-martial or for subversive activity, those with permanent geographic or climatic assignment limitations, and those whose records have been "flagged" for other reasons may also be deferred from overseas shipment.[10] Shorter, compassionate deferments are available for emergencies, such as death in the family.

Vietnam Deferments

A few deferments are available only to a soldier who has Vietnam orders. If a member of his immediate family is in military service and already in Vietnam, or is in a captured or missing status incident to service there, or is alerted on orders for shipment to Vietnam, a soldier is entitled to a deferment until the family member returns to the United States. If a soldier's wife is at least seven months pregnant, he will be deferred until the birth of the baby. Otherwise not. If a member of the soldier's immediate family has been killed or totally disabled in Vietnam (or in a hostile-fire zone in Korea), Army Regulations give him a permanent exemption from shipment to Vietnam.[11]

Applying for CO Discharge

An event that should at least postpone overseas orders is the filing of a conscientious objector claim *at the home station*. A very recent change in the regulation has eliminated the possibility of filing for CO discharge at the overseas replacement station.[12] Thus, in order to delay overseas shipment, the application must be filed at the home station *before signing out of the home unit*. This may be done even after receipt of overseas orders. On the other hand, if the soldier fails to come up with the required supporting evidence within seven days of the day he was supposed to depart from the home station, he will have to comply with the reassignment orders. See Chapter Twelve, Conscientious Objectors in the Army.

Applying for Compassionate Reassignment or Hardship Discharge

When a hardship discharge is turned down, the soldier should always consider filing a request for a compassionate reassignment. Since the Army has made it a practice to act favorably on only a small percentage of the hardship discharge applications that have been filed during the Vietnam era, the only possible relief some soldiers and their families can hope for—even in situations involving extreme distress—is a transfer to a base near home. That is what the compassionate reassignment is designed to facilitate, although here too only the most grievous situations will convince the Army to approve the request. Also, the hardship must be one which can be alleviated only by the soldier's assignment to the particular area sought. It must be of a temporary nature and not amenable to any other reasonable solution.

Both the hardship discharge and compassionate reassignment applications must be ruled on by the Army before the soldier may be shipped overseas.[13] However, if the soldier fails to apply at the home station, he stands virtually no chance of being permitted to delay shipment by filing at the overseas replacement station.

A great deal of paper work must be submitted with this request—as much as for an administrative discharge. The assistance of the clerk who handles discharges at your installation is essential. There must also be compiled a sheaf of documentary proof of the hardship, letters from friends who are familiar with the family situation, doctors' statements, and perhaps proof of financial distress. Legal Assistance should be consulted in the preparation of the paper work.

The regulation also discusses the permissive reassignment, in which the soldier himself pays for the cost of moving, and the traditional "stateside swap," which permits two soldiers who perform the same work at different bases to swap assignments. Talk to a career soldier about how to swing that one.

GETTING OUT EARLY

Apart from the administrative discharges discussed in Chapter Thirteen, Army Regulations provide for early releases from active duty ranging from thirty up to 150 days. Early releases are granted very liberally to overseas returnees, students and teachers, seasonal employees, and policemen.[14]

Overseas Returnees. It is important to time your shipment overseas (to the extent that it is within your power) so that your normal overseas duty tour will be completed, in the case of a short-tour area, such as Vietnam or Korea, within 150 days of your scheduled release from active service, known in the Army as an ETS. *When your twelve-month tour in Vietnam or thirteen-month tour in Korea is completed you will be released upon arrival in the States, even though you have 150 days left to serve.* In theory, then, you can go directly from AIT to Vietnam or Korea and, after a total of nineteen months in the Army, be released. If you return from Korea or Vietnam with 151 days or more left, you will be reassigned to another unit. If upon return from a long-tour (three years) area, such as Germany or Japan, there are thirty days or less remaining in your active-duty tour, you will be released. All paper work for these early outs must be completed at the overseas station. There is also a provision for early release of those soldiers on a temporary overseas duty tour (TDY) who have less than sixty days left to serve upon their return from overseas.

Students and Teachers. If a soldier has less than three months left to serve at the beginning of a semester, he can receive an early out for the purpose of attending or teaching at an approved educational institution, either in the United States or in a foreign country. This type of release, as well as those for seasonal employment or police work, is obtainable whether you are stationed overseas or stateside. *If you are overseas, and you will not qualify for the early out for overseas returnees because you began your duty tour too late, it is still possible to get out of the Army three months early, cutting short the overseas duty tour as well. Failure to complete a full overseas duty tour is not an acceptable reason for turning down an application for a student or teacher early out. If it is invoked against you, it is grounds for an Article 138 complaint.*

Many months must be devoted to obtaining and preparing the documentation and paper work for this type of discharge. *Plan early if you want out early.* An acceptance from the college or a letter embodying the job offer must be submitted with your own request on a DF. Be sure to contact the Early-Out Clerk and seek his help. Read the applicable regulation carefully. The local personnel office passes on these applications, unless it is a doubtful case or the school is in a foreign country. In those circumstances the applications are forwarded to Washington. You can be turned down at the local level if your services are deemed "essential to the mission" of your assigned organization, but this rarely occurs. If you are arbitrarily turned down, or discriminated against, complaint procedures are available.

Seasonal Employment. This can be extremely flexible. "As used in this regulation, the term 'employment of a seasonal nature' refers to employment that is not continuously active nor in full operation during the whole of a calendar year in the geographical area of the employment site." That language covers a pretty broad range of occupations, but there are other restrictions. The scheduled date of employment must fall within three months of your scheduled date of discharge. That, of course, can be adjusted with your potential employer. But you must also be able to show that (*a*) you will be employed "unhindered" for at least half the "season" and (*b*) it is your normal occupation or you have a "definite intent" to make it such.

Picking fruit on a farm is the classic example of seasonal employment, and fruit pickers should have no trouble getting an early release if their ETS comes up during the harvest season. However, there is no reason why the section should be so narrowly construed, and any activity that can arguably be made to fit the terms of the regulation is worth a try. Soldiers have used this regulation to get released as instructors at miniature golf courses, lifeguards, and campaign aides to candidates for congressional office. This kind of early out may take months of planning, since you have to explain the regulation to your prospective employer to assure that his letter covers every requirement. The limits of the seasonal employment early out are your imagination and the personnel officer's liberality.

Policemen. "Commanders . . . are authorized to order separation for the convenience of the government of enlisted men who have three months or less remaining in their periods of service and who submit valid application for separation evidencing employment with a legally established law enforcement agency of a city, county, state or federal government" as public police officers. Acceptance into a police training program will also suffice.

Notes

1. "Draftees' Skills Ignored in Army," *New York Times,* Nov. 3, 1969, p. 4.
2. AR 600–200, para. 3–5(b)3 (rev. 22 April 1969); other exceptions are: (4) in support of reserve summer training and (5) on special orders of DA.
3. AR 600–200, para. 2–30(a) and (b) (rev. 19 Nov. 1969).
4. See AR 614–30, para. 2–3(d)(rev. 20 Nov. 1969).

5. AR 612–2, sec. II (rev. 18 Aug. 1969). See also AR 614–30.

6. "Kvetch, Kvetch," *New Republic,* Sept. 14, 1968, p. 8.

7. See ARs 40–501, 614–30, 635–40, ch. 10.

8. AR 612–2, para. 2–66(a).

9. AR 614–30, ch. III, para. 3–2(a)1 (rev. 22 Oct. 1968). See also para. 8–1 (rev. 3 June 1969).

10. ARs 614–30, 635–89, 604–10, and 600–31.

11. AR 614–30, para. 3–5(b)2 (rev. 20 Nov. 1969).

12. AR 635–20, para. 6(a).

13. AR 612–2, para. 2–41 (rev. 18 Aug. 1969); AR 635–200, para. 6–6(a) (rev. 9 April 1968); AR 614–6 (rev. 29 Jan. 1965).

14. AR 635–200, paras. 5–14 through 5–26 (rev. 10 July 1969, 12 Nov. 1969, 21 May 1969, 9 Feb. 1970).

4

The Military Mind

"And what's all this about enlisted men? Just how the hell do they get into this act?"

The chaplain felt his face flush. "I'm sorry, sir, I just assumed you would want the enlisted men to be present, since they would be going along on the same mission."

"Well, I don't. They've got a God and a chaplain of their own, haven't they?"

"No, sir."

"What are you talking about? You mean they pray to the same God we do?"

"Yes, sir."

"And he *listens?*"

"I think so, sir."

"Well, I'll be damned."

—JOSEPH HELLER, *Catch-22*

Since hardly anyone doubts that the Military Mind really does exist, it is odd that only a few writers have paid any recent attention to it. Yet there is an urgent need for the young American recruit to understand why the modern Military Minds do what they do to him, and to understand it through the eyes of people other than his drill sergeant, his company commander, official Army propagandists, or even his father—who in the last war never dared to question.

THE AUTHORITARIAN
PERSONALITY

Military life attracts people who exhibit what psychologists have identified as authoritarian personalities. Their research has revealed:

> Certain people are eminently more suited than others to life in the armed forces. The authoritarian personality as identified by Adorno *et al.* combines the traits of conventionalism and conformity with a submissive, uncritical deference to superiors, a tendency to overassertion toward underlings, and a punitive, rejecting attitude toward those who violate conventional values; he opposes the subjective, the imaginative, and the tenderminded. His thinking is superstitious, stereotyped, and rigid; he exaggerates assertion of strength and toughness; he has . . . hostility and a lack of personal regard for others. The authoritarian personality has a tendency to attribute evil intent and actions to other groups, particularly minorities; he shows an exaggerated interest in and vigilance against sexual activity on the part of others, coupled with unconscious self-doubts about sexual adequacy.[1]

People who conform to this description can be found, naturally, in and out of the military. But they flock to the services because there they can indulge their excesses and even be rewarded for them. Every draftee encounters at least a handful of people who almost perfectly mirror the portrait of the authoritarian personality.

I remember one example, an officer, who as company commander would go to extraordinary lengths to extract tokens of deference from his men. Once he went up to a soldier who was seated on a bench waiting for a bus, his head buried in a newspaper. The officer kicked the newspaper out of the soldier's hands and asked him why he didn't salute an officer. The soldier explained that he had been reading a newspaper, which had just been kicked away, and until that point in time had not seen any officers in his vicinity. Since variations on this theme were played several times a month, the men in his company would swap stories to see who had the best one. When he suspected the lack of deference was intentional this officer would throw a temper tantrum, screaming and stamping his feet. Right after one of these sessions, and before he had fully calmed down, he started a discussion with two of his men about the gun control legislation pending in Congress at that time. He said flatly that if a strict bill were passed he would shoot anyone who tried to take his guns from him. Then he abruptly asked one of the men, "Isn't it terrible how some women are aggressive in sex?" Although he didn't say so, his guns were keeping him from being castrated, which it was his right to keep from being, except that he made life unappetizing for the men in his command.

This man was an extreme case, and you shouldn't get the idea that everyone in the Army is that crazy. In fact many career people, perhaps a majority, do not exhibit very many of the characteristics of the Military Mind. But the recruit doesn't come into contact with them on a personal basis because the system is structured to screen him away from them and toward the more militaristic types. A militaristic type is someone who thinks it is very important that the troops all look alike, standing in neat rows; he is someone who loves to walk through the ranks and have each one snap to attention in exactly the same way as he stops to inspect. He loves the ceremonies and the formalities and the customs that tell him what he can carry with him when in uniform, and in which hand he must hold it, and on which side of whom he must walk. The militaristic type still has the upper hand in the American Army over the military type, who is interested in rationally getting his job done with a minimum of ceremony. Alfred Vagts, an eminent military historian, has described the differences between the two types of approach:

> The military way is marked by a primary concentration of men and materials on winning specific objectives of power with the utmost efficiency, that is with the least expenditure of blood and treasure . . .

But

> Militarism, on the other hand, presents a vast array of customs, interests, prestige, actions and thought associated with armies and wars and yet transcending true military purposes . . . Rejecting the scientific character of the military way, militarism displays the qualities of caste and cult, authority and belief.[2]

Both styles of military thinking have succumbed to the belief that the way to make the soft American youth fierce is to humiliate and terrify him into the blind obedience that military leaders have traditionally sought and received.

HUMILIATION + FEAR = OBEDIENCE

The Military Mind believes instinctively that what makes men fight for their country is fear; even more, what keeps *everybody* in line is fear. Therefore, to accomplish his mission he must, regardless of regulations written for the benefit of public information officers, psychologically brutalize the troops. The brainwashing process is designed to make the unworldly trainee feel that if he cannot or will not do everything he is told to do he is something less than a man. Happily, an increasing number of trainees are a great deal more worldly than their sergeants.

The training films and "character guidance" sessions repeatedly hammer at this propaganda line. One such film, entitled *Authority and the Soldier,* tells the story of a foot-dragging soldier who one day is made a squad leader by his sergeant. As a result of the exercise of his new authority, the recruit (deservedly) loses all his friends. He regrets this and wants to turn in his stripes so he can get his friends back. His sergeant tells him he cannot do it, because if he did he would be letting down the President of the United States and, even worse, the astronauts.

> Sergeant: When you were picked for this Army, you were expected to be a man. To be a man, you've got to learn to respect authority.
> Recruit: But, Sarge (earnestly), what do I do? How do I begin?
> Sergeant: If you respect those stripes, you'll know.[3]

This might be called indoctrination through inspiration and example. But there's also the Fear Flick, such as the one on "military justice" shown at my reception station at Fort Jackson. It began with a brief catalogue of rights and then switched into the subject of crimes against the Uniform Code of Military Justice. Picking up momentum, it warned against the commission of capital offenses through staccato blasts of execution scenes—a noose, an electric chair, a firing squad in action. These vignettes burst upon the screen like incoming mortar fire, to make certain you wouldn't miss the point.[4] Nobody did.

What is the clear implication of these films? Certainly not to remind you that while you are a soldier you retain certain inalienable rights. *It is to create the lingering impression that the Army's authority has no limits. Or at least that you had better not try to test them.* Naturally, this view will be nowhere expressed in official literature, since it's bad for public relations. But you'll find it in realistic fiction, as in the conversation between General Cummings and his aide, Lieutenant Hearn, in Norman Mailer's novel, *The Naked and the Dead:*

> ". . . We have the highest standard of living in the world and, as one would expect, the worst individual fighting soldiers of any big power. Or at least in their natural state they are. They're comparatively wealthy, they're spoiled, and as Americans they share most of them the peculiar manifestation of our democracy. They have an exaggerated idea of the rights due themselves as individuals and no idea at all of the rights due others. It's the reverse of the peasant, and I'll tell you right now it's the peasant who makes the soldier."
>
> "So what you've got to do is break them down," Hearn said.
>
> "Exactly. Break them down. Every time an enlisted man sees an officer get an extra privilege, it breaks him down a little more."
>
> "I don't see that. It seems to me they'd hate you more."
>
> "They do. But they also fear us more. I don't care what kind of man you give me, if I have him long enough I'll make him afraid. Every time there's what you call an Army injustice, the enlisted man involved is confirmed a little more in the idea of his own inferiority . . . The Army functions best when you're frightened of the man above you, and contemptuous of your subordinates."[5]

Army Regulations take a different official view of when the Army functions best.[6] But it is evident that Army Regulations do not necessarily govern the Army in action. It is not possible to know how many high brass secretly agree with General Cummings. It is known that the Military Mind can be counted on to gloss over unpopular convictions and make them more palatable for the public. For instance, compare the fictional General Cummings' private assessment of the

American draftee as a soldier with the public one of the former Director of Military Leadership and Psychology at the United States Military Academy, who says the very same thing in nicer language:

> Decades of permissiveness in education and child rearing have led us toward a self-centered emphasis on individual autonomy and choice. Self-actualization, self-achievement, self-satisfaction and self-development have been assuming an increasing status in the spectrum of social values over those of obligation, duty and responsibility. This growing individualism has been coupled with a declining respect for established authority. Yet our society has a continuing need for a way to develop among its citizens those characteristics necessary for social cohesion and teamwork.[7]

Notice that the evaluation of what's wrong with you as a soldier, although hidden behind a sociological smokescreen, is pretty much the same as the fictional General Cummings' assessment. It does not say that you have a need to be broken down psychologically through humiliation and fear[8] but is expressed a bit more loftily. The West Point professor even disclaims any military desire to "eliminate the trainee's individuality, his opportunity to express himself . . ."[9] The soldier knows, however, that any individuality he retains is in spite of, not because of, Army training.

This self-evident fact was underscored during recent congressional hearings before the House Appropriations Committee, when Army Deputy Chief of Staff for Personnel, Lieutenant General A. O. Connor, testified before Congressman Daniel Flood of Pennsylvania:

> Gen. Connor: We are getting more kooks into the Army, for one thing . . .
> Rep. Flood: I do not see why the Army after a couple of hundred years of taking care of people like this, I never knew an outfit worthy of the name that could not take care of some

goldbrick like that. There are ways; at least there were. Are you afraid of them?

Gen. Connor [the general explained that the Army wasn't afraid, but]: The lawyers have been more active in this area, of late, sir. We don't have the same freedom we used to exercise in this area.[10]

Translated: The Army doesn't have the same freedom it once did to knock "sense" into dissident trainees, which it was always permitted and expected by certain congressmen to do. To that extent, the military and our more reactionary congressmen are becoming very frustrated. The military intellectuals have always claimed and believed that discipline (through fear) is not only a necessary technique for accomplishing a military mission but good "citizenship training" as well.[11] Of all the perversions perpetrated by the military and supported by civilians, this one could well be the most threatening to our freedom. Although it can hardly be disputed that adjustment to life in one bureaucratic organization will enable you to adjust to life in another, that isn't really all they're after. Not only do they want you to control your own desires, work blindly with others, and follow orders you dislike; they seek your compliance through the inculcation of fear and by keeping you so busy with routine chores you cannot think for yourself. This of course is "citizenship training" for fascism.[12] And although a few career officers deplore the treatment you get, there are many who think it's necessary in order to have an Army.

During their training officers are subjected to the same assortment of mortification techniques as the draftee, but the promise of salvation—*being* an officer—is dangled as an inducement to endure. Luther Charles West, a recently retired lieutenant colonel who served for seventeen years in the Army's Judge Advocate General Corps, has described the officer's motivation for absolute obedience:

Thus, at a tender age, the West Point cadet learns that military rules are sacred, and in time readily accepts them as a substitute for integrity. As he progresses through his military career, the rules remain uppermost in his code of honor. In fact, his "honor" is entwined with the rules, and so long as he obeys the rules, whatever their content, or whatever manner of man or fool may have written them, his honor is sound. The nice thing about a set of principles of this nature, of course, is that as soon as the officer himself takes command of a military unit, he can write a good many of his *own* rules, and the higher he is promoted, the more rules he can write, and the more people will be subject to his rule-making authority.[13]

COVER YOUR ASS AND THE ELUSIVE NIRVANA

Since fear is what makes the Military Mind tick, such a mind expects fear to make you tick too. After a while it does, because the only way to avoid the wrath of arbitrary authority is to be blameless. Therefore, the Army's secret motto, golden rule, and interdenominational prayer is Cover Your Ass, or as many soldiers abbreviate it in their daily conversation, CYA.

The need to be free from blame in all possible situations is so great in the career soldier—officer or enlisted man—that he occasionally resorts to comic, fantastical schemes. This insecurity pervades the entire hierarchy. Even military historians are not exempt from the desire to cover up their heroes', their nations', or their own mistakes; they are perhaps the most significant distorters:

> A very large part of military history is written, if not for express purposes of supporting an army's authority and prestige, at least with the intention of not hurting it, not revealing its secrets, avoiding the betrayal of weakness, vacillation, or distemper;

> it is usually designed with a future war in mind, in its inspiring treatment of some particular war in the past.

Further:

> The historical record of warfare is thus dependent to a large extent on the writers' desire to preserve reputations, their tendency to cliches, and confusion of history . . .[14]

If historians can't rise above their parochial or national interests, it is understandable that policy makers will deny in the face of all available evidence that the Army accidentally gassed sheep in Utah, only to admit it in the end. It is certainly not unusual for a commander to threaten to "bust" GIs in rank if they admit to congressmen that their M-16 rifles are no good.[15] And it is fairly typical for the Army to court-martial a soldier whom it orders to stay at home to await overseas shipping orders when the soldier has merely obeyed those orders.[16] In one case the Army court-martialed a doctor who wouldn't play the Army's CYA game. Stationed in Vietnam, he complained personally to General Westmoreland during the general's inspection tour of the doctor's local dispensary. Right in front of his superiors, he told the Vietnam commander that the medical facilities were rotten and supplies inadequate. Since he failed to subscribe to the CYA rule that permits your immediate superiors to cover up their mistakes also, he was court-martialed and convicted. The Board of Review threw the case out on the grounds that complaining in the way he did was within his First Amendment right to free speech.[17]

Thus the military have an odd propensity for admitting the truth only after a matter has been documented three times over and they are, once again, up against the wall. The dynamic of this process is practically unalterable because To Be Blameless is the Elusive Nirvana of the Military Mind.

CRITICISM IS ALWAYS SUSPECT

So long as criticism in the Army is directed toward relatively inessential items, such as uncomfortable living conditions, it is tolerated, perhaps even encouraged. Robert Sherrill has shrewdly observed that "to the career officers on their verandas, this traditional GI griping wafts out of the barracks and across the drill fields only as the distant, comforting drone of regimentation."[18] Nor is the soldier alone in having his criticisms either stifled or ignored. Even more than the enlisted man, the junior officer is expected to accept the role of a bland bumpkin or risk social ostracism. Consider this advice given by a retired major general, author of the latest *Officer's Guide:*

> SCORN THE HABITUAL CRITIC. You will harm your personal standing in the eyes of worthy fellow officers by associating more than casually with the continual complainer and critic. Most organizations have one or more of this type. Such individuals are almost certainly of small capacity, mediocre record, and deserve the low esteem in which held. Correct them, if they work for you. Avoid them, if they don't.[19]

Notice how neatly the Military Mind handles the problem of continual complainers. First it creates two categories for them: (1) "low capacity" and (2) "mediocre record." Then it provides only two proper alternative actions for the good officer: (1) "avoid them" or (2) "correct them." For the Military Mind a third category simply doesn't exist. If it did it might have to be something like: (3) "The continual complainer may be right." And if this third category existed, there would have to be a third alternative as well, i.e., "Join them," and that would be unthinkable. Since in the view of Army brass there cannot be *that* much wrong with the

Army, anything more than casual and occasional criticism is unwarranted, and consequently not worth listening to.[20]

"MICKEY MOUSE": THE GLORIFICATION OF TRIVIA

What the Army calls military courtesy and respect for tradition are euphemisms for the perpetuation of a caste system that is out of touch with the temper of American society and anathema to its young men and women. They are enforced on the unwilling GI through the vehicle of military discipline, but few draftees are fooled by this glorification of trivia. It is the Army's way of asserting the superiority of its way of life over that of what it regards as the money-grubbing civilian in modern society. "See," says the Military Mind, "as the guardian of your nation's past glory I am better, holier, and more patriotic than you. But by virtue of your government's grace, you now have the privilege of becoming part of this glory. Actually, you really don't know how lucky you are. Now, troop, let's see a proper salute!" That this is the stuff of militarism has not escaped the GI. The draftee has his own nonacademic and apolitical names for militarism in the American Army. In World War II it was "chicken shit." Today it's "Mickey Mouse."

Nothing illustrates militarism on the personal level more than the salute. Unbelievable amounts of time are spent in training at polishing the salute. An awesome number of post-level directives are written solely to keep the salute snappy. An enlisted man must salute an officer under most circumstances outdoors and when reporting to him indoors. Failure to do this can be a court-martial offense. But the officer's failure to acknowledge the salute with his own is merely a breach of courtesy. The salute is touted by Army propaganda as a symbol of "mutual respect" between officers and enlisted men, but no doubt lingers in anyone's mind as to who is expected to show respect to whom. On most Army installations where automobiles are permitted, enlisted men are issued red bumper decals and officers are given blue ones. Whenever an enlisted man on foot sees an officer's car approach (which he is supposed to spot by looking at the bumpers of *all* oncoming cars) he must salute, even if the car is being driven by the officer's teen-age daughter. The "mutual respect" in this case is celebrated between the enlisted man and the officer's bumper decal or, if she feels like saluting back, the officer's daughter.

It is also considered an essential expression of military courtesy for the first enlisted man who sees an officer enter a room from outdoors to shout, "Attention!" and for the others in the room to snap to attention. It is then the officer's move. He can let everyone stand at attention and absorb his Presence. Or, as is done with monotonous regularity, the officer can mumble, "At ease!" at which time people resume what they were doing. Sometimes the poor unsuspecting officer snaps to attention too and, like Major Major Major Major in *Catch-22*, is made to feel like a sad boob.

Drill and ceremonies take up vast amounts of time in Army training. In basic training, long after the troops have learned to form up in orderly fashion to march from one point to another, which is a reasonable demand, they must endlessly practice their movements —their right steps, left steps, pivot steps, and "eyes right"—all for the final review in which they march past the reviewing stand muttering to themselves things that could get them a general court-martial. For company inspections hours are spent polishing numerous brass things, taking meaningless wrinkles out of wretched bunk blankets, and arranging one's belongings in prescribed rows from right to left, until the first sergeant decides he'd rather have them in reverse order. These quasi-religious rituals are what lifers mean when they say, "It's time to soldier."

Mickey Mouse is reflected on another level in the blind veneration of custom. A uniformed soldier, rain or shine, isn't supposed to carry an open umbrella. But he may carry a *closed* umbrella. It's even more important that an officer in uniform not be seen carrying an open umbrella, since it's "unbecoming" his status as an officer. The mere carrying of a closed umbrella raises suspicion because there's always the human temptation to open it in the event of a downpour. Years ago this custom might have made sense in that an open umbrella might have inhibited the officer's battle-readiness and could have detracted from his status as a warrior. He had to be prepared to reach for his sword to defend his honor in a duel, and an open umbrella in his hand might have made his movements clumsy, thus tending to unbuckle his swash in public. Quite possibly this No Open Umbrella custom is related to the Must Salute custom, since if one is carrying an umbrella with his right hand he cannot be expected to salute. From a strictly legal viewpoint, a direct order to close one's umbrella in the middle of a rainstorm (it has happened) would be lawful and disobedience would be punishable by court-martial, since an order to comply with military custom is enforceable.

THE GLORIFICATION OF KILLING

After all, the name of the game is Kill, Kill, Kill. Although they are in a distinct minority, do not be surprised if you meet some people who live for the chance to kill—it doesn't matter whom. Once it was fashionable for officers to display their savagery to the limited public that listened to them. During World War I, a lieutenant colonel was permitted to write in the *Infantry Journal,* a professional soldier's publication sponsored by the United States Infantry Association, the following code for the bayonet fighter. It will strike a familiar chord for all who have been through basic training. This is the "Spirit of the Bayonet":

> The bayonet is, primarily, a weapon of offense; a man armed with it is not on the defensive; he must be the aggressor at all times . . . It endows its possessor with the will to destroy his antagonist at any hazard. Inspired by it, he leaps forward to the assault as to the consummation of a high desire. He is like a high-strung hound, straining on the leash and eager to be free when he scents the quarry. He is impatient of the restraint that holds him back from the final charge until the moment has arrived; and when at last the longed-for word is given he bounds towards his enemy with all the eagerness and joy of a thirst-crazed desert wanderer at the sight of cooling water. His one desire is to kill, kill, kill; his last thought is of danger to himself . . .

The Colonel was just warming up.

> [The spirit of the bayonet] is born of pride—pride in the knowledge that on the bayonet in one's hands rests the final outcome of the conflict . . . pride in the realization that all the vast and powerful machinery of modern war has been employed only to give the bayonet fighter his opportunity. *It is born of joy—joy in the conflict for itself alone;* joy in the consciousness that one is about to rid his country of an enemy; *joy in the lust of killing;* and joy in the supreme self sacrifice which pays the ultimate price if need be, for one's country. [Italics added.][21]

A public orgy of this kind would probably be frowned on in the present climate, at least by senior officers concerned with public relations. But it may be that this piece displays the kind of boldness, aggressiveness, and positive thinking the professional soldier believes is necessary to win wars. As the *Officer's Guide* emphasizes, "The 'Army Way' of undertaking a mission is to display enthusiasm, boldness, aggressiveness in getting any job done."[22] It is probable that a contemporary field-grade officer who publicly exhorted the troops to exult in "joy in the lust of killing" would today be put under observation, not in a command position. But in an Army which for an entire year covered up the Nazi-style machine gunning of unarmed civilians in a Vietnamese village,[23] we cannot be sure of that.

Difficult as it is to face, America is beginning to see itself as among the most violent of nations. Presidential commissions have confirmed that violence is, as Rap Brown has claimed, as American as cherry pie:

> In numbers of political assassinations, riots, politically relevant armed group attacks, and demonstrations, the United States since 1948 has been among the half-dozen most tumultuous nations in the world.[24]

The draftee will meet people in the Army who tell him that they had no hesitancy in torturing prisoners in Vietnam and do not regret it now; people who have thrown prisoners out of helicopters as a persuasive means of getting the others to talk; people who have mutilated Vietcong bodies, sometimes out of retaliation or rage at similar treatment to their dead buddies, sometimes for simple amusement; people who would if they could pulverize North Vietnam with nuclear weapons even at this late date, admittedly killing everybody but "saving" them from communism.[25] It even appears that the American Army's intelligence school teaches methods of assassination and torture to be used either by American officers in Vietnam or by mercenaries working closely with Americans.[26]

THE TRAGEDY OF THE
BLACK CAREER SOLDIER

Inside a dusty, peeling Mississippi shack a five-year-old Negro male cries out in bewilderment as his weeping mama thrashes his bottom good. She has just caught her son walking on the outskirts of town, holding hands with a little white girl, and this mama wants her little black boy to grow up to be a big black man.

With this lesson and others like it indelibly imprinted on his psyche there came forth the American Negro of the last generation. He went to war in a segregated regiment to fight against Nazi racism, and when he came home a grateful nation tendered its reward: the same segregated society. So he stayed in an Army that the President soon forced to desegregate, where he had enough to eat and where he had found a world in which (at least in terms of its own definitions) he was allowed to be a man.

When, therefore, as a member of a court-martial panel, the Negro officer shows less sympathy than the white officer for the black defendant, it is not surprising. And when a Negro drill sergeant is rougher on black trainees than on white trainees it makes a kind of sense. In a racist country where the black man has traditionally had to be more competent and work harder than a white man to secure the same rewards, it is no surprise that in the armed services the black man has gotten his gains by being twice as military. To get anywhere in the Army, the black man must be twice the Tom he would be on the outside.

If it is advisable to Cover Your Boss's Ass at all costs, the black man must be especially good at it. If criticism of the system is suspect, he can afford to be only half as critical as the white officer. If discipline is based, as it is, on fear and psychological brutality, he must be twice as terrifying as the white drill sergeant. And since he has succeeded in suppressing his instincts for freedom, he must naturally feel a special obligation to teach the younger black men to live according to the rules of the Army's caste system.

The tragedy, then, is in the depth of the chasm that exists between the black lifer and the black recruit. At a time when the young are discovering pride in their race, the black lifer conspires with the white lifer to crush it.

At a time when black American youth is discovering its manhood, the black lifer clings to the Army's sick cult of pseudo masculinity. In an age when the young black generation is exploding with anger at the shattered hopes and betrayed promises that dramatize the civil rights movement's failures, the black lifer is grateful to the military system for the opportunities only *it* provided when he was young. No wonder the young black soldier calls the black lifer an "Oreo" (a cookie that is black on the outside and white on the inside), and no wonder the career man doesn't like it.[27]

Probably the greatest pressures to eliminate racism in the armed forces could be generated by the black lifer, but they have come instead from civilians and black recruits. The black lifer has been quiet, still as "the black boy in the white mask,"[28] because his Military Mind is just a white man's transplant that we may hope will never sprout a single black root.

IS THE ARMY A "COMMUNIST CONSPIRACY"?

OK, let's be serious. Forgetting for a moment that the Army is not an autonomous power but limited by civilian authority, reflect on the Army way of life. Army lifers are content and comfortable in a world where they are told what kind of work they will do, where they can live and with whom, what they can own and (if living on base) where they must keep it, how many belongings they can take with them when reassigned, what they can say without fear of reprisal, what they can read or hear in a combat zone,[29] what they can wear and when they can wear it, how long they can grow their hair, and when they can carry an umbrella: a world with hundreds, thousands of other personal restrictions, important and minute. Also consider that on a military reservation there is nothing that can remotely be called privacy—at least for the enlisted man.

The incessant bombardment of his senses by mechanical Voices of Authority that the GI teaches himself to endure is not very different from life in some Communist countries:

> Every morning at 5:30 the loudspeakers began broadcasting Mao's speeches on every street corner, and they kept doing it until 11 o'clock at night. The noise was part of our lives. Whenever Chairman Mao issued a Supreme Instruction, someone from our neighborhood committee came and beat on our door, and we all had to go out and celebrate. If it was the middle of the night, you had to roll out of bed, and if you were eating, you had to put down your bowl of rice. Once, I was dead tired from working all day and some Supreme Instruction came at 2 in the morning. I tried to get back to sleep, but they caught me and accused me of being disloyal to Chairman Mao.[30]

Nor is there any genuine privacy of conscience in a system in which an officer's "honor" is defined as unquestioning loyalty to Authority. Thought control in the Army reminds us of *1984,* George Orwell's portrait of a totalitarian world. Even the advanced technique of "doublethink," in which free thought is sacrificed to the needs of the state, is an inherent feature of Army life. Army discipline can, for instance, land you in the stockade for failure to salute an officer. But once you're there you're not *permitted* to salute. On the outside it's a "duty"; on the inside it's a "privilege." On the armed forces radio and television programs in Vietnam, a mercenary is a "civilian irregular defense soldier" and a Vietcong tax collector is a "Vietcong extortionist."[31] Like everything else in the Army, language is manipulated to serve the system.

And that system envelops all of us. Since 1959 the American military establishment's "operation brainwash" has escalated even more rapidly than the defense budget. The 27.7 million dollars spent on public relations during 1969 represented a 1000 per cent increase in spending, while the total defense budget increased 60 per cent during that same period.[32]

None of this has been lost on the American draftee or reluctant enlistee. When interviewed in Vietnam by a sociologist concerned with the American soldier's attitudes toward and understanding of communism, one man replied, "Communism is something like the Army."[33]

It is instructive to point out all these deficiencies to an Army career man. In response he'll cite all the benefits you get from being in military service: free medical care from womb to tomb, guaranteed food, clothing, and shelter, free education, free transportation, guaranteed vacations, free counseling services, no unemployment, a pension, and so forth. You might ask him to explain how the various forms of communism differ from the Army's arrangement, and he might have some trouble doing that.

This kind of dialogue will underscore for you one of the great ironies of your short service: Army career people, who are among the most fanatical anti-Communists in the world, have voluntarily chosen a way of life which is much more communal and infinitely less free than yours was as a civilian. It is sobering to remember that beneath their flag-waving, apple-pieing, and country-tis-of-theeing, these Americans never chose to enjoy the freedoms they are paid to defend. They could just as easily live in a country without free speech or laws against illegal searches, and they don't know why today's draftees can't do it for the length of their tour of duty. They attribute all the political agitation to either subversion or monumental ingratitude. And yet if there should ever be a "Communist takeover" (or a Fascist takeover, for that matter) in the United States, it is likely that they would become the system's bureaucratic functionaries and that you would join the democratic guerrilla resistance.

Notes

1. *The Draft?*, a report prepared for the Peace Education Division of the American Friends Service Committee (New York: Hill & Wang, Inc., 1968), p. 10, citing: T. W. Adorno *et al.*, *The Authoritarian Personality* (New York: Harper & Bros., 1950).

2. Alfred Vagts, *A History of Militarism* (rev. ed.; New York: The Free Press, 1967), p. 13.

3. Co. E, 3rd Bn., 1st Tng. Bde., Ft. Jackson, S.C., Feb. 6, 1967.

4. Co. E, 3rd Bn., 1st Tng. Bde., Ft. Jackson, S.C., Jan. 24, 1967. A new film that emphasizes the soldier's right against self-incrimination has been introduced very recently. It is said to be a vast improvement over the one I saw.

5. Norman Mailer, *The Naked and the Dead* (New York: Rinehart and Company, Inc.; copyright, 1948, by Norman Mailer), pp. 175–76. (Reprinted by permission of the author and the author's agents, Scott Meredith Literary Agency, Inc., 580 Fifth Avenue, New York, N.Y., 10036.)

6. AR 360–81, para. 5(d); AR 600–20, para 34.

7. Samuel H. Hays, Colonel (Director of Military Leadership and Psychology at the U.S. Military Academy), "Military Training in the U.S. Today," *Current History,* July 1968, p. 51.

8. However, see an article by A. Kiev and M. B. Giffen, "Some Observations on Airmen Who Break Down During Basic Training," *American Journal of Psychiatry,* Aug. 1965, vol. 122, no. 2, pp. 184–188, quoted in *The Draft?, op. cit.* (Note 1), pp. 12–13:

> Adaptation to and development of a sense of identification with the military are the goals of basic training. To accomplish this the basic trainee initially experiences an increasing depreciation of self-esteem as a result of his inadequacy to achieve the standards of basic training . . . Earlier training in the postponement of gratification, in the toleration of negative feelings of hostility, fear and anxiety and in the acceptance of authority (arbitrary) is critical for preparing individuals to adjust to the stress of basic training.

9. Hays, *op. cit.* (Note 7), p. 12.

10. "GI Desertions, Pot Use on the Rise," *New York Post,* June 20, 1969, p. 6.

11. Hays, *op. cit.* (Note 7), p. 51: "Military training has long been perceived both here and abroad as an essential means for social and citizenship training."

12. Aldous Huxley, *Brave New World Revisited* (New York: Perennial Library, 1965), pp. 45–46. The author points out the importance of thought control to a totalitarian dictator. He quotes one of Hitler's advisers on the rationale behind the Nazi emphasis on marching (p. 57):

> Marching diverts men's thoughts. Marching kills thought . . . Marching is the indispensable magic stroke performed in order to accustom the people to a mechanical, quasi-ritualistic activity until it becomes second nature.

13. Luther Charles West, *The Command Domination of the Military Judicial Process,* Ph.D. Thesis, George Washington University Law School, p. 364 (1970), portions to be published in the *UCLA Law Review* and a book sponsored by the Clergy and Laymen Concerned about Vietnam.

14. Vagts, *op. cit.* (Note 2), pp. 25 and 27.

15. "GIs Report Threat on Rifle Complaint," *New York Times,* July 26, 1967, p. 15.

16. "GI Fined for Remaining at Home for Two Years," *New York Times,* July 9, 1968, p. 44.

17. *U.S. v. Wolfson,* 36 CMR 722 (1966). This case is also discussed in Chapter Five, The Soldier's First Amendment Rights.

18. Robert Sherrill, "Must the Citizen Give Up His Civil Liberties When He Joins the Army?" *New York Times Magazine,* May 18, 1969, p. 25.

19. Maj. Gen. Russel B. Reynolds, U.S. Army, Retired, *Officer's Guide* (33rd ed.; Harrisburg, Pa.: Stackpole Books, 1968), p. 31.

20. In this respect the Army merely reflects, in gargantuan proportions, a shortcoming of all bureaucracies. As Professor Galbraith has reminded us, "One of the perquisites of great power is that its use need not be defended." John Kenneth Galbraith, "How To Control the Military," *Harper's Magazine,* June 1969, p. 43.

21. Lt. Col. Paul H. McCook, "Spirit of the Bayonet," *Infantry Journal,* June 1917–June 1918, vol. 14, p. 780.

22. Reynolds, *op. cit.* (Note 19), p. 12.

23. "Ex-GI's Letter Accused Officer," *New York Times,*

Nov. 14, 1969, p. 17; "GI Says He Saw Vietnam Massacre," *New York Times,* Nov. 20, 1969, p. 1.

24. H. D. Graham and T. R. Gurr, *Violence in America— Historical and Comparative Perspectives,* a staff report to the National Commission on the Causes and Prevention of Violence, June 1969, vol. II, p. 628.

25. The top sergeant major of an overseas Army command once indicated that in his opinion there was no other reasonable solution. All he needed was a general to give the order and the Button.

26. Judith Coburn and Geoffrey Cowan, "Training for Terror: A Deliberate Policy?," *The Village Voice,* Dec. 11, 1969, p. 5.

27. "Newer Negro Marines Are Looking for Identity with Blackness," *New York Times,* Dec. 21, 1969, p. 44.

28. Steven Morris, "How Blacks Upset the Marine Corps," *Ebony,* December 1969, p. 58.

29. "Military in Vietnam Accused of Censoring GI's News," *New York Times,* Oct. 14, 1969, p. 12. And compare AR 360–65, Establishment and Conduct of Field Press Censorship in Combat Areas (rev. 1 April 1966), with "Radio-TV Censoring Denied by Pentagon," *New York Times,* Jan. 17, 1970.

30. Chinese factory worker, quoted in *Newsweek,* Oct. 13, 1969, p. 50.

31. See *New York Times* articles (Note 29).

32. "Fulbright Exposes the Pentagon's Multi-Million-Dollar Operation Brainwash," *I. F. Stone's Weekly,* Dec. 15, 1969, p. 3. See also "GIs in War To Be Told About 'Silent Majority,' " *New York Times,* Dec. 18, 1969, p. 14.

33. Charles C. Moskos, Jr., "A Sociologist Appraises the GI," *War, an Anthology,* Edward and Elizabeth Huberman, eds. (New York: Washington Square Press, 1969), p. 160.

5

The Soldier's First Amendment Rights: Freedom of Expression

"why talk of beauty what could be more beau-
tiful than these heroic happy dead
who rushed like lions to the roaring slaughter
they did not stop to think they died instead
then shall the voice of liberty be mute?"

He spoke. And drank rapidly a glass of water

—e. e. cummings,
"next to of course god america i love you"

I think, but dare not speak.

—SHAKESPEARE, *Macbeth*

In an article for a military journal on the soldier's right to free speech, a career Army lawyer introduced his topic this way:

On the other hand, what of the uproar generated by the multi-hued domestic bohemian, the pseudo-intellectual, and the dissenter who can be heard today on nearly any issue that divides men's minds? It is in this atmosphere that our youth are reared and from this environment that they enter into the military service. It is, therefore, not unexpected that there is today occasionally heard a dissenting voice raised from military ranks.[1]

This portrait of the critic of our national ills and social illnesses may sound a little odd, even to the unihued, entirely conventional, and truly intellectual reader. But it does accentuate for the conscript an obvious if easily forgettable truth: It is the conviction of our Military Minds—civilian and military—that practically all the multihued antiwar dissent in the United States is a fundamentally foreign blend of many shades of Red.[2] *Accordingly, any meaningful attempt to exercise your First Amendment rights to criticize the war or the military system can be a dangerous activity.*

THE MILITARY MIND
AND DISSENTERS

Like the American Negro, the American GI has traditionally "known his place." A high-minded pat on the head and a friendly "Good boy" were enough to make the day for both of them. And very much like the white civilian of the 1960s, the Army officer reacts with fear and confusion now that his military underlings are demanding their rights.

Dr. Robert Coles, a Harvard psychiatrist, has compared the white man's fear of black power advocacy (the black man's demand to be treated as a man and to control his own destiny) to the parent's anger at a child who begins to talk back and become disobedient.[3] The military's reaction to the GI's refusal to be treated like a retarded person, a child, or a thing is not dissimilar. The parent, the white man, and the career officer or NCO display similar psychological reactions toward their respective rebels: They feel hurt because of the underling's ingratitude "after all we've done for him." The career officer feels, by and large, that the honor of wearing the Uniform has been bestowed and the Blessings of Paternalism have been showered upon the GI. Yet he is still complaining, and this time it's not only about things he's always complained of—bad food, petty harassment, and the like. Now there is something more serious afoot. Today's GI is actually talking and writing about things he's not even supposed to be *thinking* about: the morality and legality of the war, the inhumanity of dropping bombs on peasants who don't like the rulers we are fighting for, and whether or not the only right thing to do is to go to jail. He is attacking the war as only one more atrocity committed by a society born in idealism, dedicated to freedom, scourged by racism, insensitized by greed, and condemned perhaps to death for betraying its highest ideals. Even more significantly, GIs are getting organized!

On a personal level the GI is daily repelled by the Army's caste system, with its elaborate code of behavior that has nothing to do with defending one's country in modern warfare. He is not at all convinced that saluting a cannon in the dusk will do anything to fire his patriotism. Nor can he believe that being forced to listen to tripe printed in the Pentagon on "purity," "loyalty," and "courage" will do anything to uplift his character when the message is brought by a chaplain who worships the commanding general over God. The GI will no longer be persuaded, if he ever was, that discipline will crumble and anarchy reign if he should be afforded the elementary right to take a simple crap in the officers' latrine. But the GI is no longer content to complain solely about these "little" issues. He wants the right to rap on the big ones.

BACKGROUND OF FREE SPEECH IN THE MILITARY

The notion of free speech for American soldiers has a very short history. Some commanding generals are amazed and confounded by directives from above that soldiers have a right to "dissent" and that this right should be respected when military discipline is not directly threatened.[4] Withdrawal of the power to crush criticism from below has been as bewildering and painful a shock to them as basic training is for the draftee. *In fact, some commanders have ignored the soldier's right to dissent, no matter what the directives said.*

The failure of local commanders to recognize GIs' constitutional rights must be a source of considerable frustration to the highest civilian authorities within the defense establishment who have begun to read the prevailing sentiment of the American people in the opinions of federal court judges who, for the first time in many areas, are interfering with military decisions.

Although judges, like other lawyers, are cautious, conservative, and slow at catching up with developments in society in general, they have recently embarked upon new paths of control over military oppression. The highest military authorities are getting the message and are attempting to pass it down the chain of command: "Cool it—until the heat wave is over." They have made no permanent commitment to the proposition that free speech for the conscripted soldier is a good thing for the country. Their reluctant recognition of the rights of GIs is surely the direct result of America's sudden discovery that it's been had, that it's been etherized by ingratiating militarists into accepting a cautiously graduated *coup d'état.*[5] Though at first sealed off to a trickle by the "responsible" media, the truth has finally flowed home in torrents of blood.

In both world wars public expression of disillusionment and dissent was limited, controlled, and prosecuted. The government today is having a more difficult time; in fact what is happening is unique. As was apparent from the reversal of the convictions of Dr. Spock and his fellow defendants for their antiwar "call to resist illegitimate authority," it is not receiving the full "cooperation" of the courts.[6] Further, hundreds of officials, thousands of editorialists, and millions of citizens have publicly uttered the kinds of things for which people went to jail during World War I under the Espionage Act of 1917. This law prohibited not only spying but any attempt to cause "insubordination, disloyalty, mutiny, or refusal of duty in the military or naval forces of the United States."[7] The Act was amended in 1918 to include saying anything to obstruct the sale of United States bonds, except bona fide and loyal advice!

It was also unlawful to promote the cause of America's enemies or to employ "any disloyal, profane, scurrilous, or abusive language, or language intended to cause contempt, scorn, contumely or disrepute regarding the form of government of the United States, the Constitution, the flag, or the uniform of the Army or Navy," or to urge "curtailment of production of any things necessary to the prosecution of the war with intent to hinder its prosecution," or to support or defend anyone who urged or said those things.[8]

Under these statutes and others enacted by the states, thousands of prosecutions were instituted and upheld. Professor Zechariah Chafee, who was one of the most respected authorities on free speech, indicated the extent to which it was punished during World War I:

> It became criminal to advocate heavier taxation instead of bond issues, to state that conscription was unconstitutional though the Supreme Court had not yet held it valid, to say that the sinking of merchant ships was legal, to urge that a referendum should have preceded our declaration of war, to say that war was contrary to the teaching of Christ. Men have been punished for criticizing the Red Cross and the Y.M.C.A., while under the Minnesota Espionage Act it has been held a crime to discourage women from knitting by the remark, "No soldier ever sees those socks."[9]

Essentially for the first time, the Supreme Court of the United States began to explore the meaning of the First Amendment's mandate in the course of reviewing several wartime convictions. *In every case it upheld the conviction.* In 1919, in the course of deciding the now famous case of *Schenck v. United States,*[10] the Supreme Court set forth the "clear and present danger" test of whether certain speech was permissible:

> The question in every case is whether the words used are used in such circumstances and are of such a nature as to create a clear and present danger that they will bring about the substantive evils that Congress has a right to prevent.[11]

In the *Schenck* case the defendant was accused of conspiring with others to obstruct recruiting and to cause insubordination in the armed forces. He had distributed pamphlets to draftees which condemned conscription as the despotism of "cunning politicians and a mercenary capitalist press." The most inflammatory exhortation was, "You must do your share to maintain, support and uphold the rights of the people of this country." Applying the newly formulated test quoted above, the Court found that Congress had the power to prevent the "substantive evil" of insubordination in the armed forces, and that the pamphlet created a clear and present danger of the evil's being brought about. No further proof was necessary, in the Court's opinion.

Even less promising for the civil libertarian was the case of *Debs v. United States.*[12] As leader of the Socialist Party, Eugene Debs made a speech in which he denounced the war and voiced support of those socialists who had been convicted for refusing induction. In the course of the speech he said, "You need to know that you are fit for something better than slavery and cannon fodder."[13] For that one speech Debs was sentenced to ten years in jail.

In such a desert of intolerance it would have been expecting too much to discover free speech rights for those in the military. Unsurprisingly, there were none.

In those days enlisted men were subject to court-martial for uttering contemptuous words against the President, the Congress, and other civilian officials. Today only officers may be punished under the "contemptuous words" article (88), *but the Army has evaded the clear intention of Congress and has used the general article (134) to punish intemperate remarks against congressmen when uttered by enlisted men.* (A detailed discussion of this abuse appears later in this chapter.) As a sampling, here are some of the statements for which soldiers were court-martialed during World War I: "Woodrow Wilson is no more a Christian than you fellows, as no Christian would go to war."[14] "The United States had no business to enter this war."[15] "God damn President Wilson, William Jennings Bryan is smarter than he is; I am as smart as he is."[16]

Although the Supreme Court had begun to take a somewhat more lenient attitude toward unconventional political speech during the early 1940s,[17] soldiers were still court-martialed for offhand remarks during World War II, although the sentences were a little lower. It was a court-martial offense to say that Roosevelt was "the biggest gangster in the world, next to Stalin"[18] and to ask, referring to Roosevelt, "What has that son of a bitch done now?" Army Regulations which suggested that private remarks made in a political discussion should not be punishable were simply ignored.[19] And apart from a case in which the statement "You can take the whole God damned Army and shove it up your fat fanny" was held *not* to be disloyal,[20] a soldier's right to criticize civilian or military authority in strong terms seems to have been up to the discretion of his commander. It cannot be said, then, that any First Amendment right to free speech in the military was recognized prior to the passage of the Uniform Code of Military

Justice in 1951, either by civilian or military courts. Because of a growing appreciation of its importance, it *is* recognized today.

THE IMPORTANCE OF FREE SPEECH

The First Amendment states:

Congress shall make no law . . . abridging the freedom of speech, or of the press; or the right of the people peaceably to assemble, and to petition the Government for a redress of grievances.

In more recent decisions of the Supreme Court, the First Amendment has occupied a "preferred position" over other important protections in the Constitution, and for very good reasons.

Vehicle for Democracy

The First Amendment has been recognized as the very lifeblood of democracy. No matter what else may be wrong with a particular country or society at any particular time in its history, the absence of freedom of speech could well be the worst evil. Only through freedom of speech can the mechanisms for peaceful change, like free elections, be expected to work. There is no sense in voting if free discussion of the issues is prohibited. A society that lacks either free elections or free speech must maintain its stability by resorting to dehumanizing methods of suppression.

Human Dignity

Because the framers of our Constitution believed that human life could never be enriched by suppressive or despotic methods, a commitment was made in the Bill of Rights (the first ten amendments) to protect the dignity of the individual. This justification for maintaining freedom of speech is perhaps the most fundamental, because implied in the right to speak, publish, assemble, and associate freely is the right to *think* freely about things and in ways disapproved of by society and government. The moral responsibility of an individual for his own actions is thus tied in with the freedom of speech.

Skepticism Toward Absolute Truth

There is the additional implication in the First Amendment that absolute truth can never be found. Any system that would substitute a State Authorized Truth for competing truths would be inimical to the values embodied in the Constitution, and one of these values is skepticism toward absolute truths. Therefore, even speech which advocates the abolition of these very protections in the Constitution is constitutionally protected.

At the same time, it has always been recognized by political theorists—except anarchists—that even democratically structured societies have a right and obligation to protect themselves from direct threats to overthrow the existing system and to substitute one that would snuff out the freedoms that do flourish. The dilemma facing courts in free speech cases has been to balance society's need for self-protection against the values embodied in the First Amendment, *without destroying those very values in the process.* Although the First Amendment's prohibition appears to be absolute, the courts have never held that free speech cannot in some circumstances be curtailed. What they have tried to do—with excruciating difficulty—is find a useful test for determining when people can be lawfully punished for saying or publishing something considered by the government to be offensive. The highest Court in the country is still engrossed in this search, which is one reason why the limits of military free speech cannot now be predicted.

MILITARY MURK IN THE MIDDLE
OF A MUDDLE

The other reason why the limits of free speech in the military may not be known for some time is that the appellate military courts have ignored the most significant and liberating decisions of the civilian courts. In the free speech area military courts will bow when they must, and not before. *In the meantime they can be expected to follow the older, more restrictive cases in order to uphold convictions for offensive political speech. The "political" soldier should be aware of this risk.*

An example is the court-martial of Lieutenant Henry Howe, Jr., for conduct unbecoming an officer and for using contemptuous words against former President Lyndon Johnson. It was the first reported prosecution under Article 88 of the UCMJ since it went into effect. In 1965 Howe participated in an antiwar demonstration near Fort Bliss, Texas, in civilian clothing and on his own time, in accordance with Army Regulations. He carried a placard that read:

> LET'S HAVE MORE THAN A CHOICE BETWEEN
> PETTY IGNORANT FASCISTS IN 1968
>
> END JOHNSON'S FASCIST AGGRESSION IN VIETNAM

The defense made the argument, among others, that the article forbidding conduct unbecoming an officer (133) was so vague that it violated Howe's First Amendment right not to be deprived of his liberty without due process of law. (The civilian courts had developed a body of law by which some statutes were declared to be void because of vagueness and failure to give fair notice of what conduct was considered criminal.) The American Civil Liberties Union lawyers who represented Howe also argued that the prosecution violated his First Amendment right to free speech. In affirming the conviction, the Court of Military Appeals held that a clear and present danger of insubordination and impairment of discipline of the troops was created by an officer carrying such an offensive placard:

> That in the present times and circumstances such conduct by an officer constitutes a clear and present danger to discipline within our armed services, under the precedents established by the Supreme Court, seems to require no argument.[21]

By asserting that the central constitutional issue "requires no argument" the Court avoided a difficult discussion of the reason *why* no argument was required. The *Howe* case unfortunately symbolizes the military approach to any statement traditionally punishable during the barbaric "preconstitutional" days of World Wars I and II, when almost any critical remark could be punished as "contemptuous" or "disloyal." Many lawyers have been troubled by the Court of Military Appeals' summary treatment of such a significant constitutional claim. For one thing, it is not entirely clear that the Supreme Court would today adhere to the doctrine laid down in the nineteen-year-old case by which the Court of Military Appeals chose to be guided.[22]

If the "substantive evil" (impairment of discipline) which the military had a right to protect itself against was extremely unlikely to result from Lieutenant Howe's activity, then perhaps the clear and present danger test was not met. To determine whether a clear and present danger exists in civilian cases, the courts have in the past weighed the *gravity of the evil* which Congress sought to legislate against. For instance, if the evil is the violent overthrow of the government, it is considered so grave that, in order to prohibit speech threatening it, no immediate or imminent danger need be shown. The possibility of the speaker's actually fulfilling his evil intention may be very remote, but the speech may be prohibited. However, if the evil is less grave—such as impairment of discipline at Fort Bliss— then there should be a requirement of a higher degree of probability that the evil would actually come to pass before the speech can be prohibited. But the Court did not attempt to rationalize its decision even within this traditional conceptual framework.

More than that was wrong with the court's approach. *It is far from certain that the Supreme Court would today apply any variation of the clear and present danger test.* Some legal writers think it has been effectively discarded in the search for a test that would protect more speech more often. The Court of Military Appeals did not even entertain this possibility. Nor did it consider the possible application of recent Supreme Court free speech decisions to the military, decisions which have clearly extended the civilian's right to dissent beyond what it was during the two world wars. Obviously Howe could not have been prosecuted for sedition or any other offense if he had been a civilian. The Supreme Court has stated that *an attack on a public official must be made with actual malice or reckless disregard for the truth in order for the speaker or publicist to be subject to civil or criminal penalties.*[23] Actual malice doesn't necessarily mean ill will, hatred, or nastiness, but actual lying, which is very hard to prove.[24] The same standard of protection seems to have been extended by the federal courts to statements not only about public officials but about all public figures.[25] The Supreme Court has reminded us in these cases that in the long run only discussion which is permitted to be "uninhibited, robust, and wide open" can enrich the democratic process.

The Court of Military Appeals also failed to weigh the possible impact of the important Supreme Court case of *Bond v. Floyd.*[26] The Georgia House of Representatives had refused to seat Julian Bond, a black legislator, because of his antiwar statements and those of the Student Nonviolent Coordinating Committee, of which he was communications director. Included in the SNCC statement was a condemnation of American policy overseas and a general call to resist the draft:

> Vietnamese are murdered because the United States is pursuing an aggressive policy in violation of international law . . . We are in sympathy with, and support, the men in this country who are unwilling to respond to a military draft which would compel them to contribute their lives to United States aggression in Viet Nam in the name of "freedom" we find so false in this country.[27]

In a unanimous decision the Supreme Court held that the Georgia legislature had deprived Bond of his First Amendment right to free speech. It did not employ the clear and present danger test, or any other test which it had seemed to use in the past. It did say that Bond's statements did *not* amount to "any incitement to violation of law." And in a subsequent decision in 1969 the Court held that even a general incitement to break the law is protected if it amounts to no more than the "mere abstract teaching of the moral propriety or even moral necessity for a resort to force and violence . . ."[28]

Meanwhile, back at the stockade, the military has been putting dissenting soldiers away for criticism of the Vietnam war which was no more provocative than Bond's. *Yet no military court seems prepared to consider whether any genuine "military necessity" exists for jailing such dissenters.* The issues have been made murkier still by the military's careful avoidance of a direct confrontation with federal courts over the propriety of placing dissenting soldiers in pretrial confinement on trumped-up charges. When a federal court indicated it would inquire into the legality of the pretrial confinement of a group of soldiers at Fort Jackson, South Carolina—the Fort Jackson Eight—by the commanding general (on petitions for writs of habeas corpus filed by civilian lawyers in the soldiers' behalf), the general simply let them all out of the stockade and dropped the pending charges, thereby avoiding a federal court precedent against the Army.[29]

It is against this confused, impermanent backdrop that we embark on an investigation of your specific free speech rights.

A MINI-FREEDOM: THE RIGHT TO GRIPE

Like all large organizations, the Army prizes its internal complaint system. Like all bureaucracies, the Army doesn't appreciate any outside scrutiny of its nicely functioning flow of un-information. Griping and filing complaints with the Inspector General have traditionally had a proper slot in the system, since they give the people who run the system the chance to correct the deficiencies they choose to see. And when claims cannot be substantiated, the system can threaten to prosecute for lying to the IG.[30] *Unhappily for the military, Congress has passed two statutes which take the discretion to act on some complaints out of military hands.* One is Article 138 of the UCMJ, which requires that an official report be forwarded to the Secretary of the Army by the commanding general. The other is a federal statute that gives *any* soldier the right to communicate with *any* member of Congress about *any* subject. (In all probability the courts would make an exception for some security matters.) Specific advice on when and how to use these statutes is in Chapter Seven, How To File a Complaint or Bring Charges.

Practically all the decisions by Boards of Review and the Court of Military Appeals in which free speech has been upheld involved an assertion of the right to gripe about traditionally accepted inadequacies. Two recent cases concern complaints about mismanagement and poor living and working conditions in the Army.

The Threat To Pursue One's Rights

An Army enlisted man who had written his congressman about poor food and bad living conditions at Fort

Riley, Kansas, was subsequently told he was going to be punished under Article 15 (see Chapter Nine) for having complained. The soldier then drew up a news release which proclaimed: "FORT RILEY SOLDIER RECEIVED PUNISHMENT FOR EXERCISING RIGHTS."

He showed it to his commanding officer and said that if he got the Article 15 he would release the story to the press. Infuriated by the GI's threatened assertion of his right to protest the deprivation of another right, the officer brought court-martial charges against him for extortion and wrongful communication of a threat! Of course, the soldier was convicted. The Court of Military Appeals, however, reversed the conviction and condemned the practice of punishing soldiers for exercising their right to complain to Congress or to the press. The Court felt that there was no criminal intent in the accused's mind, since:

> The appellant felt he was being persecuted for having exercised a right fully protected by statute, a right deeply rooted in the American concept of representative government.[31]

In a concurring opinion, Judge Ferguson said:

> When, therefore, it appears that an accused has announced he intends to expose to public view the unlawful and unjust measures which have been taken against him in reprisal for his resort to a right expressly granted by statute, his fair statement of the course he intends to pursue . . . does not amount to an unlawful threat or an extortionate communication . . .
>
> It was also open to him respectfully to make known his intention to air his just grievance publicly, without being subjected to adjudication as a blackmailer.[32]

Two things should be remembered from this case: (1) A threat to do something lawful, such as the exercise of a First Amendment right, may not legally be used as the basis for a criminal prosecution or any administrative sanction. (2) A soldier may "respectfully make known his intention to air his just grievance publicly." A *disrespectful* manner of doing this may subject the soldier to prosecution for disrespect toward a superior officer or for insubordination toward an NCO.

Unauthorized Complaining

Dr. Wolfson was an Army doctor who complained a lot about the inadequate medical facilities and supplies furnished him in Vietnam. He decided during an inspection tour conducted by General Westmoreland, commander of all American forces in Vietnam, to complain personally to the general. The doctor thus embarrassed his commander, who brought charges against him for conduct unbecoming an officer and breaking the chain of command. A Board of Review threw out the conviction, stating: "The right to complain is undoubtedly within the protection of the First Amendment of the Constitution of the United States guaranteeing freedom of speech."[33]

Restrictions on Nonpolitical Speech

The only other reported case in which free speech was upheld concerned a sergeant who had been given a blanket order not to talk with any of the men in his company either on or off duty. The officer's reason for giving the order was to keep the sergeant from creating dissension in the company and from interfering with an investigation of sexual misconduct between members of the company and the sergeant's family. Because the order "sought to place the accused in a tight vacuum completely sealed off from all normal communicative exchange with those with whom he would be most likely to converse," *the Court held that the order was overly broad and unenforceable.* However, the Court seemed to rely more on interference with the sergeant's personal rights, and didn't even mention the First Amendment.[34] In no other reported military case has a conviction been reversed on First Amendment grounds.[35]

Now let's see what happens when your "bitching" is cast in political or intemperate rhetoric.

THREATS, INSULTS, AND DISRESPECTFUL REMARKS

The Supreme Court has stated that threats, insults, and "fighting words" that are likely to induce a breach of the peace are *not* constitutionally protected speech. One of the older opinions gives the rationale:

> It has been well observed that such utterances are no essential part of any exposition of ideas, and are of such slight social value as a step to truth that any benefit that may be derived from them is clearly outweighed by the social interest in order and morality.[36]

A more recent and very influential Supreme Court decision, however, heralds the contemporary commitment to freedom of speech and may well have undermined the government's ability to prosecute civilians for "breach of peace" merely for using strong language that offends some listeners. The Court pointed out that our country has:

> a profound national commitment to the principle that debate on public issues should be uninhibited, robust, and wide open, and that it may well include vehement, caustic and sometimes unpleasantly sharp attacks on government and public officials.[37]

Since the Court of Military Appeals has long ago determined that "the protections in the Bill of Rights, except those . . . expressly or by necessary implication inapplicable, are available to members of our Armed Forces,"[38] the soldier should have the right to say or publish everything a civilian may say or publish, unless a genuine military necessity can be conjured up to require a restriction of that right. In practice, there are a great many restrictions on what you may say or do, many of which are required by the nature of any military organization and are constitutionally sanctioned. *Other restrictions are not required by any military necessity but are enforced by the military only because nobody has ever tried very hard to stop them.*

In several of the pending test cases discussed in this chapter, soldiers and sailors are arguing that their imprisonments are illegal because the statements for which they are being punished are protected by the First Amendment. Their cases may be reversed on appeal, but in the meantime they are very much in jail. *Many soldiers protesting the war and publishing underground newspapers are seriously risking prosecution under present circumstances, at least until the federal courts provide some concrete guidelines for determining the outer limits of free speech in the Army.*

No precise guideline can be given on what language will be considered disrespectful. Some epithets, such as "fascist pig" or the more traditional "SOB," if directed at particular NCOs or officers, would clearly give rise to sustainable court-martial convictions. On the other hand, to accuse one's superior officer of being "rigid" or "irrational" or "extremely unfair" or "discriminatory" or even, when appropriate, "racist" should not give rise to prosecution for making disrespectful remarks. It is possible for the soldier to state his opinion or case without resort to the popular but patently offensive names that could get him in trouble.

Friends, Acquaintances, and the "Lower Four" Ranks. If you call your buddy or someone of equal or lower rank an SOB or a fascist pig, you probably cannot legally be court-martialed for that alone, even if he is moved to take a swing at you. Although it is a crime in the UCMJ to use "provoking and reproachful words or gestures" toward *anybody else in the military,* this is a rarely used article. The constitutionality of its application could probably be successfully attacked, especially if the defendant showed that provocative words similar to those he used were generally used by others in the command and that *he alone* had been selected for prosecution. This would raise not only a First Amendment question but also the issue of whether the defendant was being discriminated against for any reason, in deprivation of his right to equal protection of the laws under the Fourteenth Amendment.[39] For instance, NCOs and officers regularly violate this article, especially in training situations, and it is extremely improbable that any prosecutions against them have ever taken place when the lower-ranking GI was on the receiving end of the provoking word or reproachful gesture.

NCOs and Warrant Officers. If you call a sergeant a disrespectful name, it is clear that you can be punished without any abridgment of your constitutional rights. Since this is the most direct kind of affront to military discipline, the courts can correctly find a military necessity for punishing, under Article 91, someone who "treats with contempt or is disrespectful in language or deportment toward a warrant officer, noncommissioned officer or petty officer in the execution of his office." The contempt need not be verbally expressed. For example, spitting at the feet of a sergeant constitutes an offense. But the prosecution must show that two factors existed, according to the *Manual for Courts-Martial:* (1) *The affront must be within the "sight or hearing" of the person offended.* If you say to your friends, "I think Sergeant P. is an SOB," and he later hears about it, he can keep an eye out to get you on something else, but you cannot lawfully be court-martialed for making that statement in those circumstances. (2) *The NCO must be "in the execution of his office."* If you bump into him at the local bar and say, "You know, Sarge, you're a dope," you cannot be court-martialed under Article 91. Of course, the authorities could resort to Article 117, which prohibits provoking words and gestures, but your constitutional arguments would then be available. Actually, what Article 117 seems to do is to extend the disrespect to NCOs article to situations where the NCO is *not* in the execution of his office. *Such a statement to*

an NCO in public might also be "service discrediting"
against Article 134, so it is best to hold your tongue and
avoid direct insults to NCOs and warrant officers.

Officers. Calling an officer superior in rank or command a disrespectful name, in his presence or not, and
whether or not he is in the execution of his office, is an
offense under Article 89, which prohibits disrespect to
officers. It is noteworthy, though, that the *Manual for
Courts-Martial,* paragraph 168, says: "It is considered
objectionable to hold one accountable under this article
for what was said or done by him in a purely private
conversation." If in a small bull session in the barracks
you referred to your commanding officer or commanding general by a disrespectful name, you might be called
to account by Article 134, the general article (whose
constitutionality is questionable). But if the statement
were made at a formation or at a barracks meeting, the
remark would surely be punishable. Remarks about
one's *identifiable* superior officers may be constitutionally curtailed, since there is assumed to be a direct
military necessity for preventing such direct assaults on
respect within a unit. *Even expressions of disdain in less
blunt language could, if uttered in public, be made the
basis for court-martial.* If you stated to your own
company in formation that your commanding officer
was, for instance, on the impoverished side of intelligence, that too might be a sufficient and legal basis for
an Article 89 offense. However, if your CO made the
mistake of asking you what you think of him and your
response was, "I think, sir, you are a dummy," you
might arguably have the defense of "entrapment."[40]
But it would be safer to resist the temptation.

In addition to words, acts expressing "marked disdain, indifference, insolence, impertinence, undue famil-
iarity, or other rudeness in the presence of the superior
officer" can be punished under Article 89. But the
government must prove the accused's intent. A case in
which no criminal intent was found arose when, at a
squadron party at the officers' club, an airman got drunk

and began to threaten an officer who was stripped to the waist and acting as bartender. When the officer refused to acknowledge the airman's claim that his thirst remained unquenched, the EM said, "Hey, Tip, let's fall out on the green." Instead, the airman fell into the stockade (with a little bit of help) and was court-martialed for violating Article 89. The Court of Military Appeals held that the words and behavior of the accused were not disrespectful under the informal conditions in which the remark was made.[41] Commenting on the case, the chief judge of the Court later wrote, "At the core of the decision is a reconciliation of the right of the individual to speak freely within the necessities of military life."[42]

As a final thought, it is possible that the Chairman of the Joint Chiefs of Staff is *not* the "superior commissioned officer" of any serviceman and that any statement made about him cannot be made the basis of an Article 89 charge. Such an argument was made by David Rein, civilian counsel for Seaman Roger Priest, the Navy journalist who, as publisher of *OM—The Serviceman's Newspaper*, was recently given a general court-martial for various free-speech-related offenses.[43] Priest's battle is still raging at the time of this writing, but if the argument is upheld, then no serviceman will be subject to court-martial for disrespectful remarks made about the Joint Chiefs of Staff Chairman. The reason being urged is that the Chairman is, by law, outside the chain of command.

Civilian Officials. Article 88 makes it a court-martial offense *for an officer* to use contemptuous words against the President, the Vice-President, Congress, the Secretary of Defense or Secretary of a military department, the Secretary of the Treasury,[44] or the governor or legislature of any state in which the soldier happens to be at the time the words are said. *No enlisted man may be tried under this article. To evade the mandate of Congress in removing enlisted men from the purview of Article 88, the military has accused servicemen of*

uttering "disloyal statements" against Article 134. If an
enlisted man called the President an abusive name, it
would probably amount to a deprivation of his constitutional free speech rights to punish him for it. It's
essentially a political statement and only in the most
remote way threatens discipline in the Army. *But this
right has not yet been vindicated in the courts, and the
best policy is to avoid using such inflammatory language.*

Since 1951, Article 88 has been invoked only in the
Howe case, where it was perverted from its original
function into an instrument of repression. When first
enacted, its purpose was to minimize the threat of
highly placed military officers undermining civilian authority. Instead it has been added to the arsenal of
articles that can be invoked to enforce internal discipline. In fact, generals do, in more subtle ways and in
more effective language, criticize civilian officials and
policies and get away with it. *Meanwhile, lower-ranking
officers are silenced by Article 88, and lower-ranking
enlisted men are silenced by Article 134.*

One of the charges originally brought against Seaman
Priest was an Article 134 specification of making disloyal statements about a civilian official, South Carolina
Congressman L. Mendel Rivers, a strong supporter of
the military establishment and chairman of the House
Armed Services Committee. Priest reprinted in his
newspaper a parable by the Black Panther leader,
Bobby Seale, in which America's political "stream" was
depicted as being "polluted" by the power structure's
continual urinating and defecating in the stream.
Priest's newspaper printed the parable and added the
following words: "L. MENDEL RIVERS, GET YOUR ASS
OUT OF THAT STREAM. YOU HEAR, BOY?" As disrespectful
and crude as the language may have been, Priest had a
constitutional right to ridicule the Congressman. Recognizing this, the Navy subsequently dropped that particular charge.

It seems fairly clear, then, that *your right to criticize*

civilian officials is as broad as it is for civilians. And in order to convict a civilian of criminal libel, a showing must be made that the statements were made with actual knowledge of their falsehood or a reckless disregard for their truth. Satirical statements like the one above, no matter how tasteless, should be protected. Again, that doesn't mean they will be.

CRITICISM OF AMERICAN SOCIETY, THE MILITARY SYSTEM, AND THE WAR

Unlike direct insults against NCOs and officers, which could be argued to have some bearing on discipline in the ranks, generalized criticism of society and the military system is less of an immediate threat to the Army's legitimate needs and more the kind of speech which is needed for reform. A soldier should be free to make statements at least as critical as what is said in this book, and he should be constitutionally protected, if not necessarily appreciated. But for making relatively mild political statements, soldiers are today suffering vindictively long prison terms. These courageous young soldiers have been convicted for making supposedly "disloyal statements with intent to promote disaffection among the troops," punishable by Article 134, the catch-all that means everything and nothing. *So far, the military appellate courts have rubber-stamped military determinations of what constitutes "disloyalty"—just the opposite of what courts have done in a civilian context.*

To compound the irony, the Army now claims to permit soldiers to criticize American society, the military system, and the war. The latest Department of Defense directive states that "the service member's right of expression should be preserved to the maximum extent possible, consistent with good order and discipline and the national security."[45] An earlier Army letter on dissent said pretty much the same thing, although it revealed a somewhat deeper appreciation of the right to free speech than the subsequent DOD directive:

> *Complaining personnel must not be treated as "enemies of the system."*
> ... However, in applying any such statutes and regulations ... it is important to remember that freedom of expression is a fundamental right secured by the Constitution ... Severe disciplinary action in response to a relatively insignificant manifestation of dissent can have a counter-productive effect on other members of the command, because the reaction appears out of proportion to the threat which the dissent represents. [Italics added.][46]

Unfortunately, unless you have a civilian lawyer ready to file a habeas corpus petition for you in federal court, you have no guarantee that your particular installation commander will follow the spirit of the directive. *It might be a long haul before your rights are vindicated, if ever. Convictions which are in clear contravention of the directive have not been erased or expunged by higher authorities in any of the armed services, and the victims are still in jail.* By making reasoned statements (like those above) for the record, the Army hopes to quiet public criticism of its endemic, everyday lawlessness. At the same time, military commanders pick off GIs who write for the underground newspapers, and get illegal convictions as easily as they were obtained by the commanders of the doctor in Vietnam, or the Fort Riley soldier who wrote his congressman.

This threat has become even more immediate, now that the more moderate voices in the office of the Secretary of the Army have been attacked by influential members of the House Armed Services Committee, one of whom considers the letter quoted above "nauseating." In closed hearings that took place in the summer of 1969, Florida Congressman Charles E. Bennett stated:

> The dissent paper concerns me more than anything
> I have ever read from the Army . . . It is just
> nauseating to me to think that such a publication
> would be possible from the Army.[47]

Secretary of the Army Stanley R. Resor explained
that the guidelines were

> our best judgment as to what the Constitution
> means, applied to these circumstances . . . I think
> it is very important to the Army that we adopt a
> position that appears to the public as a wholly rea-
> sonable position and not an arbitrary one . . .[48]

Congressman Rivers didn't agree with Resor, and
even suggested that a constitutional amendment be
passed, if necessary, to stifle GI dissent. In September
1969, after the hearings, the more restrictive DOD
guidelines were issued. At the moment the Army seems
to be taking the position that its own earlier guidelines
are not in conflict with the DOD's, but in the next few
years this power struggle within the military establishment is fairly certain to involve the civilian population,
who will have to decide how free the American GI
shall be.

For now, the risks can be as high as they were for
two soldiers at Fort Ord, California, who decided that
their country was pursuing a disastrous course in Vietnam. They drew up a statement entitled, "WE PROTEST,"
signed their names—Pfc Daniel Amick and Private Kenneth Stolte, Jr.—had it mimeographed, and distributed
it on post. It said in part:

> We protest the war in Vietnam . . . War cannot
> be rationalized, justified, or condoned. If you want
> to fight for peace, stop killing people . . . You as
> a human being with a free will have the right, if
> not the obligation, to speak out against these
> atrocities . . . If you really want to work for
> peace and freedom, then join us in our opposition.
> We are organizing a union in order to express our
> dissension and grievances.

Nowhere in the statement did they call for "victory" for North Vietnam. Nowhere did they call for soldiers to refuse duty or to disobey any orders. Nowhere did they vilify any individual. In May 1969 they were given a general court-martial on charges of making disloyal statements with design to promote disaffection among the troops and the civilian populace and with conspiring with each other to do so. They did not deny anything, except to state that the statement was not disloyal and did not "disaffect" any troops and that it could not have done so. Amick testified that he had read similar statements by Generals Gavin and Shoup and it was far beyond his imagination that such statements could be considered disloyal to the United States. The military court duly deliberated. Amick and Stolte were duly convicted. They received sentences of dishonorable discharges and four years in prison. The convening authority reduced the sentences to three years. That was military justice.

It's no different in the Marines. Lance Corporal Thomas Met and Private Young Claude Gray took unauthorized absences and made a joint statement in a church near their base. In it they described the brutality of life in the Marines and their complete disillusionment with the Corps. They criticized the military legal system as being oppressive and unfair and they criticized the military caste system. They also attacked the war:

> We can no longer cooperate with these practices or with the war in Vietnam. We are not deserting; we are simply taking a stand to help others like us . . . This is where we stand, and we hope that other men in the Armed Forces who know that we speak the truth will stand with us.

Again, there was no call to disobey any order, to be insubordinate, to mutiny, or to do any illegal act. For this speech they were both convicted under the same article as Amick and Stolte and were sentenced to dishonorable discharges and jail terms. These prosecutions of two thoughtful (now there's the crime!) Marines—like those of Amick and Stolte—were illegal and unconstitutional infringements on their right to free speech.[49] The American Civil Liberties Union is presently representing all four servicemen in their appeals.

One obvious reason why their convictions were illegal is that the statute under which they were charged fails to come up to the standards of "specificity" long required by civilian courts to insure fairness in the application of civilian criminal codes. *The crime of making "disloyal statements with a design to promote disaffection among the troops" is so vague as to mean anything a commander and his hand-selected court want it to mean.* That this violates our most basic notions of fairness and justice has long been recognized by the Supreme Court:

> . . . a statute which either forbids or requires the doing of an act in terms so vague that men of common intelligence must necessarily guess at its meaning and differ as to its application, violates the first essential of due process of law.[50]

The vague crime has been a useful tool for suppression of freedom in many fascistic and communistic regimes. Statements "disloyal" to the United States are as handy a vehicle for suppression of political freedom here as are "anti-Soviet" statements in the Soviet Union. The Military Mind is no invention of the American Army.[51]

The difficulty if not impossibility of defining the scope of "disloyal statements" was urged by the ACLU lawyers who are representing Met and Gray in their appeals:

> It may be disloyal to say, "I hate the United States," but is it a crime under Article 134? Is it a crime to say that life might be better in Russia? In Tahiti?[52]

Other examples of disloyal statements which appear in the *Manual for Courts-Martial* are "praising the enemy" and "attacking the war aims of the United States." These too create constitutionally insurmountable problems.

> Who is the enemy? Is it a country with whom the United States is engaged in a declared war? If not, how is a serviceman to know which countries might be considered "the enemy"? Is North Vietnam the enemy? Russia? Communist China? Cuba? East Germany? Poland? Syria and Egypt? What constitutes praise? Can one applaud the peace efforts of the Soviet Union in the Indian-Pakistan dispute? Can he praise the educational programs of Premier Castro? . . . Can a serviceman be sure what the war aims of the United States are? . . . Do statements calling for a coalition government constitute a crime?[53]

With the administration of the "law" at its present lawless stage, what can the serviceman do? *He can, of course, keep quiet, or keep his speech within the limits of militarily approved dissent, or he can take the risk of a protracted political battle which he may lose.* This "chilling effect" on speech is precisely what the Supreme Court in recent years has sought to discourage. Without hesitation, it has struck down laws of Congress[54] and the states[55] whenever there was the real possibility that First Amendment rights would be "chilled" by vague laws that sought to punish citizens with unpopular views. No court has yet specifically prevented the military from "chilling" antiwar or otherwise officially discredited speech, but the confrontation is imminent.

COUNSELING, ADVOCATING, OR INCITING OTHERS TO BREAK THE LAW

Some lawyers have suggested that all civilian speech should be protected on the theory that the dangers of inflammatory speech are outweighed by the social dangers created by its suppression. In the area of racial violence, a study of ghetto uprisings between 1964 and 1967 reveals that in ninety-three per cent of the cases no black power advocacy was involved.[56] The conclusion was drawn that social conditions are much more likely to produce violence than advocacy. The argument has also been made that speech is merely a verbal *activity* through which an opinion is expressed, and that other actions which *essentially* express opinions—such as the burning of one's draft card—should be protected as "symbolic speech."[57] But the Supreme Court has rejected these arguments,[58] and many other actions expressing opinions that produce no inherent social harm—such as flying the flag upside down—are made criminal by the states.[59] Even outside military society, not all speech or all actions amounting to speech are protected.

It is illegal for either civilians or soldiers to urge soldiers to mutiny, desert, or refuse duty. However, the courts have created safeguards protecting constitutional speech which have never been applied to soldiers. Although the original Espionage Act of 1917 has been given an extended life by Congress,[60] the major statute providing peacetime criminal penalties in this area is the Smith Act of 1940, which makes it illegal

> . . . for any person, with intent to interfere with, impair, or influence the loyalty, morale or discipline of the military or naval forces of the United States—
>
> (1) to advise, counsel, urge or in any manner cause or attempt to cause insubordination, disloyalty, mutiny, or refusal of duty by any member of the military or naval forces of the United States; or
>
> (2) to distribute any written or printed matter which advises, counsels or urges insubordination, disloyalty, mutiny, or refusal of duty by any member of the military or naval forces of the United States.[61]

It is also a crime under the Smith Act to advocate violent overthrow of the government or to attempt to cause insubordination.[62] Other laws make it criminal to help someone evade the draft by illegal means,[63] or to entice desertion or harbor deserters.[64] In interpreting these statutes *the Supreme Court has set up high standards of proof to prevent defendants from being convicted for speech which is unpopular but not prohibited.*[65] It has recently emphasized that even the advocacy of violence is not always prohibited:

> The constitutional guarantees of free speech and free press do not permit a State to forbid or proscribe advocacy of the use of force or of law violation except when such advocacy is directed to inciting or producing imminent lawless action and is likely to incite or produce such action . . . "the mere abstract teaching of the moral propriety or even moral necessity for a resort to force and violence, is not the same as preparing a group for violent action and steeling it to such action."[66]

If in racy radical rhetoric a GI should say or write, "KILL THE PIGS! SMASH THE STATE! POWER TO THE PEOPLE!" in circumstances where it was clear that nobody expected anyone to take any such action, his speech should be protected under present Supreme Court interpretations of the scope of the First Amendment. A soldier may be tried by military court-martial, however, for committing any of the *federal* offenses quoted or cited above, under the "crimes and offenses not capital" clause of the general article (134). *This means that a soldier may be tried by a military court for military crimes and for some federal crimes.*[67] But sometimes the military authorities do not have sufficient proof to sustain a conviction under the federal statutes and the courts' guidelines. *In these cases the military falls back on other sections of the UCMJ, sections which lack the necessary elements for fairness and due process of law.*

In one of the most outrageous military prosecutions
of recent years, two black Marines, Pfc George Daniels
and Lance Corporal William L. Harvey, were court-
martialed and convicted for making "disloyal statements" to other Marines and were given jail sentences
of ten and six years. All they had done was express their
anger at having been ordered to Vietnam to fight in
what they considered a white man's war, suggest
vaguely to their buddies that no black soldier should
fight there, and urge everyone present at the bull session
to "request mast"—demand the right to complain to the
commanding officer directly. Their sentences were later
reduced, but the Board of Review affirmed their convictions and the case is now pending in the Court of Military Appeals. The brief filed by ACLU lawyers raises a
number of serious constitutional questions.

When *civilian* laws have been as vague and amenable
to abuse as Article 134, the courts have often struck
them down.[68] *But vague military statutes have almost
always been upheld.* Besides the "disloyal statements"
specification under the general article, there is the vague
military crime of "soliciting" others to mutiny, desert,
or commit sedition against Article 82 or to commit any
other offense under the general article. One of the
Navy's charges against Seaman Roger Priest was solicitation of desertion. His newspaper said:

> BE FREE GO CANADA—Deserters from the U.S.
> military can still find refuge in Canada contrary to
> recent misleading reports in the Establishment
> press.

Included were names and addresses of various deserters' committees in Canada, together with suggestions
on personal items potential deserters should take along
with them. Priest was also charged with soliciting sedition for printing this:

> WE MUST STOP THE CAPITALIST CORPORATE POWER
> STRUCTURE FROM KILLING US, TAXING US, DIVID-

ING US AND RULING US. WHY DO WE HAVE CAPITAL-
ISM, IMPERIALISM AND AN ECONOMY BASED ON
MILITARISM? THE TIME HAS COME TO FAIL THE
SYSTEM. IT ONLY USES US TO PERPETUATE ITSELF.
TO SERVE THE SYSTEM IS TREASON. SMASH THE
STATE. POWER TO THE PEOPLE . . .[69]

If the civilian decisions mentioned above were fully
applied to the facts in Seaman Priest's case, it is
probable that no valid conviction could be obtained; but
there is absolutely no certainty that the courts will
extend First Amendment protections available to civilian radicals to those in the military. The same criticisms
of capitalism, imperialism, and militarism can be made,
perhaps with more effectiveness, when calls to violent
action are absent. *Unless you are prepared to take substantial risks, neither your verbal statements nor your
publications should counsel or urge illegal action of any
kind.*

The possibility exists that published solicitations to
the civilian public to engage in illegal actions may not
be punishable as a matter of military law. Solicitation
cases in the military have indicated that the accused
solicited *"a certain person or persons."*[70] Another argument made by Priest's civilian counsel, David Rein, was
that the high standard of "specific intent" must be met
by the government in military as well as in civilian free
speech cases. Lastly, the Supreme Court might forbid
military authorities—as it has refused to permit civilian
agencies—to punish speech which merely justifies the
abstract use of violence at an indefinite future time.

To summarize: *Under military law as it is presently
applied, any statement which suggests, implies, or even
vaguely hints that at some indefinite future time soldiers
should refuse duty, go AWOL, commit insubordination,
violence, mutiny, or any other illegal act can be made
the basis for a court-martial. But the constitutionality of
at least some of these proceedings is doubtful.*

SPEECH BEARING ON NATIONAL SECURITY

There used to be regulations which required that everything a soldier wanted to publish be submitted for official censorship and approval.[71] This would include even a letter from a basic trainee to his hometown newspaper in which he complained of bad food for breakfast. If the soldier sent the letter without first obtaining Army approval, he had technically violated a general regulation. Needless to say, the regulation was enforced only when important matters were at stake. In the case of *United States v. Voorhees,*[72] a lieutenant colonel was court-martialed for publishing a book about his experiences as a public information officer during the Korean war. The colonel had submitted it according to regulations but had refused to delete sections that were unflattering to his commander, General Douglas MacArthur. He was then refused permission to publish it but went ahead anyway. Although each judge on the Court of Military Appeals wrote a separate opinion, the thrust of the decision was that *the Army has a right to require submission for censorship only on the ground of national security, not on the ground of enforcing conformity with "policy" or "propriety."* Since very few soldiers—even those with access to security information—ever attempt to complain about classified matters, or to disclose information received by virtue of a security clearance, prior censorship of everything each soldier writes would seem to be ludicrous and unenforceable. The recent directives on dissent literature appear to have recognized this fact.

There are several other security-related restrictions on the soldier's right to free speech, all of which are lawful. The offense of treason, punishable by death, is of course the most serious crime that involves elements of speech. However, treason may be committed only in time of a *declared war* and must involve something more than

merely expression. These are constitutional requirements and cannot be changed by act of Congress or
Army Regulation.[73] Other provisions of the UCMJ
punish speech in specific situations typically involving
combat. It is a crime to attempt to compel one's
commander to surrender to the enemy.[74] It is a crime
to reveal a countersign to someone not entitled to receive it,[75] to aid the enemy as one who "communicates
with or holds any intercourse with the enemy,"[76] or to
give away information obtained as an enemy spy.[77]

In a Korean war case involving an American prisoner
of war, a Board of Review held that the First Amendment was no defense when the defendant had recorded
speeches praising the Communists for their treatment of
POWs, criticized the United States and the United
Nations as aggressors in Korea, and urged the people of
the United States to stop the war.[78] In 1969 the United
States government officially admitted and apologized for
an intrusion upon North Korean sovereignty by an
American naval spy ship, the *Pueblo,* in order to secure
the release of the ship's crew a year after they'd been
captured. The government then immediately repudiated
its admission. To what extent these actions will undermine future prosecutions like the Korean POW case
remains to be seen. But the morality of enforcing two
different standards—one for the government and another for individual servicemen—is certain to be raised
by defense counsel. *May the government knowingly
provide grist for the enemy's propaganda mill and
punish individual servicemen who do the same thing?*
Nobody knows.

TECHNICAL CRIMES AND
FREE SPEECH

To discourage the distribution of GI underground
newspapers on post, the military has authorized its local
commanders (1) to require a submission of each edition
for screening and (2) to delay on-post distribution

while the Army is deciding whether the publication presents a clear and present danger to discipline and morale.[79] If this power is not abused it may be held constitutional. But extensive litigation is almost a certainty, since the very notion of a GI underground press in which official policy is criticized constitutes, to many a Military Mind, a direct threat to discipline and morale.[80] *Anyone caught distributing a publication for which no prior approval has been received is subject to court-martial for violating a local regulation of which he has knowledge.* Whether the mere handing over to a friend of an underground paper received in the mail is "distributing" has yet to be settled by the courts, military or otherwise. But men have been court-martialed for doing just that, and in one case the soldier, a member of the American Servicemen's Union, was turned in by the chaplain![81]

Soldiers have been prosecuted as well for failing to print in their newspapers a disclaimer stating that the views contained therein do not reflect the opinions of the military establishment. (The disclaimer is supposed to prevent other soldiers and the public from thinking the military has approved the contents.) Courts-martial have also been used to punish GI organizers, like Andy Stapp of the American Servicemen's Union, for refusing to open their wall lockers and turn over their literature. Even if the order is designed to accomplish an illegal purpose—such as the confiscation of allegedly "subversive" materials—it is very likely that a military court would find some other military necessity for the order. If the person giving the order really wants to get in, he'll break open the locker anyway. *The best thing to do in this situation is protest strenuously, say that you deem the order to be an infringement on your constitutional rights, state that you will pursue the appropriate legal remedies, and obey the order.* An order to turn over a specific item of literature would probably be valid, if your CO or someone higher in the chain of command had not already examined it. However, you would be entitled to have it returned within a reasonable period of time. *To deprive you of a critical guide, such as this one, to military life and law would violate your constitutional rights. There exists no valid military purpose in prohibiting its possession or use.* If you don't get your property back within two days, go to the Legal Assistance Office. If that doesn't work, follow one or several of the ways of filing complaints presented in detail in Chapter Seven, How To File a Complaint or Bring Charges.

PORNOGRAPHY AND OBSCENITY

Like other traditional institutions in our society, the Army has peculiar feelings about pornography. It thinks, in fact, that pornography is the same thing as obscenity, and that they both have exclusively to do with sexy words and filthy pictures. In actuality, the word "obscenity" covers a much broader range of activities. It has surely escaped the attention of the military establishment that the bulk of "Brand PX" war movies exhibited at Army theaters rate among the most obscene examples of American cinematic offal. Not only has this knowledge evaded them, but no doubt such a statement would be hotly contested, in the first place, by Army film censors and military establishmentarians.

That's just the point. A judgment as to what is obscene must be a personal one, based on everything the individual has been exposed to during his lifetime. To many Americans naked bodies doing natural things together on a movie screen constitute instant obscenity. To other Americans the war flicks that are endemic to Army theaters should be burned at the stake. To them war itself is and always has been the ultimate human obscenity.

Fortunately for those who value freedom of artistic expression as an important aspect of freedom of speech, the Supreme Court has in recent years shared this judgment. Obscenity is still said by the courts to fall outside the shelter of the First Amendment, and people are still prosecuted for trafficking in obscene books, films, photographs, performances, and broadcasts. To determine what is obscene, a jury-boxful of verbal tests has been experimented with by the Supreme Court. But from the pens of the justices there has flowed no magic in obscenity cases, since precision in matters of taste is impossible to achieve. The trend has been to allow increasing amounts of things that once titillated enough people enough to be considered obscene. A classic formula which is still used by the Court is

> whether to the average person, applying contemporary community standards, the dominant theme of the material taken as a whole appeals to prurient interest.[82]

Don't bother to look up the word "prurient." Nobody's sure what it means, least of all the Supreme Court. The important thing to remember is that practically every magazine that is available on the seediest newspaper stands in our seediest towns will, because of the First Amendment and its defenders on the Court, withstand legal attack on its right to exist. *This includes many publications that are savagely disapproved of by the military establishment, but there is nothing they can legally do to prevent you from possessing them. "Contemporary community standards" are national standards, not military standards.* There is no military necessity for applying a different test. No PX has to carry a publication the Army doesn't like, but that is about the only direct control it has. *In fact, specific issues of an approved publication, such as the August, 1968, issue of* Esquire *magazine that carried a feature story about the American Servicemen's Union and its defiance of the brass, may not lawfully be banned by a local commander.* The commanders who tried to ban that issue of *Esquire* ultimately failed.

Another factor the courts take into consideration in determining whether a publication is obscene is whether it has any "redeeming social value." In practice, the Supreme Court has often upheld the right to distribute materials which in the opinion of most people had very little redeeming social value. What a majority of the American people would permit to be circulated in a hypothetical poll is not controlling on the Court. *It is important to remember this when threatened by your CO or sergeant with confiscation of your personal literature merely because it contains some four-letter words.*

Nobody can tell in advance exactly what material will be deemed obscene by a higher court, but remember that, because of the important function it performs in a democracy, *political literature has the highest social value.* It is today a significant political reality that four-letter words have become a vehicle for the expression of some very important ideas about contemporary society. The employment of shocking and outrageous language, like the shedding of conventional forms of dress, carries an urgent message from a substantial minority of Americans—a message of anger and disgust with the carefully measured doses of American arrogance that have been injected into the lifeblood of weaker nations. Accordingly, when a popular magazine prints a story by a political activist which happens to be called something like "Up Against the Wall, Mother-fucker," the writer should be given his forum—not a jail cell. Because these considerations have figured in one way or another in judicial decisions, the Army cannot, on the pretext of "obscenity," lawfully confiscate your essentially political literature.

PROTEST DEMONSTRATIONS

One of the precious rights enumerated in the First Amendment is "the right of the people peaceably to assemble." It has been reaffirmed on many occasions by courts throughout the nation, and includes access to most public places, such as large bus terminals,[83] state capitol grounds,[84] and streets and parks.[85] Governmental authorities may place reasonable restrictions on the time and place of a demonstration, and a permit may lawfully be required. But if an authority exercises its discretion to refuse a permit for a particular time and place on grounds other than community health, safety, and convenience, the action may be an invalid restriction on First Amendment rights. In deciding what is reasonable the courts weigh the degree of public inconvenience that would result from the exercise of the right. In the public bus terminal case, the probability that the terminal would be littered by commuters throwing away the fliers distributed by antiwar protesters was not a sufficient reason for impeding the protesters' access to the terminal. On the other hand, the denial of a permit for a nighttime demonstration in a residential neighborhood would probably be reasonable. In one Supreme Court case, civil rights demonstrators were held *not* to have a right to demonstrate on the grounds of a Florida county jail because jails are built specifically for security purposes.[86] This argument cannot properly be applied to most military installations, since they are "open bases" where the public moves freely.

According to Army Regulations, there remains for the soldier merely the shell of his right peaceably to assemble. The Army's restrictions have not been tested very much in the courts, and it is not known yet whether portions of them violate the Constitution. At any rate, the restrictions in AR 600–20, paragraph 46, are "the law" for now:

> Participation in picket lines or any other public demonstrations . . . is prohibited—
> a. During the hours they [soldiers] are required to be present for duty.
> b. When they are in uniform.
> c. When they are on a military reservation.

    d. When they are in a foreign country.

    e. When their activities constitute a breach of law and order.

    f. When violence is reasonably likely to result.

So far as on-post demonstrations go, the military may not lawfully discriminate between groups because it prefers the views of one over those of another. Just as public transit authorities may not refuse political advertising because they do not like its ideological orientation,[87] the military may not lawfully permit prowar bumper stickers on automobiles and ban antiwar stickers.[88] Surprisingly enough, some installation commanders have permitted a few small antiwar demonstrations to take place on post, but no uniform practice has yet been established.

With respect to the restrictions in the AR, the prohibition against demonstrating during duty hours is legitimate on its face. It can be manipulated, however, to prevent soldiers from participating in civilian-organized protests. In fact it has been so manipulated and the practice may be unconstitutional.[89] Nobody has yet obtained speedy relief in federal court for this kind of abuse, but lawsuits are pending to restrain commanders from persecuting dissenting soldiers.

There is little doubt that the military can forbid a soldier to wear his uniform at antiwar rallies, even though it permits the use of the uniform at prowar rallies or other community activities.[90] Nobody knows whether the ban on participating in demonstrations in foreign countries is constitutional or not. There may be reasons of military necessity—mainly diplomatic considerations—that would require tighter control on protest activities overseas. But which protest activities? During the November 1969 Moratorium for Peace, Air Force Captain David I. Greenly, a doctor, took part in a peace vigil in front of the American Embassy in Ankara, Turkey, where he was stationed. He received an official reprimand for the action, and in a letter of protest Melvin L. Wulf, legal director of the ACLU, wrote the Air Force:

> Finally, not only was the action taken against the Captain a violation of his protected constitutional liberties, but it performed a great disservice to the democratic principles for whose furtherance we profess to maintain our far-flung military establishment. We hardly advance the struggle for "the hearts and minds of men" by punishing the type of gentle protest exhibited here.

The Air Force rejected the ACLU position, and this issue too will in time have to be decided by the courts.

There is really no demonstrable need for the ban on activities which "constitute a breach of law and order," since illegal conduct is punishable anyway, by either civilian or military authorities. Moreover, just because the military gratuitously forbids what is illegal anyway, it does not automatically acquire the power to punish a soldier for *any* breach of law and order, such as an "occupation" of a university's administration offices. It is entirely possible that, under present Supreme Court doctrine requiring that there be a connection between a military interest and the crime, only local authorities would have jurisdiction over GIs for breach of peace or criminal trespass offenses.

Nor is the last restriction in the AR essential or necessarily valid. To the extent that it merely overlaps the "breach of law and order" restriction, it may be. To the extent that it seeks to prevent GIs from exercising their constitutional rights just because violence might result due to factors beyond *their* control and to which they have not personally contributed, it might, in a test case, be held unconstitutional. But there are no reported cases so far.

New variations on old protest techniques are beginning to appear in the armed forces. At a hospital in Pleiku, Vietnam, over two hundred soldiers signed an

open letter to the President protesting American participation in the war and declaring that they would give up
their turkey dinners and fast on Thanksgiving Day
because "we have very little for which to be thankful."
They requested that their Thanksgiving rations "be
redistributed among the poor of the United States and
Vietnam."[91] Other soldiers in different units throughout Vietnam protested by petitioning in the same manner. The military authorities took no legal action against
the protesters, partly because fasting for one day would
not be likely to give rise to a military offense, and partly
because repression of so mild a form of protest could
have created an uproar back home.

"POLITICAL" ACTIVITIES

Federal civil service employees are forbidden by the
Hatch Act,[92] an antiquated hodgepodge of frequently
silly restrictions, to participate in certain political activities. They cannot serve as delegates to party conventions,
or solicit contributions, or distribute campaign literature, or become a candidate for public office, or even
drive someone to the polls.

Political activities of the armed forces are restricted
by a special group of statutes.[93] Army Regulations
which implement these laws are designed to preserve the
political neutrality of the military establishment and to
prevent the use of pressure from above to influence
votes of those below. *AR 600–20, paragraph 42, even
restricts active duty personnel from expressing their
political opinions except "privately and informally."
This is no longer taken seriously and has more or less
been admitted to be unconstitutional by the Department
of Defense directives permitting some dissent activities.*[94] Behind these laws is the fear of a military takeover. But we know that even laws restricting the use of
government-appropriated funds for lobbying have not
prevented military officers from "snowing" Congress
with justifications for ever higher military appropria-

tions; nor have they stopped the high brass from using the massive public information machinery available to them for the purpose of "educating" the public to the military point of view.[95]

Further restrictions in the AR state that service members

> may not participate in political management or be members of political committees, nor may they take an active part in other political activities, including but not limited to political conventions and campaigns, political speeches, the publication of articles, and any other public activity designed to influence the outcome of an election or solicit votes for themselves or others. Members participating in activities not prohibited by this paragraph will not publicize their rank or military affiliation.

When read in conjunction with other ARs, this paragraph should be interpreted to restrict only your right to work for *particular political parties. You may still try to influence votes in an indirect manner by expressing your opinions on the issues of the day in the variety of ways mentioned in this chapter.* Some lawyers have questioned the constitutionality of these restrictions—even as interpreted to limit only political party and election campaign activities. But here as elsewhere in the field of constitutional rights for soldiers, the law is not only unsettled but, like the terrain before an earthquake, it is impermanent and trembling in its depths.

THE RIGHT TO FREE
ASSOCIATION: CIVILIANS

The right to keep the company of anyone you please and to join any organization you like is guaranteed to all citizens by the First Amendment. As a civilian you can hang around with drug addicts, atheists, Ku Klux Klansmen, coffeehouse radicals, Legionnaires, Communists, Daughters of the American Revolution, sex perverts, and consumers of cyclamates. So long as you don't *do* anything illegal you have the right to associate with, talk to, and read the literature of *any* group you want. You can even be a member of an organization that advocates the violent overthrow of the government without being subject to prosecution.

Under recent decisions of the Supreme Court, no governmental body can punish, directly or indirectly, someone who joins an organization with knowledge of its illegal purpose unless the government can show *also* that the individual *actively shares* the illegal purpose. This protection has been provided by the Court because many organizations expressing political attitudes have both legal and illegal purposes. In depriving *active* members of unpopular organizations of certain rights, such as public employment[96] or a passport,[97] the government is put to a very high standard of proof. It must show a "specific intent" to commit the unlawful act with which the individual is charged. To do this, the government must produce evidence that the individual actively supported the illegal purposes of the group. For instance, if someone joins the Communist party primarily because it favors racial equality, he cannot be prosecuted. Racial equality is not an illegal goal in this country. *But if he joins the party with specific intent to advance the violent overthrow of the government in the immediate future, he may be prosecuted for conspiring to overthrow the government.*

To obtain the proof necessary to sustain convictions, state and federal agencies have begun to rely increasingly on the use of confidential informants. They have been used extensively to infiltrate the peace movement, including groups peaceful and not so peaceful. Government agents pose as revolutionaries or hippies and gain the confidence of the groups. By later testifying to conversations with the accused, they supply the proof necessary to prove specific intent to cause violence or riot.[98] This is not the only area where the government uses agents. They are also employed to obtain convictions against nonpolitical defendants, such as homosexuals, narcotics pushers, and people the government may have been trying to "get" on something for a long time.[99] These agents frequently carry hidden microphones—"bugging" devices—which are capable of transmitting and recording a suspect's private conversations for future use at trial. Sometimes an agent is actually an *agent provocateur,* an instigator of crime.

If an investigator seizes evidence from someone's home without a warrant, it will usually be excluded from the trial as evidence obtained in violation of the Fourth Amendment. Yet recorded conversations that take place in a suspect's home between a bugged federal agent and himself (without his knowing the agent's identity) are admissible.[100] Through his "misplaced confidence" the defendant is considered to have "waived" his constitutional rights under the Fourth and Fifth Amendments, even though he is *not aware* of any such waiver. *That such a waiver clearly stifles the exercise of the First Amendment right of free association as well has disturbed constitutional lawyers, and they have argued that the use of informant testimony be greatly curtailed by the courts.*[101] *But court approval of secret agents is still the law of the land.*

Also extremely threatening to the freedom of Americans is the use of telephone wiretapping by the FBI.[102] The use of recording devices to "seize" information that is transmitted by telephone is prohibited in most cases unless the agents have obtained a warrant from a judge,[103] but in Congress' latest attempt to beef up the FBI's investigative arsenal, it may well have passed an unconstitutional law.[104] Many practices which seem odious to Americans, such as eavesdropping on attorney-client communications, may increase with each cry for more "law 'n order." In the case of Roger Priest, who lived off post, even the Washington, D.C., garbage men cooperated with the FBI by permitting agents to go through his discarded mail to get evidence for court-martial proceedings. GIs involved in political activities should take note.

FREE ASSOCIATION IN THE MILITARY

It is far from clear that as a soldier you can belong to any domestic organization you choose. Joining a foreign political group while stationed overseas is especially dangerous, since if it is found that the group is an arm of the "enemy" you could conceivably be court-martialed. In one case an American soldier was tried for "affiliating" with the East German Communists, and the conviction was upheld even though the government did not seek to prove the accused's "specific intent" to advance the Communists' objectives.[105] (A civilian could not constitutionally be convicted of such an offense.)

If the military should attempt to prosecute GIs for associating with or becoming members of the more militant domestic political groups, there is no doubt that it will try to justify more stringent rules than govern civilians. The military may attempt to show that mere knowing membership in an organization like the Communist party—without any further proof of the individual's acceptance of its illegal goals—will be sufficient to sustain a conviction for service-discrediting behavior under the general article. Whether the courts will find a sufficient "military necessity" to justify a departure from the protections afforded civilians cannot be predicted. As with the other unsettled issues, the answer will depend significantly on who is appointed to the Supreme Court.

The military does appear to have recognized your right to belong to such groups as the American Servicemen's Union, the GIs United Against the War, and others, since no attempt was made in the DOD directive on dissent to outlaw them. Rather, it simply informs commanders that they are not authorized to engage in collective bargaining with servicemen's unions. *The military can restrict your activities for these organizations during your duty hours, but it may not lawfully discriminate against you in any way for your membership in them. Do not forget, however, that the military can and does use the same techniques as civilian law enforcement agencies—including undercover agents.* In the case of the Fort Jackson Eight, when some soldiers in GIs United were restricted or confined to the stockade for antiwar dissent (until their civilian lawyer secured their release through habeas corpus proceedings), it was disclosed that one of those originally arrested, "a certain Private Huffman," had been acting as a government informant.[106] He apparently heard no illegal speech and saw no illegal actions during the spontaneous antiwar "speak-out" for which the GIs were jailed, since, rather than justify their pretrial confinement, the commanding general dropped all charges against all remaining defendants and instituted administrative discharge proceedings instead.

Because the radically oriented coffeehouses have been so successful in communicating with GIs, the military is seeking ways to combat them. In Columbia, South Carolina (the home state of Mendel Rivers), the country's first GI coffeehouse, the UFO, was closed down by local authorities as a "public nuisance." In Tacoma, Washington, an Armed Forces Disciplinary Control Board, consisting of officers of all services, has attempted to place the Shelter Half coffeehouse "off limits" for being "a source of dissident counseling and literature and other activities inimical to good morale, order and discipline within the Armed Services."[107] The "other activities" were never enumerated, and "dissident counseling and literature" is, even under the Army's own regulations, perfectly legal. After a show of massive support for the coffeehouse, the hearing at which a final decision was to be made was suddenly postponed. At the time of this writing it appears that the coffeehouse battle too will soon move to the courts.

THE SECURITY PROGRAM

If the Army could *prove* that the Fort Jackson Eight or any other group of soldiers actively adhered to an organization's illegal doctrines—such as the violent overthrow of the government—*it could resort to court-martial for conspiracy, which is punishable by Article 81.* The Army could prove no such thing against the Fort Jackson soldiers, but it did have an alternative. It got rid of some of them as "security risks," with discharges less than honorable. *There seems to be little question that the Army can discharge from active duty anyone it wants to for almost any reason, but it may be prevented by the Constitution from labeling someone a security risk and from giving him an undesirable discharge unless it meets the same standards of proof that are required for a criminal conspiracy prosecution.* This issue too will probably be litigated. The Army used to discharge people with less than honorable discharges for *preservice* political activities, but the Supreme Court put a stop to that.[108]

Ostensibly in pursuit of its obligation to prevent enemy agents from sabotaging our defense system, the military has established a security program. It involves a security check on every soldier who is inducted into the armed services, and background investigations for all officers and higher NCOs, who must have SECRET security clearances. The basic security check, the National Agency Check (NAC), involves an examination of the files of government agencies like the FBI to see if the GI has a criminal record. If the record is clean, the soldier can be granted a SECRET or CONFIDENTIAL clearance.

No soldier has a right to receive a security clearance. But before one can be taken away, if the soldier objects, he is entitled to a hearing on the reasons for which it is being removed.[109] To some soldiers the removal of a clearance might mean removal from a more interesting job and placement in one infinitely less interesting—like infantry.

One simple way the military has of determining whether someone is a subversive is to ask him if he belongs to an organization appearing on what is known as the "Attorney General's list." Used by all government agencies, it lists several hundred right-wing and left-wing organizations, many of them out of existence for years, that are deemed to be devoted to illegal ends. Some years ago the National Lawyers Guild, a group of lawyers active in civil liberties cases, brought suit against the federal government to prevent it from placing their organization on the list without a hearing. The government finally gave up its attempt to list them, and since that time very few organizations have been added to the list. It is more or less irrelevant today, except that if you refused to answer the questions attached to the list when you were inducted into the Army a special investigation of your record was undoubtedly begun.

Of course, you were not automatically discharged. In very extreme situations the Army discharges organizers within its ranks, but it has generally withheld the "privilege" because it knows that, if discharges become that easy, every draftee will be a potential organizer.

To sum up, you may associate with anyone you want and join almost any organization you wish with safety, and you cannot properly be subjected to court-martial. However, there is no way to prevent the government from trailing you just for the purpose of "getting" you on other charges. The offense of marijuana possession is typical. Most offenders get off with a light sentence. But one active and vocal antiwar publicist, Bruce Peterson, the founder of Fatigue Press, an antiwar GI newspaper at Fort Hood, Texas, received an eight-year prison sentence for possession of an amount of marijuana so minuscule that, after laboratory testing, there wasn't any left to introduce as evidence at the trial!

The United States learned in the aftermath of Mc-

Carthyism that crazed preoccupation with internal subversion had destroyed thousands of innocent people. No
single institution in society—the Supreme Court included—can prevent this from happening again. We
must insure that the people we trust with power will
listen to the Court's warning:

> Yet this concept of "national defense" cannot be
> deemed an end in itself, justifying any exercise of
> legislative power designed to promote such a goal.
> *Implicit in the term "national defense" is the no-*
> *tion of defending those values and ideals which*
> *set this Nation apart . . .* It would indeed be
> ironic if in the name of national defense, we
> would sanction the subversion of one of those
> liberties—the freedom of association—which
> makes the defense of the Nation worthwhile.
> [Italics added.][110]

Notes

1. Maj. Jerome X. Lewis, II, "Freedom of Speech—An Examination of the Civilian Test for Constitutionality and Its
Application to the Military," 41 *Military Law Review* 55
(1968), p. 56.
2. The military view of the "multi-hued domestic bohemian"
as an active or unwitting Communist agent is not without
congressional support. Commenting on a national antiwar
protest in 1967, the House Un-American Activities Committee ["Communist Origin and Manipulation of Vietnam
Week," H.R. Doc. No. 186, 90th Congress, 1st Session, 2
(1967)] stated:

> The real objective of Vietnam Week is not the expres-
> sion of honest dissent to promote the best interest of
> the American people and their Government but to do
> injury and damage to the United States and to give aid
> and comfort to its enemies.

3. His conclusions and their relation to the law of black
power advocacy are discussed by Paul Harris in: "Black

Power Advocacy: Criminal Anarchy or Free Speech," 56 *California Law Review* 702 (1968), p. 742, Note 222.

4. Department of Defense Directive No. 1325.6 (12 Sept. 1969), Guidelines for Handling Dissent and Protest Activities Among Members of the Armed Forces. Also, Letter from Army Maj. Gen. Kenneth G. Wickham, Adjutant General, to all commands, "Guidance on Dissent" (27 May 1969).

5. See Juan Bosch, *Pentagonism—A Substitute for Imperialism* (New York: Grove Press, 1968), especially pp. 92 and 125.

6. *U.S. v. Spock,* 2 SSLR 3090 (1969).

7. Act of June 15, 1917, sec. 3, 40 Stat. 219, as amended, 18 USC 2388(a) (1964).

8. Z. Chafee, *Free Speech in the United States* (1941), pp. 40–41, summarized by Thomas I. Emerson, "Freedom of Expression in Wartime," 116 *University of Pennsylvania Law Review* 975 (1968), p. 981.

9. *Ibid.,* pp. 51–52, quoted in Emerson, p. 981.

10. 249 U.S. 47 (1919).

11. *Ibid.,* p. 52.

12. 249 U.S. 211 (1919).

13. *Ibid.,* p. 214.

14. John G. Kester, "Soldiers Who Insult the President: An Uneasy Look at Article 88 of the UCMJ," 81 *Harvard Law Review* 1697 (1969), p. 1725, Note 176.

15. *Ibid.,* p. 1727, Note 188.

16. *Ibid.,* p. 1738.

17. The Supreme Court struck down a state sedition law in *Taylor v. Mississippi,* 319 U.S. 583 (1943).

18. Kester, *op. cit.* (Note 14), pp. 1730–31, Note 214.

19. *Ibid.,* p. 1738.

20. *U.S. v. Peterson,* 39 B.R. 291 (1944). This should still be good law.

21. *U.S. v. Howe,* 17 USCMA 165, 37 CMR 429 (1967), p. 438. The ACLU has filed suit in Howe's behalf to have his conviction declared unconstitutional and to have him restored to duty and awarded back pay and allowances. *Howe v. Clifford* (Dist. Ct. D.C.), Civ. Action 622–68.

22. *Dennis v. U.S.,* 341 U.S. 494 (1951). Justice Douglas concurring in *Brandenburg v. Ohio,* 395 U.S. 444, 23 L.Ed.2d 430, 438 (1969):

> When one reads the opinions closely and sees when and how the "clear and present danger" test has been applied, great misgivings are aroused. First, the threats were often loud but always puny and made serious

only by judges so wedded to the status quo that critical analysis made them nervous. Second, the test was so twisted and perverted in *Dennis* as to make the trial of those teachers of Marxism an all-out political trial which was part and parcel of the Cold War that has eroded substantial parts of the First Amendment.

23. *New York Times v. Sullivan,* 376 U.S. 254 (1964).

24. *St. Amant v. Thompson,* 390 U.S. 727 (1968).

25. *Curtis Publishing Company v. Butts,* 388 U.S. 130 (1967).

26. 385 U.S. 116 (1966).

27. *Ibid.,* pp. 119–120.

28. *Brandenburg v. Ohio,* 395 U.S. 444, 454 (1969).

29. *Chapparro v. Resor,* 412 F.2d 443 (4th Cir., 1969).

30. AR 20–1 (rev. 22 Aug. 1968), Inspections and Investigations, para. 3–4, "Liability of Individuals Knowingly Making Untruthful Statements."

31. *U.S. v. Schmidt,* 16 USCMA 57, 36 CMR 213, 216 (1966).

32. *Ibid.,* p. 217.

33. *U.S. v. Wolfson,* 36 CMR 722 (1966).

34. *U.S. v. Wysong,* 9 USCMA 249, 26 CMR 29 (1958).

35. In *U.S. v. Voorhees,* 4 USCMA 509, 16 CMR 83 (1954), the Court of Military Appeals did reverse an Army lieutenant colonel's convictions for failing to comply with censorship regulations, but it did not clearly hold that requiring submission of writings for censorship on the grounds of policy and propriety was prohibited by the First Amendment. See also *U.S. v. Bayes,* 22 CMR 487 (1956), petition denied, 23 CMR 421 (1957).

36. *Chaplinsky v. New Hampshire,* 315 U.S. 568, 572 (1942).

37. *New York Times v. Sullivan* (Note 23), p. 270.

38. *U.S. v. Jacoby,* 11 USCMA 428, 29 CMR 244, 246–47 (1960).

39. The equal protection clause of the Fourteenth Amendment, which applies to the states only, has been read into the due process clause of the Fifth Amendment, which applies to the federal government. *Bolling v. Sharpe,* 347 U.S. 497 (1954).

40. *MCM,* para. 216(e).

41. *U.S. v. Noriega,* 7 USCMA 196, 21 CMR 322 (1956).

42. Robert E. Quinn, "The U.S. Court of Military Appeals and Individual Rights in the Military," 34 *Notre Dame Lawyer* 491 (1960), p. 499.

43. *U.S. v. Priest.* Memorandum of Law submitted by Lt. Gary Brown and civilian attorney David Rein.

44. The Coast Guard used to come under the jurisdiction of the Treasury Department but is now under the Department of Transportation.

45. DOD Directive No. 1325.6 (12 Sept. 1969).

46. Wickham, "Guidance on Dissent" (Note 4).

47. "Crackdown on G.I. Dissent," *Washington Post,* Nov. 10, 1969, p. A–6.

48. *Ibid.*

49. They had pleaded guilty to the offenses of unauthorized absence and possession of marijuana, which, for nondissenters, are usually referred to special courts-martial.

50. *Connally v. General Construction Company,* 269 U.S. 385, 391 (1926).

51. See discussion of similarities between Communist regimes and internal military government in Chapter Four, The Military Mind.

52. Brief of accused Thomas Met, submitted to Board of Review by the ACLU, and prepared by Melvin L. Wulf, Brook Hart, Edward F. Sherman, and Lt. Scott M. Feldman, July 1, 1969. On file at ACLU, New York.

53. *Ibid.*

54. *U.S. v. Robel,* 389 U.S. 258 (1967).

55. *Dombrowski v. Pfister,* 380 U.S. 479 (1965).

56. Harris, *op. cit.* (Note 3), p. 726, ftn. 150.

57. Emerson, *op. cit.* (Note 8).

58. *U.S. v. O'Brien,* 391 U.S. 367, 88 S.Ct. 1673 (1968).

59. "Long Island Veteran Is Fined $50 for an Upside Down Flag," *New York Times,* Oct. 16, 1969, p. 21.

60. It was extended in 1953 until "six months after the termination of the national emergency proclaimed by the president on December 16, 1950 . . ." 18 USC, sec. 2391. The "national emergency" has never been terminated.

61. Act of June 28, 1940, ch. 439, sec. 1-a, 54 Stat. 670, as amended 18 USC 2387 (1964).

62. 18 USC, sec. 2388.

63. 50 USC, sec. 462.

64. 18 USC, sec. 1381.

65. *Yates v. U.S.,* 354 U.S. 298 (1957); see also *U.S. v. Spock,* 2 SSLR 3090 (1969).

66. *Brandenburg v. Ohio,* 395 U.S. 444, 447–48 (1969), reaffirming *Noto v. U.S.,* 367 U.S. 290 (1961).

67. The question is open whether, under the doctrine of

O'Callahan v. Parker, 37 U.S.L.W. 4465, 2 SSLR 3068 (1969), crimes under the Smith Act can still be tried in military courts.

68. *Keyishian v. Board of Regents,* 385 U.S. 589 (1967); *Ware v. Nichols,* 266 F. Supp. 564 (N.D. Miss. 1967); *Carmichael v. Allen,* 267 F. Supp. 985 (N.D. Ga. 1967).

69. The solicitation of sedition and solicitation of desertion charges were dismissed by the military judge, after which the convening authority restored the charges. Priest's defense counsel believed this was illegal and asked the Court of Military Appeals by extraordinary writ to forbid the convening authority from interfering with the proceedings. The Court ruled in favor of the government, and at the time of this writing the case is proceeding with the charges reinstated.

70. *U.S. v. Morris,* 31 CMR 535 (1955); *U.S. v. Jackson,* 8 CMR 215 (1952).

71. DOD Directive 5230.9. Also AR 360–5, before its revision.

72. 4 USCMA 509, 16 CMR 83 (1954).

73. U.S. Constitution, Article III, sec. 3; *Cramer v. U.S.,* 325 U.S. 1 (1945).

74. Article 100.

75. Article 101.

76. Article 104.

77. Article 106.

78. Article 104; *U.S. v. Bayes* (Note 35).

79. AR 210–10, para. 5–5 (rev. 10 March 1969); DOD Directive No. 1325.6 (12 Sept. 1969), sec. III-A-1.

80. In an application made in federal court to enjoin the commander of Fort Bragg, North Carolina, from interfering with the distribution of *Bragg Briefs,* a newspaper published by GIs, Leonard Boudin, the soldiers' civilian counsel, argued that prior restraints on the press imposed under the authority of the post regulation (and by implication AR 210–10) violate the First Amendment of the Constitution. *Yahr v. Resor,* No. 876 Civ. (E.D. N.C., 10 Nov. 1969). The district court ruled in favor of the Army, and the decision has been appealed.

81. Summary court-martial of Pvt. Hal Muscat, Fort Dix, New Jersey, 1969.

82. *Jacobellis v. Ohio,* 378 U.S. 184 (1964), in which the Court restated the test of *U.S. v. Roth,* 354 U.S. 476 (1957). To be suppressed as "obscene," material must (1) "appeal to the prurient interest," (2) be "patently offensive," and (3)

be "utterly without redeeming social value." *Memoirs v. Massachusetts,* 383 U.S. 413, 418 (1966).

83. *Wolin v. Port of New York Authority,* 392 F.2d 83 (2nd Cir., 1968).

84. *Edwards v. South Carolina,* 372 U.S. 229 (1963).

85. *Hague v. C.I.O.,* 307 U.S. 496 (1939).

86. *U.S. v. Adderley,* 385 U.S. 39 (1966).

87. *Wirta v. Alameda-Contra Costa Transit District,* 64 Cal. Repr. 430, 434, P.2d 982 (1967); *Kissinger v. NYC Transit Authority,* 274 F. Supp. 438 (S.D. N.Y. 1967).

88. The Army has recently reversed its policy, and political bumper stickers are now permissible. *New York Times,* March 23, 1969, p. 10.

89. "Army Memorandum Tells of Plans To Prevent Five Soldiers from Participating in Antiwar Protest," *New York Times,* Nov. 7, 1969, p. 13. Many units in the Washington, D.C., area rescinded all passes for the weekend of the historic Moratorium peace march in November 1969. Other units throughout the country found a sudden need for inspections and drill. "G.I. Communication," *New Republic,* Dec. 6, 1969, pp. 29–30.

90. One court has so held, *Locks v. Laird,* 300 F. Supp. 915 (N.D. Calif. 1969).

91. "Protesting GIs in Pleiku To Fast on Thanksgiving," *New York Times,* Nov. 24, 1969, p. 3.

92. 5 USC, sec. 1501.

93. 5 USC, sec. 2195; 18 USC, sec. 602, 607. However, it has been suggested that the Hatch Act may apply to officers.

94. See Note 4.

95. "Major Held Five Years by Vietcong Wages Fight on Doves in Congress," *Washington Post,* Nov. 23, 1969, p. A-1.

96. *Elfbrandt v. Russell,* 384 U.S. 11 (1966).

97. *Aptheker v. Secretary of State,* 378 U.S. 500 (1964).

98. This method was used at the notorious Chicago conspiracy trial of several militant leaders of the 1968 Chicago Democratic Convention protests.

99. *Hoffa v. U.S.,* 385 U.S. 293 (1966). For a recitation of the dangers to democracy inherent in the use of government informers, see Justice Douglas' dissenting opinion in *Osborn v. U.S.,* 87 S.Ct. 439 (1966).

100. *Ibid.*

101. Note: "Police Undercover Agents: New Threat to First Amendment Freedoms," 37 *George Washington Law Review* 634 (1969). The author suggests that there should be a "presumption of illegality" whenever police agents are

used against political groups (p. 663). The ACLU has filed suit to enjoin the Attorney General of New Jersey from maintaining a reporting system whereby intelligence would be collected on gatherings of groups the police consider suspicious and disseminated to police authorities throughout the state. The court held that the system violated the First Amendment and directed that it be discontinued. The Attorney General and various law enforcement agencies have appealed. *Anderson v. Sills* (Super. Ct., Hudson County, Docket No. C-215-68), decided July 30, 1969.

102. The FBI lied to a congressional committee when it claimed to have wiretapped only in national security cases. Herman Schwartz, "The Legitimation of Electronic Eavesdropping: The Politics of 'Law and Order.'" 67 *Michigan Law Review* 455 (1969), p. 478, Note 109.

103. *Katz v. U.S.,* 389 U.S. 347 (1967).

104. Title III of the Omnibus Crime Control and Safe Streets Act of 1968 authorizes electronic eavesdropping by federal and state officials with very loose controls.

105. *U.S. v. Blevens,* 5 USCMA 480, 18 CMR 104 (1955).

106. See Note 29 and related discussion in text.

107. Letter from naval Captain H. W. Stauffacher, of HQ, 13th Naval Dist., Seattle, Washington, to the Shelter Half Coffeehouse, Dec. 11, 1969, *New York Times,* Jan. 22, 1970, p. 13.

108. *Harmon v. Brucker,* 355 U.S. 579 (1958).

109. AR 604–10 (rev. 15 Nov. 1969).

110. *U.S. v. Robel,* 389 U.S. 258, 264 (1967).

6

The Soldier's Right to Privacy

Persons in the military service are neither puppets nor
robots. They are not subject to the willy-nilly push or
pull of a capricious superior, at least so far as trial
and punishment by court-martial is concerned. In that
area they are human beings endowed with legal and
personal rights which are not subject to military order.
—CHIEF JUDGE ROBERT E. QUINN,
U.S. v. Milldebrandt

With the blessings of technology have come its night-
mares—electronic snoopers, government data banks,
and the fear that privacy and freedom may be in peril of
extinction.[1] A heightened urgency has been brought to
the ceaseless search for what it is that the "right of privacy" is supposed to protect. The right itself has been
called "the right to be let alone,"[2] the power to control
information about ourselves,[3] and the right of "inviolate
personality."[4] Whatever expression is used, we recognize
that human dignity is in some way enhanced by placing
limits on the kinds of things governmental authority or

the public may find out about us, or do to us, or require us to do or refrain from doing. When there are no limits, we know from experience what happens:

> The man who is compelled to live every minute of his life among others and whose every need, thought, desire, fancy or gratification is subject to public scrutiny, has been deprived of his individuality and human dignity. Such an individual merges with the mass . . . he is not an individual.[5]

If the recruit gets the intended message in basic training, he forgets about being an individual and never entertains a thought about privacy in the Army. As the Military Mind views it, the greatest obstacle to turning a civilian into a soldier is his self-image as an individual with human dignity. *Therefore, specialized training in the skills of warfare is only secondary to the role of indoctrination, which is designed to convince the trainee not only that he is no better than, but that he is no different from, the fellow next to him, and that neither of them is worth very much in the first place.*[6] Fortunately, the brainwashing of the basic trainee gradually wears off as he moves into a less totalitarian environment, that of a permanent duty station.

The high-ranking NCO and especially the officer are allowed much more privacy than the low-ranking enlisted man. No officer need live with his fellows in a single bay with up to sixty bunks and no partitions. No officer is required to use bathroom facilities where all sinks, showers, toilets, and urinals are in a single, stinking, open space, but this is the typical enlisted barracks arrangement. This physical arrangement is maintained not only for reasons of economy but because of the psychological "benefits" that accrue to the Army. It's easier to get you to behave like an animal if you are treated like one.

NCOs usually have their own rooms to which they can retreat. An officer can almost always elect to live off post, while a low-ranking enlisted man may do so only if he is married and obtains permission. By labeling the commonly accepted accouterments of dignity as "privileges," the Army attempts to reserve the right of privacy, by and large, for the enjoyment of the officer class. *But the private, too, has some privacy rights, and more than the morsels the Army has thrown him.* This chapter attempts to spell out how far the Army can go in limiting the privacy you enjoyed as a civilian.

This is one area of the law where there could be a rapid expansion of soldiers' rights by the courts as a result of the Supreme Court's *O'Callahan v. Parker*[7] decision, which held that the military has no jurisdiction to court-martial a soldier when his actions are not service-connected. Because henceforth the Army will have to show a military necessity for regulating his off-post, off-duty activities, a soldier's privacy will be intertwined with court determinations of "service connectedness."

Even after this legal development has run its course, however, there will still be very few areas that the Army cannot regulate in some way. Since the military commander is responsible for the welfare, safety, morale, and effectiveness of all his men, the courts grant him great leeway in the kinds and extent of activities he can control by resort to court-martial. Those regulations which the courts do on rare occasions nullify are invalidated because they are too broad and unlimited and encroach a little *too* much on a soldier's private affairs. It is nearly impossible to delineate with precision the outer legal limits of a given regulation before a judge decides what it means in the context of a case. *The soldier is cautioned to go through complaint procedures rather than take the risk of disobeying a regulation that appears to encroach too much on his privacy.* Remember also that in overseas commands a commander has broader powers than he exercises stateside because of the additional factors of diplomatic obligations, special security problems, and the absence of civilian laws.

PRIVACY IN MILITARY QUARTERS

In law, at least, the soldier enjoys a right to privacy in his own quarters. This right was firmly established by the Court of Military Appeals in the celebrated case of *United States v. Adams,*[8] in which the accused was convicted of murder for shooting an armed intruder in his own tent. The Court decided the accused was under no obligation to retreat (as he would have been had he been outdoors or in someone else's home) so long as he was in his own tent. The accused, like a civilian in his own home, had a right to stand his ground and use what force was necessary to protect himself:

> Generally a military person's place of abode is the place where he bunks and keeps his few private possessions. His home is the particular place where the necessities of the service force him to live. This may be a barracks, a tent, or even a foxhole. Whatever the name of his place of abode, it is his sanctuary against unlawful intrusion; it is his "castle." And he is there entitled to stand his ground against a trespasser to the same extent that a civilian is entitled to stand fast in his civilian home.[9]

In an article discussing the case Chief Judge Quinn later elaborated on this right:

> Implicit in *Adams* is the fact that subordination of rank or grade does not qualify the right of privacy. The recruit has the same right to be free from illegal intrusion as does the general or flag officer.[10]

But the Court indicated in another case that a disturbance will justify the intrusion into a man's quarters on a military installation, although "the military authorities do not have the right to enter at will and without legitimate reason."[11]

Of course, announcing the law and living it are two

different things, and most soldiers will be surprised to discover that the noble rules set forth by the Court actually apply to them. Nobody seems to have told the Army's company commanders and sergeants that conscripts have privacy rights. And despite the urgings of lonely voices in the military wilderness that it may be time to educate the leaders on the limits of their powers,[12] the Army has not yet undertaken the extraordinary effort that will be needed to change the habits of centuries.

ROUTINE AND "SHAKEDOWN" INSPECTIONS

Next to the induction physical, the greatest imposition on a soldier's privacy is the foot- and wall-locker inspection. The military has always claimed the necessity for this inspection, and the courts have never seriously questioned its legality.

Unless he finds an off-post refuge, all a soldier's personal belongings are kept in his foot and wall lockers, which are in the barracks next to his bunk. At any moment, and totally on the whim of his commanding officer (or first sergeant), it can be determined that the time is "ripe" for a "routine" inspection of the men and their foot and wall lockers.

Periodic inspections are conducted to insure that barracks are clean, field gear in usable condition, and uniforms neat. When these inspections are unannounced, they are called "shakedown" inspections. They are authorized on the ground of military necessity, as one of the methods by which a commander keeps proper control of his company's discipline, safety, and morale. Knives and "dirty books" are frequently confiscated, in the interest of making the company a more "effective" unit. Of course it is deadly to morale when a company is harassed by repeated and unnecessary inspections. The remedy in such situations is for the men in the company to file complaints (see Chapter Seven, How To File a Complaint or Bring Charges). *Refusal of an order on the ground of "too much harassment" would be self-defeating.*

"INSPECTION" AS EXCUSE FOR ILLEGAL SEARCH

Only legal inspections have been discussed so far, but there are illegal ones too. *It is illegal for a commanding officer to conduct a search, under the guise of a "shake-down" inspection, for the fruits of a crime he merely suspects has been committed.*[13] He must have information amounting to "probable cause" for believing that a crime has been committed *in a particular location.*

In both civil and military courts this "probable cause" requirement has been used to declare police searches illegal when the authorities merely suspect someone of having committed a crime. The founders of our country valued privacy so much that when they wrote the Constitution they made it illegal for police authorities to search people, homes, or belongings unless they first had some pretty good information that the person to be searched had committed some crime. Since it was impossible to determine for all time how much and what kind of information the police must possess before they could lawfully search a citizen's home, they used the phrase "probable cause" and counted on the courts to come up with reasonable interpretations in particular cases. Thus the Fourth Amendment reads:

> The right of the people to be secure in their persons, houses, papers, and effects, against unreasonable searches and seizures, shall not be violated, and no Warrants shall issue, but upon probable cause, supported by Oath or affirmation, and particularly describing the place to be searched, and the persons or things to be seized.

Civilian Searches

In civilian life, an arrest without a warrant may be made when a police officer has probable cause to believe either (1) that a felony has been or is being committed, whether or not in his presence, or (2) that a misdemeanor is being or has just been committed in his presence. Pursuant to such an arrest an incidental search may be made, and anything found within the proper scope of the search may be used against the person arrested. However, the courts are very strict in requiring police officers to obtain search warrants, especially for searching premises, and will exclude from a trial any evidence seized as the result of a warrantless search when it is clear the police had time to obtain it. To obtain a warrant, the law enforcement officer must go before a judge or magistrate and present some proof, by affidavit or otherwise, that criminal evidence may be found at a particular place. The judge then inquires into the facts and circumstances and makes a determination as to whether "probable cause" exists. If a warrant is issued, it will specify the persons to be searched (if known), the specific location, the time the search is to take place, and the items which are to be sought. *The searching officer is given no discretion in determining whether the search should include other persons or additional locations.* If the police officers go beyond the legal limits of their warrant, anything seized as a result will be excluded from evidence against the accused in any trial. This is the Supreme Court's established device for punishing police violations of citizens' Fourth Amendment rights; it is, in fact, the only effective control on illegal searches and seizures.[14]

Military Searches

The same rules are supposed to be applied to the military. The difference in procedure is that the commanding officer of the area or persons to be searched performs the equivalent function of the magistrate: He is supposed to determine whether the information presented to him indicates there is probable cause for believing a crime has been committed. If he does so determine, he issues his order to search the particular location involved. *The CO's order is the military "warrant," and it is supposed to be as limited in time and scope as a civilian warrant. However, since this power is combined with the CO's responsibility to conduct "routine" inspections to maintain the safety and efficiency of his unit, the soldier has a great deal more difficulty in proving that a particular shakedown inspection is not routine but a device for searching the soldier's locker on mere suspicion.* Since the police and other public authorities do not have the power to conduct "routine inspections" of our homes, they must *always* establish probable cause to conduct a legal search.[15] The military commander can, for the reason just stated, easily get around this. Yet the courts and military writers continue to assert that Fourth Amendment protections are enjoyed by soldiers.

Even when there is probable cause to believe a crime has been committed, the civilian warrant must be specific: it must have "particularity." When it is too vague or too broad, a court can later exclude evidence obtained under its authority. *This is another problem that the military commander, as a matter of actual practice, doesn't have to worry about. Since he acts as the "military magistrate," he alone decides whether there is "probable cause" to search any area or man under his command.* Only if a case later gets as far as a court-martial, and the defense counsel tries to exclude any evidence obtained from the commanding officer's search, does the soldier's Fourth Amendment right to privacy receive any vindication. If an illegal search fails to turn up incriminating information against a soldier forced to undergo it, and he subsequently complains to the Inspector General that his constitutional rights have been violated, he is likely to be asked, "So what do you want me to do about it?" Therefore, in this area, forget about the IG.

It is very likely that the military method of "issuing a warrant" for a search, that is, allowing the commanding officer to decide whether there is "probable cause," fails to meet constitutional standards. The Court of Military Appeals is uneasy about this strong possibility and it has "encouraged" commanders to require written applications for military warrants[16] so that later the courts will at least be able to determine realistically the legality of search orders in the way that civilian courts determine the legality of search warrants, by looking to the recitation of facts in the application for the warrant. But only a few scattered commands have followed the suggestion. Perhaps the military will begin to use the new military judges as magistrates for the purpose of issuing military warrants before the federal courts invalidate the present scheme.[17]

But for now, at least, the "routine" shakedown inspection is still legal, and the search ordered by a commanding officer upon probable cause is still legal. Since the facts that constitute probable cause depend on very subtle legal distinctions that are ultimately drawn only months or years later by appellate courts, the soldier cannot safely disobey an order to submit to a search under any circumstances. He cannot know whether the order will be held legal or illegal. It is best to state one's objections, obey the order, and pursue one's complaint procedures or legal remedies later.

The military has still another way to circumvent legally the constitutional protection of privacy enjoyed by civilians. Assume a commander has suspicions that an individual has contraband in his lockers. If he can manage to get the soldier into the stockade on another charge, the soldier's lockers may be "inventoried" by his sergeant as part of his "routine military duties," and anything found inside can legally be used against the soldier to establish new court-martial charges. So long as the motive for a search is to perform routine military duties, the search will be upheld by the courts.[18] This could not be done lawfully in civilian life. If a suspect is in jail awaiting trial, the police have no authority to go into his home, "inventory" his belongings, and use anything they find as a basis for additional criminal prosecutions.

LEGAL SEARCHES THAT BECOME ILLEGAL

It is possible for an otherwise legal search to become tainted with illegality when its scope is unreasonably broad. This is true both for searches incident to valid arrests and for those conducted on probable cause and the commanding officer's order. An arrest at one point, for example, does not justify a search by military police of an automobile located elsewhere, unless there is a logical connection between the two locations.[19] In contrast, the Court of Military Appeals has upheld the legality of a search ranging over an area of twenty-five buildings when a dead body and a trail of blood had been found.[20] Thus what would be outrageous in some circumstances would be reasonable in others.

It is when the military appellate courts feel that the authorities were looking for evidence of additional, unknown crimes that they will strike down such forays as illegal. *For a search to be reasonable it must "not go beyond the limits imposed by the necessities of the case."*[21] It appears, however, that the proper scope of a search incident to a lawful arrest has been greatly restricted by a recent Supreme Court opinion which said that a search without a warrant may not extend beyond the individual's person or the area within which he might be hiding a weapon or evidence.[22] The precise impact of this decision on military law is not yet clear, but ultimately it will mean that some searches formerly considered legal will become illegal.[23]

WHO MAY CONDUCT A SEARCH

Only the commanding officer or someone acting with his authorization can legally conduct a search in the company area. Criminal Investigation Detachment investigators and military police are not permitted, without the suspect's consent, to search and seize items from his foot and wall lockers. They are supposed to present enough evidence to the CO for him to make an independent determination that probable cause exists that a particular person has committed a crime and that evidence of the crime may be found in the suspect's locker.[24] When the CID conduct the search on their own without consulting the commanding officer, it should be held illegal.[25] Although the *Manual for Courts-Martial* seems to require that a specific authorization to act in his behalf be made before someone else in the command may substitute for the CO, the courts have upheld a number of searches conducted by first sergeants or by people acting on the sergeants' orders alone.[26] This has usually been done when the missing item was easily hidden or disposable—money, for example—and the CO was nowhere around. And although a search by an executive officer of a company was recently declared illegal because the CO was nearby and could easily have been consulted, *the soldier still cannot safely refuse an order to open his foot or wall locker when the order is from his first sergeant or executive officer.*[27]

SEARCHES BY "CONSENT"

Although it is wise to comply with a direct order to open one's foot and wall lockers, or to empty one's pockets, the soldier need never give his "consent." On or off post, if the soldier's consent is asked for and refused there is always the possibility that those who want to make the search know they have no legal grounds for it and will simply go away. This has happened many times when military authorities have sought to search a soldier's apartment off post. *When you share a room, apartment, or house with someone else, be sure to remind this person of your rights.* If a roommate, wife, or girl friend consents to a search that turns up incriminating evidence against the soldier with whom the premises are shared, the evidence cannot usually be suppressed thereafter, even if the soldier clearly would have refused to allow the search.[28] On the other hand, if the authorities use the implied threat of force,[29] or obtain consent by trickery,[30] the search is illegal. Also, evidence obtained as a result of unauthorized physical penetration of the suspect's premises will be excluded. In a landmark Supreme Court case[31] federal agents had driven a "spike mike" through the wall of the accused's premises, where it made contact with a heating duct and picked up incriminating conversations. The Court held that the conversations were overheard through an illegal search and seizure in violation of the Fourth Amendment. But in a case where the listening device did not actually penetrate the suspect's wall, the Court held there was no illegal search.[32] And when a suspect engages in conversations with an undercover agent who is wearing a hidden transmitting device, any evidence obtained can be used against the accused.[33]

"SEARCHES" THAT VIOLATE THE FIFTH AMENDMENT OR ARTICLE 31

Sometimes what appears to be a search is really an "interrogation" and the "things" produced are actually "nonverbal statements." When a suspect is asked to identify his property, and the identification is to be used as evidence against him in a criminal case, it is required that his Article 31 rights first be read to him. This is because even the act of identification—pointing to a duffel bag, for instance—is a statement. It is the equivalent of saying, "That's mine." The accused is entitled to be *reminded* that the government must prove its case against him without his help.[34]

An interesting twist on this rule occurs when an MP who *already suspects* that a soldier is not carrying a pass requests to see the pass without first reading Article 31 aloud. In such a situation the evidence resulting from the request has been obtained illegally and may be excluded.[35] However, when the MP requests to see the pass merely as a *matter of routine,* the statement, "I don't have it," may be admitted into evidence against the accused. Similarly, when an MP, on mere suspicion that a soldier is a "head," orders him to turn over marijuana cigarettes, without first reading the Article 31 warning, any marijuana obtained is excluded from evidence in the subsequent trial.[36] As soon as someone becomes a suspect, the police, military or civilian, must inform him of his rights.

SEARCHES IN FOREIGN LANDS

The rules that govern searches and seizures in the United States also govern them on American installations overseas. But when the search takes place off the installation, problems arise. A search that is legal under the law of the host country, and is conducted by its investigating authority in pursuit of the country's *independent interest,* will not be held illegal by an American court—even if the search did not come up to American "probable cause" standards.[37] Evidence obtained thereby, which would have been excludable had it been obtained by American investigators in the same manner, will be admitted into American courts-martial proceedings. However, when the use of foreign investigators is *merely a subterfuge for a strictly American investigation,* the requirements of the Fourth Amendment will be adhered to and illegally obtained evidence will be excluded. This happened in a Vietnam wartime case, when American probable cause requirements were applied to a search in Saigon of a serviceman who was suspected of illegal currency transactions.[38] However, some doubt has recently been cast by a member of the Court of Military Appeals on whether the Fourth Amendment's strict requirements will be imposed on military authorities in areas, such as Vietnam, which the Court considers to be "strife-torn."[39] For the most part, though, the protections of the Constitution follow the serviceman throughout the world.[40]

SEARCH AND SEIZURE OF MAIL

Army Regulations presently forbid any interference with or inspection of a soldier's mail, except in very unusual circumstances:

> a. The secrecy of the mail is inviolable. Military postal personnel will not break, nor permit to be broken, the seal of any First Class mail while in military channels . . . Articles mailed at the Second, Third or Fourth Class rate and believed to contain matter prohibited in the mail by provision of law, treaty or the Postal Manual, may be opened by a postal officer in the presence of a witness . . .[41]
>
> Except pursuant to a legal search or seizure (see paragraph 152, MCM, 1969), mail in the custody of unit mail clerks will not be subject to delay, interception, seizure, rifling, or confiscation by any person . . .[42]

When incoming mail reaches the mail room of the unit it is addressed to, the mail is no longer considered to be in a military postal channel. At this point the mail may be seized, but under the same rules and constitutional standards by which all other searches and seizures are governed. If the authorities do not have sufficient information (amounting to "probable cause") about the commission of a crime to justify the seizure of mail, they do not have the authority to confiscate or withhold it or delay its delivery to the addressee.[43] Violations of these sections by military postal clerks or officials are punishable as federal crimes.

There are also very strict rules governing the dissemination of information on addresses, postmarks, and records of registered, insured, and certified mail, as well as the use of "mail covers." A mail cover involves, at the very least, keeping a record of all the return addresses on an individual's mail. A soldier engaged in political organizing activities within the Army should be aware of its existence. The AR authorizes the use of mail covers only to (1) protect the national security, (2) locate a fugitive, and (3) obtain information regarding the commission or "attempted commission" of crime,[44] which is to say that if any appropriate authority should decide that a mail cover on anyone involved in organizing activity would be desirable, he would not have much trouble getting the necessary approval.

LEAVES, PASSES, DRINKING, AND DRUGS

As soon as he is immersed in training, the draftee gets the impression that his body belongs to the commanding officer twenty-four hours a day and that freedom to leave post for an hour, a weekend, or a month is solely within the discretion of the commander. It's not so, in spite of the AR's pronouncement that "passes are not a right to which one is specifically entitled, but a privilege to be awarded to deserving individuals by their commanders."[45] It is true that the privilege of a pass may be withheld in special circumstances, such as in overseas commands and during basic training, but in a company composed of permanent-party soldiers where the routine issuance of passes is customary, if the CO or first sergeant should arbitrarily deprive a group or an individual of a pass on a repeated basis, there might well be grounds for an Article 138 complaint. (This is the kind of abuse that the IG staff pooh-poohs, because they think the CO has a right to be arbitrary in this area.

However, trying the IG first always helps to bolster an Article 138 complaint.)

Even overseas, in restricting a serviceman to post the commander must be fulfilling a justifiable military purpose or the order is illegal. This became clear when an airman in Japan was accused of breach of restriction under Article 134 for disobeying his CO's order to stay within the limits of Misawa Air Base. The airman had previously been convicted of wrongful appropriation of property. When he completed his sentence to confinement, his CO ordered him to stay out of town because he "would continue to do the same thing if the opportunity presented itself." The Court held that since the airman was not under charges, investigation, or suspicion of a crime, and since the restriction was not for purposes of training, discipline, or medical quarantine, the order was an illegal restraint on his liberty.[46]

While on leave, a soldier has almost an absolute right to freedom of action in the United States, within the limits of civilian laws. It appears, however, that the Army can require a soldier who wants to travel to a foreign country to obtain official approval first or be subject to court-martial.[47]

In a case involving the *nature* of leave status, a commanding officer permitted an enlisted man to take a thirty-day leave to straighten out his financial situation. However, the EM was ordered to telephone and report his financial status once a week. In declaring the order invalid because it was too much of an infringement on the soldier's liberty and inconsistent with his leave status, the Court of Military Appeals said: "When an enlisted man is granted leave, he ought not to be subject to orders requiring him to perform strictly military duties unless their performance is compelled by the presence of some grave danger or unusual circumstance."[48]

A soldier has no vested right to receive leave when he wants it, but if the reasons for wanting it at a particular time are especially pressing and the CO denies the leave arbitrarily, there may be grounds for a complaint. Many soldiers who have complained to higher authority in such circumstances have achieved rapid results. A statute requires that the soldier be given thirty days' leave a year, and if the individual has not taken leave for over a year his case is even stronger.[49]

Soldiers' activities while on pass and leave are likely to give the military a chronic legal headache for a long time to come. A constitutional shroud (the military would say "cloud") has been placed over a great many off-post activities by the Supreme Court's *O'Callahan*[50] decision (see Chapter Nine, The Framework of Military Law), which has invited civilian courts to entertain writs of habeas corpus when a soldier is punished for a purely personal, off-post act. For example, it was assumed in the past that the military could prohibit GIs from hitchhiking, making television appearances, going to whorehouses, traveling beyond a specified distance while on pass, or venturing downtown without collars on their shirts. Since civilian standards now govern conduct off post (in the United States) which is not "service-connected," there are many things a soldier may do that he could not do before *O'Callahan*. The problem is that no one knows what conduct is prohibitable and what is not, although decisions should be made against the background of older cases. In one, a soldier was ordered "not to drink liquor" without any limitations on the order. The Court simply said, "In the absence of circumstances tending to show its connection to military needs, an order which is so broadly restrictive of a private right of an individual is arbitrary and illegal."[51]

Imagine what would happen if a state court should decide that the prohibition of mere possession of marijuana is an unconstitutional invasion of the right to privacy—a position that has recently been urged in legal journals.[52] Since a state court once decided that a city could not forbid cigarette smoking within the city limits,[53] the argument might also be made that the use of marijuana falls within the citizen's constitutional right "to be let alone." Could a commander of an installation in a state which accepts that argument order his men not to smoke pot while off duty and off post and enforce the order by resort to court-martial? For now, at least, he has the power, and it may seem far-fetched to suggest that some day he may lose it.[54] But in a recent California case a state court held that the First and Fourth Amendments prohibited the government from forbidding the use of peyote, a drug, as a sacramental substance by Indians.[55] Since freedom of religion is involved, it is doubtful that a military commander could forbid the use of peyote under such circumstances by a member of his command. Is the use of one drug any more or less "service-connected" than the use of another? In the next few years the courts should have a field day with this and other novel legal questions. Meanwhile, the Army's drug regulations are enforceable by court-martial.

MARRIAGE AND SEXUAL RELATIONSHIPS

The Army recognizes that it has no right to prohibit a soldier outright from marrying while he is in the United States. Not too many years ago Army Regulations required that lower-rank EMs receive their regimental commanders' permission to marry, but the only punishment for noncompliance was denial of the right to reenlist.[56] Overseas marriages can legally be regulated, and by implication prohibited, so long as restrictions are not overbroad and are related to a military interest. In a well-known case in the Philippines, the Court of Military Appeals invalidated a Navy Regulation governing marriage to foreign nationals in an overseas area on the ground that it was an unreasonable restraint on the freedom of the individual. The regulation required, among other things, that the seaman "cool off" for six months after filing his application for permission before the Navy would even begin to act on it. (This was the Navy's simple way of deterring impetuous marriages.) The Court opted for romance:

> For a commander to restrain the free exercise of a serviceman's right to marry the woman of his choice for six months just so he might better reconsider his decision is an arbitrary and unreasonable interference with the latter's personal affairs which cannot be supported by the claim that the morale, discipline, and good order of the command require control of overseas marriages.[57]

The Court soon made it clear, though, that not all regulations of overseas marriages were illegal, upholding a conviction where essentially the same regulation had been redrafted to eliminate the waiting period.[58] And despite the uplifting language of the first decision, Army Regulations still require a soldier in a Far Eastern command to go through a tremendously burdensome and expensive procedure before he can get his application approved.[59] In—Korea and Vietnam the process usually takes the better part of a year, and frequently longer. The prospective bride must be checked by her own government as well as by the American military authorities for associations that might make her a security risk. She must be checked not only for the presence of communicable diseases but for good moral character; a clean record must be obtained from the local police authorities. The applicant has to show that he can afford to transport his bride back to the States. The paper work, required interviews, and background investigations take many months and are defended on the ground that approval of the marriage would be senseless if the woman should be found. ineligible to immigrate to the United States.

The question of whether the act of marrying in defiance of an official denial of permission could legally be made a court-martial offense has never been squarely faced by the courts. All the cases so far have involved failure to abide by the various procedures for *delay*. It is possible that although overseas marriages may legally be delayed, they may not constitutionally be prohibited outright.

But for other sexual relationships it's a different story. The Army has long assumed the power to create standards of morality and to provide sanctions for their breach. On post, the commander's powers are probably still intact, although constitutional developments in civilian society are bound to affect military practice as well. One recent example is the case of *Griswold v. Connecticut*,[60] in which the Supreme Court invalidated a Connecticut law prohibiting the distribution of birth-control information and contraceptive devices. The Court felt that the practice of birth control was too personal a matter to be prohibited by the state. The Court posed and answered in the negative its own question: "Would we allow police to search the sacred precincts of marital bedrooms for telltale signs of the use of contraceptives?" It is fairly certain that no "military necessity" could be dredged up to justify prohibition of birth control on military bases, although there is one report of its having been attempted.[61]

With respect to off-post sexual activities, the *O'Callahan* case promises to reverberate for years ahead. There are a great many activities which are crimes under the laws of most states: adultery, incest, fornication, indecent exposure, pandering, sodomy, and various "lewd and lascivious" acts. Since the *O'Callahan* decision removed the crime of rape from any perceivable military interest, it is likely that the military lacks jurisdiction to try any of the above offenses as well, unless of course they take place on military property (or perhaps while the perpetrator is in military uniform).[62] There are also a great many activities which are *not* criminal, at least not yet, under civilian laws, but which the military can clearly prohibit on military installations. These too should be beyond the reach of military jurisdiction when engaged in off post. (For this purpose, there should be no difference between pass status and leave status.) For instance, participation in an organization which practices sexual freedom in the form of public or private orgies or partner-swapping arrangements would no doubt be labeled "conduct of a nature to bring discredit upon the armed forces" and punishable under Article 134. But the *O'Callahan* decision raises jurisdictional doubts.

Prohibition by the state of Tennessee of the establishment of a nudist colony was recently struck down by a federal court as an unconstitutional restriction on the nudists' right of privacy.[63] Prior to *O'Callahan,* a commander might have had the power to prohibit his troops from spending their leave in a nudist colony, but it seems fairly clear that he cannot do so now. (But lawyers might consider whether the "shedding of the military uniform" under circumstances that would discredit the armed forces could be made a court-martial offense.)

Consensual homosexual acts between adults are crimes under military as well as civilian law. Preinduction homosexual conduct, together with present tendencies, may be enough to secure an administrative discharge for the enlisted man or a resignation "for the good of the service" for the officer. Postinduction homosexual activity is a court-martial offense, but in the absence of force, fraud, violence, or acts involving children it is usually dealt with administratively. The military has always regarded homosexual activity as a grave threat to discipline, morale, and military security. The security aspect may result in the military courts' retaining jurisdiction over some categories of off-post homosexual acts, since an argument could be made that the military has a strong interest in weeding out homosexuals no matter where the acts take place.[64]

With the exception of homosexual activities, the Army has in practice taken a live-and-let-live attitude toward the sex lives of all its members. Most criminal actions have probably been instituted when a commander was trying to "get" a man on any charge and finally found the opportunity, or when behavior was considered outrageously indiscreet.[65] An unusual example of such activity came to light in a recent case that involved two servicemen allegedly enticed into being prostitutes for women. Although the Court of Military Appeals reversed their convictions because there was no proof that the men had been paid, it did hold that despite "public indifference to the individual doing his 'own thing,' . . . commercialized copulation" would continue to be dealt with in the military as conduct to the prejudice of good order and discipline in the armed forces.[66] The only other area in which the Army's regulatory arsenal has been used to control sexual activity is that of venereal disease; here the military has given up on morality and turned to medicine.

The power to place houses of prostitution off limits is not used very often any more. Instead, the military takes an active interest, especially in South Korea and South Vietnam, in host government inspection and registration procedures for prostitutes. In recent years American puritanism has given grudging way to realism, and the offense of "contracting a loathsome disease" has been eliminated from the military's criminal codes. The purpose of this remarkable exercise in military largesse was to encourage soldiers to go to the clinics for treatment of VD instead of trying to hide it. Although this wasn't done with the Vietnam war in mind, one may now speculate whether the war effort might have been mired in a bog of courts-martial if getting gonorrhea were still a crime.

There is still a great deal of harassment for soldiers who seek treatment for VD, and it does deter some for long periods of time. In Korea it is not unusual for a dispensary sergeant to announce to the morning turnout at sick call, "All right! All you guys with the drip to my left—all the rest to my right!" After public exposure comes an occasional denunciation by orderlies and doctors. Back at the company, it is the practice to put the soldier on restriction to prevent him from "catching a relapse." This kind of invasion of privacy, probably legal, would never be inflicted on an officer, though his strain of VD be just as virulent. In Korea, and no doubt elsewhere, the secretiveness of the officer would vary in direct proportion with his rank. The "cooperative" doctor who would dispense the necessary drugs to a colonel or a general while keeping evidence of the grievous misdeed out of his medical records would collect more gratitude during one tour of duty than his imagination could conjure ways to use.

There are occasions when the families of military men fare no better than the GIs themselves. Wives of career officers and enlisted men are made constantly aware of their obligation to digest, reflect, and exude the social mores of their respective castes. That is, if they want their husbands to be promoted. Complaining about the indignities, inconveniences, and absence of privacy to which they are sometimes subjected by the Army will not help their husbands, and might even be considered a trifle unpatriotic. One wonders how the sergeant's wife felt when, in order to be treated at the Fort Jackson hospital, she had to undress not only in front of the doctor but with several Special Forces aidmen-in-training looking on.[67] When she complained, the hospital's response was that if she wanted to use the Army's facilities she had to take them as she found them.

FAMILY LIFE AND OBLIGATIONS

When a disgruntled wife writes a letter to her enlisted husband's commanding officer and enumerates his defaults and derelictions, the Army considers this to be *its* business:

> The Army will not be a haven or refuge for personnel who disregard or evade their obligations to their families . . . This includes the requirement that

they provide adequate and continuous support for
their legal dependents and comply with the terms
of separation agreements and court orders . . . [68]

It used to be that the Army didn't care about what
enlisted men did to, with, or for their dependents, since
such responsibilities were expected to be fulfilled only
by officers. But as the Army grew larger during World
War I, measures were instituted to make sure soldiers
supported their families. It is a court-martial offense to
fail to support one's family, but courts-martial proceedings are invoked only rarely. The Army has adopted the
mandatory allotment for enlisted men in the lower pay
grades and a voluntary system for the senior enlisted
pay grades. (Actually, the mandatory allotment would
seem to be even more necessary for the career enlisted
men. After the law was changed eliminating mandatory
allotments for senior enlisted men, the number of non-
support complaints increased sixfold.)[69] It is still virtually impossible to cut off an allotment (which includes
a deduction from one's pay) to a wife who has aban-
doned or deserted a soldier unless a copy of a divorce
decree can be produced on demand of the finance office.

AUTOMOBILES

The Army cannot prohibit a soldier from owning an
automobile. It can and does regulate its use and can
prevent a soldier from transporting one to an overseas
command. When a car is allowed overseas, the requirement of liability insurance can be made a prerequisite to
the right to operate it on post.[70] A local commander
anywhere can prohibit driving after drinking any time
on the same day![71] He can prescribe rules of the road
for driving on post. Naturally, the military can require
that nobody may drive a vehicle without a valid driver's
license.[72] It can require registration of the car with the
local provost marshal's office. One military writer points
out that the power to regulate automobiles is so broad

that "no judicial opinion from any board of review or the Court of Military Appeals has ever cast doubt" on it.[73] Overseas, the American military commander even has the power to prescribe off-post rules of the road and speed limits for American soldiers—if the host country does not object.[74]

THE SOLDIER AS CONSUMER AND DEBTOR

An Army Regulation states:

> Commanding officers will not tolerate actions of irresponsibility, gross carelessness, neglect, dishonesty, or evasiveness in the private indebtedness and financial obligations of their personnel.[75]

The commanding officer is directed to make his own determination whether a claim against a member of his command is just, and to recommend disciplinary action if he believes the individual has dishonorably failed to pay his just debts. Fortunately, most COs do not like to be put in the position of judging commercial disputes and refer the man to the Legal Assistance Office for competent advice.

The justification for court-martialing a soldier is actually not "military necessity" but "civilian necessity." Servicemen are transferred so often that it is difficult to pin them down long enough to collect a debt through the state courts. To bolster its public image as a professional group of responsible persons, the Army uses the court-martial threat as an aid to commercial creditors.

But a commanding officer is not a collection agent. When a CO ordered one of his men not to leave base until he paid a certain civilian creditor, the order was held to be illegal:

> A commanding officer is not invested with paternal power and dominion over the enlisted men of his

command. He does not stand in loco parentis . . . commanding officers are not required to act as agents for creditors in debt matters.[76]

No one may legally be court-martialed for mere negligent failure to pay debts; the failure has got to be wrongful and willful.[77] Additionally, the Army has no authority to prohibit a soldier from purchasing anything he wants (except contraband), no matter how foolish the purchase may be and no matter how probable it is that the soldier will not be able to afford it.

EMPLOYMENT AND EXPLOITATION

The Army has the power to prohibit the buying and selling of military duties, but in certain areas of work the prohibitory regulations are rarely enforced. KP, CQ runner, fire guard, and other company duties have always been sold, and so long as a body is on the job nobody cares very much.[78] This almost universal willingness to look the other way is a healthy and wise way of siphoning off discontent in the ranks and of creating a greater amount of personal freedom than would exist if the duty rosters were rigidly adhered to. When attempts are made to restrict the practice, the troops get angry.

A soldier has a right to take an off-post job in his spare time if it does not interfere with his military duties. Some local commands require by regulation that permission be obtained before anyone can take a non-military job. If the local commander thought the work would lend itself to abuse—for example, if a soldier planned to sell mutual funds to other servicemen—he could deny permission. Another restriction on the soldier's right to hold a civilian job is contained in a federal statute that forbids soldiers to pursue employment when it would take jobs away from civilians.[79]

Fortunes have been made in the Army by enterprising

low-ranking soldiers. Most of them have been come by in a manner not approved of by the Army—such as the sale of overseas assignments by clerks, before the Army took this power away from the post and restored it to the Pentagon. Most of the better money-making schemes are illegal, and it takes the Army less time to catch up with the lower-ranking operators than with the bigger ones. That's because there's no one around to snuff out an investigation of a Pfc or Spec/4, and it's easier to do it if you know a couple of generals and you're on your way to becoming the Sergeant Major of the Army.

Regulations preventing exploitation between soldiers are legal and enforceable. A regulation setting the maximum rates of return on loans by soldiers to others has been upheld,[80] but in the absence of a regulation no soldier may be court-martialed for charging unconscionable interest rates.[81] Regulations designed to prevent exploitation by one group over a weaker group are also valid. Hospital orderlies can be prohibited from borrowing money from patients,[82] and training cadre can be forbidden to borrow from basic trainees.[83]

A great many more measures are used overseas to protect host nations from economic damage resulting from the influx of duty-free American goods into PXs and commissaries and the black-marketing activities that inevitably follow. The courts have usually assumed the validity of regulations controlling the amount of money that can be brought into a host country from abroad,[84] restricting the conversion of military payment certificates to dollars,[85] and prohibiting the purchase of MPCs from unauthorized sources.[86] The overseas commander can also restrict the soldier's right to sell something he has bought in the PX to someone who would not be authorized to buy it there.[87] A regulation may even deny the soldier the right to remove customs-free items from the military installation.[88] A direct personal order to a Navy seaman not to take more than a limited amount of cigarettes off the ship in the Philippines was said to be legal on the ground that it related to black-market prevention.[89] The validity of rationing has also been assumed.

RELIGIOUS PRACTICES

Although freedom of religion is protected in the First Amendment, not all religious *practices* are invulnerable to prohibition. The Supreme Court has upheld the outlawing of polygamy, even though it was central to the religious belief of those who practiced it.[90] Compulsory vaccination has also been upheld, even though it violated religious scruples.[91] Public safety, health, and welfare have been used to justify these decisions. In the Army, the added makeweight of "military necessity" is thrown in, and the result is more restrictions on religious practice.

People who wish to marry overseas must submit to an interview with the chaplain, who advises them on the "sanctity of marriage, the seriousness of the marriage contract, and . . . the potential difficulties in interracial marriages." No matter how offensive this procedure may be to the beliefs of some soldiers seeking permission to marry, it has been upheld.[92] Further, a soldier must, if ordered, perform military duty on his sabbath,[93] and he must submit to inoculations even if they are forbidden by his religion.[94] A Jehovah's Witness may be punished for refusing to salute the flag, even though he considers it worshiping idols,[95] and even though the Supreme Court has held that it is unconstitutional to require civilian Jehovah's Witnesses to salute the flag,[96] and has indicated in later decisions a willingness to protect *acts* based on religious belief.

In military courts the "military necessity" for such symbolic gestures of respect is considered overriding in importance. But with the increasing pressure to apply First Amendment freedoms to the military, and the growing recognition of the futility of using compulsory measures as unifying devices, perhaps the courts will some day permit refusal to salute the flag on religious grounds. One example of this pressure is the recent successful attack against the Army's "character guidance" program. This attempt at religious brainwashing will, it seems, be given up in the future, however reluctantly. Perhaps the armed forces will also cease to discriminate against those young Americans who have become Black Muslims or embraced Buddhism in preference to the prepackaged Christianity that characterizes the military's efforts at religious propaganda.

As American social mores continue to change, the Army's attempts to regulate private morality and personal endeavors will come under increasing attack. The military will not be able to exist indefinitely as an authoritarian enclave, isolated from the social energies generated by the society it is supposed to serve.

Notes

1. The ability of a sophisticated data center to generate a comprehensive womb-to-tomb dossier on an individual and transmit it over a national network is one of the most graphic threats of the computer revolution.

Arthur M. Miller, "Personal Privacy in the Computer Age: The Challenge of a New Technology in an Information-Oriented Society," 67 *Michigan Law Review* 1089 (1969), p. 1119.

2. *Olmstead v. U.S.*, 277 U.S. 438 (1928).

3. Hyman Gross, "The Concept of Privacy," 42 *NYU Law Review* 34 (1967); Charles Fried, "Privacy," 77 *Yale Law Journal* 475 (1968), pp. 475–476:

Existing technology can produce devices capable of monitoring not only a person's location, but . . . his temperature, pulse rate, blood pressure, the alcoholic content of his blood . . . what he says and what is said to him . . . and perhaps in the not too distant future even the pattern of his brain waves.

4. Warren and Brandeis, "The Right of Privacy," 4 *Harvard Law Review* 193 (1890), p. 205.

5. Edward J. Bloustein, "Privacy as an Aspect of Human Dignity: An Answer to Dean Prosser," 39 *NYU Law Review* 962 (1964), p. 1003.

6. See Chapter Two, Basic and Advanced Individual Training, and Chapter Four, The Military Mind.

7. 395 U.S. 258, 2 SSLR 3068 (1969). See discussion of this case in Chapter Nine, The Framework of Military Law.

8. 5 USCMA 563, 18 CMR 187, 194 (1955).

9. *U.S. v. Adams* (Note 8).

10. Robert E. Quinn, "The U.S. Court of Military Appeals and Individual Rights in the Military Service," 35 *Notre Dame Lawyer* 491 (1960), p. 496.

11. *Ibid.*, p. 497; *U.S. v. Hines,* 21 CMR 201 (1956).

12. Arthur A. Murphy, "The Soldier's Right to a Private Life," 24 *Military Law Review* 97 (1964). This could be the only published article in a military journal in which a military lawyer urges other military lawyers to educate their lay commanders on the importance of GIs' privacy rights.

Stanley R. Resor, Secretary of the Army, recently expressed an awareness of the problem in an address to the Association of the U.S. Army, 22 October 1969. Unfortunately, Mr. Resor's sentiments are not shared by professional soldiers, who don't really pay much attention to any civilian when it comes to running the Army:

> Retention of one's individuality, and resentment of seemingly arbitrary exercises of power, are today foremost concerns of enlisted men of both races. The soldier continues to show a willingness to bear great hardship, when he understands the reason for it. On the other hand, he may balk at small things which appear to discomfort or demean him unnecessarily. Such matters as living conditions, minor restrictions, administrative procedures, all can be sources of discontent, sometimes out of proportion to the positive ends being served.

13. *U.S. v. Lange,* 14 USCMA 486, 35 CMR 458 (1965).

14. *Mapp v. Ohio,* 367 U.S. 643 (1961).

15. *Camara v. Municipal Court,* 387 U.S. 523 (1967). This includes public health authorities who want to enforce local health and regulatory codes. However, the *standards for probable cause* may be somewhat relaxed when the authority is not a criminal enforcement agency and wants only

to enforce codes that affect the health and safety of adjoining residents. *But even then, a warrant must be obtained before a search may lawfully be conducted.*

16. Robert E. Quinn, "Some Comparisons Between Courts-Martial and Civilian Practice," 15 *UCLA Law Review* 1240 (1968), pp. 1254–55.

17. *MCM* (1969), para. 152.

18. *U.S. v. Kazmierczak,* 16 USCMA 594, 37 CMR 214 (1967). See also *U.S. v. Rosado-Marrero,* 32 CMR 583 (1962).

19. *U.S. v. Decker,* 16 USCMA 397, 37 CMR 17 (1966).

20. *U.S. v. Schafer,* 13 USCMA 83, 32 CMR 83 (1962).

21. *U.S. v. Ross,* 13 USCMA 432, 32 CMR 432, 438 (1963).

22. *Chimel v. California,* 395 U.S. 752 (1969). Followed in *Pullen,* CM 420039, 29 Jan. 1970.

23. See Note 39 and related discussion in text.

24. Until 1967 the Supreme Court excluded "mere evidence" from the category of seizable items, but now just about anything reasonably related to the crime may be sought and introduced into evidence. *Warden v. Hayden,* 387 U.S. 294 (1967), overruling *Gouled v. U.S.,* 255 U.S. 298 (1921); followed by military courts: *U.S. v. Whisenhant,* 17 USCMA 117, 37 CMR 381 (1967).

25. *U.S. v. Waller,* 28 CMR 484, affirmed 29 CMR 111 (1960).

26. *U.S. v. Davis,* 4 USCMA 577, 16 CMR 151 (1954); *U.S. v. Swanson,* 3 USCMA 671, 14 CMR 89 (1954).

27. *Gionet,* CM 419742 (10 Oct. 1969).

28. *U.S. v. Mathis,* 37 CMR 797 (1966), affirmed 16 USCMA 522, 37 CMR 142 (1967).

29. *McDonald v. U.S.,* 335 U.S. 451 (1948).

30. *Gouled v. U.S.,* 255 U.S. 298 (1921).

31. *Silverman v. U.S.,* 365 U.S. 505 (1961).

32. *Goldman v. U.S.,* 316 U.S. 129 (1942).

33. *On Lee v. U.S.,* 343 U.S. 747 (1952).

34. *U.S. v. Williams,* 10 USCMA 578, 28 CMR 144 (1959); *U.S. v. Holmes,* 6 USCMA 151, 19 CMR 277 (1955).

35. *U.S. v. Nowling,* 25 CMR 362 (1958).

36. *U.S. v. Corson,* 18 USCMA 34, 39 CMR 34 (1968).

37. *U.S. v. DeLeo,* 5 USCMA 148, 17 CMR 148 (1954).

38. *U.S. v. Price,* 17 USCMA 566, 38 CMR 364 (1968).

39. *U.S. v. Goldman,* 18 USCMA 516, 517, 40 CMR 228 (1969)..

40. However, very delicate problems of diplomacy arise when American soldiers are tried in host countries for crimes

against their citizens by local courts that lack the safeguards of American courts. See "Due Process Challenge to the Korean Status of Forces Agreement," 57 *Georgetown Law Journal* 1097 (1969).

41. AR 65–1, para. 8–3 (rev. 12 Dec. 1968).

42. AR 65–75, para. 6 (rev. 26 Sept. 1967).

43. AR 65–1, para. 8–4(b).

44. AR 65–1, para. 8–5.

45. AR 630–5, para. 10–1 (29 Dec. 1969).

46. *U.S. v. Haynes,* 15 USCMA 122, 35 CMR 94 (1964).

47. *U.S. v. Porter,* 11 USCMA 170, 28 CMR 394 (1960). It also appears that the Army can require all soldiers on leave in foreign countries to notify the U.S. Army commander or Army attaché of their whereabouts. AR 630–5, Appendix B (29 Dec. 1969). But see Note 48 and related discussion in text. For civilians the right to travel is part of liberty guaranteed by the Fifth Amendment: *Kent v. Dulles,* 357 U.S. 116, 125–127 (1958). The *O'Callahan* case (Note 50) may possibly undercut some of the Army's authority to prohibit foreign travel.

48. *U.S. v. Milldebrandt,* 8 USCMA 635, 25 CMR 139, 142 (1958).

49. See 10 USC sec. 701.

50. *O'Callahan v. Parker,* 2 SSLR 3068 (1969).

51. *U.S. v. Wilson,* 12 USCMA 165, 30 CMR 165, 166 (1961).

52. Stephen Wizner and Jonathan Weiss, "Pot, Prayer, Politics and Privacy: The Right To Cut Your Own Throat in Your Own Way," 54 *Iowa Law Review* 709 (1969); David Wallenstein, "Marijuana Possession as an Aspect of the Right of Privacy" 5 *Criminal Law Bulletin* 59 (1969).

53. *Hershberg v. City of Barbourville,* 142 Ky. 60, 133 S.W. 985 (1911).

54. *U.S. v. Beeker,* 18 USCMA 563, 40 CMR 275. But see *Moylan v. Laird,* Civ. Act. No. 4179 (D.C. R.I. 20 Oct. 1969), and Chapter Nine, The Framework of Military Law.

55. *People v. Woody,* 40 Calif. Reptr. 69, 394 P.2d 813 (1964).

56. Murphy, *op. cit.* (Note 12), p. 103.

57. *U.S. v. Nation,* 9 USCMA 724, 727, 26 CMR 504 (1958).

58. *U.S. v. Wheeler,* 12 USCMA 387, 30 CMR 387 (1961).

59. AR 600–240 (17 Dec. 1965). Area commanders are authorized to issue additional regulations.

60. 381 U.S. 479 (1965).

61. An attempt to prohibit the importation into Okinawa of contraceptive devices and pills (merely because they were banned by federal customs statutes) was squelched just in time, according to Maj. Wayne E. Alley, writing in 37 *Military Law Review* 57 (1967), "The Overseas Commander's Power To Regulate the Private Life," p. 114:

> With a nervous eye on the probable reactions of dependent wives joining their sponsors after a separation of at least several weeks . . . the Army urged that there was no military interest in rummaging through luggage for such items.

62. See discussion of *O'Callahan* and sex offenses in Chapter Nine, The Framework of Military Law.
63. *Roberts v. Clement,* 252 F. Supp. 835 (E.D. Tenn. 1966).
64. But the Court of Military Appeals chose to follow *O'Callahan* when the homosexual act was sodomy between a serviceman and a child: *U.S. v. Shockley,* 18 USCMA 610, 40 CMR 322 (1969). Whether it will find a service connection when the relationship involves a possible breach of security, through blackmail or otherwise, remains to be seen. It is probable that the doctrine of *U.S. v. Yeast,* 36 CMR 890 (1966), which held that an officer can be court-martialed for conduct unbecoming an officer when he openly associates with a known homosexual, will still be the law in the *O'Callahan* era.
65. *U.S. v. McGlone,* ACM 9462 (1954).
66. *U.S. v. Adams,* 18 USCMA 310, 40 CMR 22 (1969).
67. Brief of petitioner *Levy v. Parker et al.* (Dist. Ct. M.D. Pa.), p. 179; on file at ACLU, New York.
68. AR 600–20, para. 37 (rev. 31 Jan. 1967).
69. Murphy, *op. cit.* (Note 12), p. 108, at ftn. 63.
70. *U.S. v. Boone,* 18 CMR 572 (1954).
71. *U.S. v. Day,* 4 CMR 278 (1952).
72. *U.S. v. Bridges,* 30 CMR 96 (1961).
73. Alley, *op. cit.* (Note 61), p. 101.
74. Murphy, *op. cit.* (Note 12), p. 118, ftnt. 122.
75. AR 600–20, para. 36(b) (rev. 31 Jan. 1967).
76. *U.S. v. England,* 30 CMR 733, 734–35 (Coast Guard, 1960).
77. *U.S. v. Kirksey,* 6 USCMA 556, 20 CMR 272 (1955).
78. See Chapter Three, Life as Permanent Party.
79. 10 USC sec. 3635; AR 600–50, para. 12(b) (rev. 29 June 1966).
80. *U.S. v. Giordano,* 15 USCMA 163, 35 CMR 135 (1964).

81. *U.S. v. Day,* 11 USCMA 549, 29 CMR 365 (1960).

82. *U.S. v. Hill,* 5 CMR 665 (1952).

83. *U.S. v. Hooks,* 7 CMR 629, petition denied, 2 USCMA 680, 7 CMR 84 (1952).

84. *U.S. v. Mallow,* 21 CMR 242 (1956).

85. *U.S. v. Blau,* 17 CMR 232 (1954).

86. *U.S. v. Gehring,* 20 CMR 373 (1956).

87. *U.S. v. Silva,* 26 CMR 200 (1958).

88. *U.S. v. Barnes,* 12 CMR 204 (1953).

89. *U.S. v. Martin,* 1 USCMA 674, 5 CMR 102 (1952).

90. *Reynolds v. U.S.,* 98 U.S. 145 (1878).

91. *Jacobson v. Massachusetts,* 197 U.S. 11 (1905).

92. *U.S. v. Wheeler,* 12 USCMA 387, 30 CMR 387 (1961).

93. *U.S. v. Burry,* 36 CMR 829 (1966).

94. *U.S. v. Chadwell,* 36 CMR 741 (1965). See related discussion in Chapter Two, Basic and Advanced Individual Training.

95. *U.S. v. Cupp,* 24 CMR 565 (1956).

96. *West Virginia State Board of Education v. Barnette,* 319 U.S. 624 (1943).

7

How To File a Complaint or Bring Charges

> Fury said to a mouse,
> That he met in the house,
> "Let us both go to law:
> *I* will prosecute *you*.—
> Come, I'll take no denial;
> We must have a trial:
> For really this morning
> I've nothing to do."
> Said the mouse to the cur,
> "Such a trial, dear sir,
> With no jury or judge,
> Would be wasting our breath."
> "I'll be judge, I'll be jury,"
> Said cunning old Fury;
> "I'll try the whole cause,
> and condemn you to death."
> —LEWIS CARROLL, *Alice in Wonderland*

There are many ways to air complaints in the Army. No one can tell in advance when a particular tactic is the best one to use. It must depend on the nature of the abuse you are complaining about; its severity; the personalities of the people involved as perpetrators, witnesses, victims, and interested parties; the amount of evidence available to sustain your position; your own commitment to seeing something through; and primarily, your instincts and ultimate purposes.

Sometimes the most advisable procedure is to seek a solution on the company level and to drop the matter if success is not achieved. In other situations you might pull out all the stops. If, for instance, you've been denied an emergency leave and your only object is to get the leave fast, that is a simply defined and limited goal. If, however, you've been victimized in a serious way, such as through physical abuse, and you want not only to protect yourself in the future but to see the responsible individuals brought to justice, you might pursue the more direct of several methods about to be described—or all of them at once. And if you have mustered up the courage to dramatize an especially grotesque situation and the case is a strong one, you might, together with your fellow draftees, take the offensive and make it more difficult for the system to preserve its fading image as the embodiment of public virtue.

Every quiet injustice that becomes public knowledge is officially explained as a "rare exception," but the civilian public is becoming increasingly aware that the Army, especially on the lower levels, continues to function as a lawless institution. *Only through the collective and joint action of GIs and civilians of conscience can the shabby camouflage of the "rare exception" be shattered.*

THE CHAIN OF COMMAND: A STALLING TACTIC

On the lowest level, the all-pervasive response during basic training toward the private's request to visit the finance office, Legal Assistance, the chaplain, the psychiatrist, or the Inspector General is the "stall." Since almost every instant of your time in basic or AIT must be accounted for, this becomes an effective method of discouragement and control. If they do not let you go, you may be AWOL if you leave your company to complain that they would not let you go. Usually, with polite insistence on your rights it is possible to obtain permission to consult with whomever you wish on post.

One of the stalling methods is the "appointment" ploy. You are told that no appointment is available for two or three weeks, when the sergeant himself knows that all you have to do is drop in and wait your turn, which is what he himself invariably does when he needs legal assistance. Since some offices operate, tacitly at least, on an appointment basis, play that game with them, but a two- or three-day wait should be the limit, even if your problem is not urgent. If you are having a lot of trouble being heard, you might point out AR 600–20, para. 34(e), to your CO or first sergeant. It presents the Army's idea of the ideal relationship between the recruit and his superiors:

> Authority will impose its weight by the professional competence of leaders at all echelons rather than by the arbitrary or despotic methods of martinets . . .
>
> Commissioned officers [and NCOs] will keep in close touch with personnel within their command, will take an interest in their organizational life, will hear their complaints, and will endeavor on all occasions to remove those causes which make for dissatisfaction. Leaders will strive to maintain such relations of confidence and sympathy as will insure that personnel of their command will feel free to approach them for counsel and assistance, not only with regard to military and organizational matters, but with matters which may be contributing to personal or family distress or perplexity. This relationship may be gained and maintained without relaxation of the bonds of discipline and with great benefit to the service as a whole.

If you have a problem that you would like to settle on the company level, you might try to get your CO to act in the spirit of the AR. *Notice that it imposes the obligation on your company commander to concern himself with your welfare, but imposes no obligation on you to bring your complaints directly to him if you have no faith that he will deal with you fairly, or if the matter, in your opinion, is beyond his competence. No AR or post regulation can legally impose such an obligation on you. Even though some regulations strongly urge you to, you are not required to do more than make an attempt to go through the chain of command in registering a complaint.* If your sergeant has screened you from the CO, then you have a perfectly good excuse for not having talked a problem over with him before going to the IG or, perhaps, filing an Article 138 complaint. And when you do go through the chain of command in order to get permission to see another counselor on post, such as the lawyer at Legal Assistance or the chaplain, you cannot lawfully be stalled indefinitely or refused permission just because you don't want to discuss the details of the problem with your sergeant or CO. But as a practical matter, to protect yourself and insure that your complaint will be taken seriously by higher authorities, it is wise first to make at least one attempt to secure relief on the lowest levels.

THE DRAFTEE'S HIDDEN WEAPON: ARTICLE 138

Article 138 of the UCMJ is part of a federal law governing the conduct of everybody in the military. Of all the complaint procedures, it is the strongest, because unlike many ARs, *it is not merely a statement of broad policy but a statutory right, a mandate from higher authority which the brass are compelled to follow.* Generally speaking, only lifers ever use it, but it provides the GI with a potentially powerful internal vehicle for insuring that his rights are not trampled upon. Article 138 states in its entirety:

> Any member of the armed forces who believes himself wronged by his commanding officer, and who, upon due application to that commanding officer, is refused redress, may complain to any superior commissioned officer, who shall forward the complaint to the officer exercising general court-martial jurisdiction over the officer against whom it is made. The officer exercising general court-martial jurisdiction shall examine into the complaint and take proper measures for redressing the wrong complained of; and he shall, as soon as possible, send to the Secretary concerned a true statement of that complaint, with the proceedings had thereon.

If your company commander has "wronged" you and has "refused redress," you can apply to *any* superior officer (in a different unit on post, or at the Pentagon, or at an installation near your home during leave, etc.), and he must forward your complaint to the person exercising general court-martial jurisdiction over the company commander, usually the commanding general of the installation. *The person to whom you complain need not be in the chain of command directly over your company commander.* He can be the Staff Judge Advocate, or someone you just happen to know. This officer *must* forward the complaint to the commanding general, who *must,* after an investigation, forward it to the Secretary of the Army together with a record of the "proceedings had thereon." The advantage to you of resorting to this article of the UCMJ is that *its provisions for informing higher authority are mandatory, and cannot be covered up as IG complaints can be.* One additional way to assure that it won't be covered up is to write your congressman simultaneously, telling him what steps you have initiated, and let the authorities know exactly what you have done.

The important thing to remember about the Article 138 complaint is that nobody has any clear understanding of its scope, since it has almost never been tested in court. The reason for this is that there is no provision for direct judicial review of an officer's alleged noncompliance with its provisions. Perhaps a federal declaratory judgment or injunction proceeding will be resorted to in this area, as it has had to be used in others for soldiers to vindicate their rights.

According to one military lawyer, *the article could possibly be used to deal with almost any matter other than discipline.* This includes claims that a commanding officer deprived a soldier of a "property right," or "abused his command discretion," or "otherwise dealt with him unjustly in a field other than discipline."[1] The obvious problem with such a definition is that in some remote way discipline is tied up with everything else in the Army, including "property rights." As an illustration, assume that a soldier while on a weekend pass gets picked up by civilian police and is kept in a jail cell for three weeks, after which he is released and all civilian charges are dropped. In the meantime his discharge date (ETS) has passed. When he returns to military authority, his commanding officer has his records "flagged" and places an "administrative hold" on the soldier, the practical effect of which is to prevent him from getting out of the Army. Since he has a clear defense to any AWOL charge (incarceration by civilian police without a subsequent conviction is deemed to be beyond the soldier's control and without fault on his part), there is no good reason for holding him. It may be said that the CO is "abusing his command discretion" and that he is depriving the soldier of his "property rights" to earn a living *as a civilian* as well as his liberty. In such a case, an Article 138 complaint should be filed, *in writing,* and should be accepted. The only time it would clearly appear to be inappropriate is when it is used as a substitute for appeal channels in a court-martial situation.

The lawyer also says that your CO's failure to take

disciplinary action against another soldier who has wronged you would not be a proper subject for an Article 138 complaint. But since no court has yet stated that such a use of the complaint is improper, you might be well advised to resort to it anyway, especially if the situation is as clear-cut as it was in the case of the sergeant who threw a lump of coal at a trainee (see Chapter Two, Basic and Advanced Individual Training), and you happen to have been that trainee.

If you are informed that your formal Article 138 complaint (which incidentally need *not* be prepared in any particular format) is deemed inappropriate and is not going to be forwarded as required by its terms, *you can follow the matter up by filing a new Article 138 complaint, stating that those who failed to accept the first one violated Article 98 as well, which punishes deliberate failure to enforce or comply with the UCMJ.* Then you might also write the Secretary of the Army and request that a Court of Inquiry be convened under Article 135 to investigate your commanding general's refusal to forward your Article 138 complaint. Or you might send a copy of the second complaint to a congressman. Don't be surprised if no Court of Inquiry is convened, but expect swift attention to your problem.

As a bystander, you cannot properly file an Article 138 complaint about a wrong done to someone else. Nor will a joint complaint be accepted, since it is inconsistent with the traditional military method of isolating each soldier from the other. *However, a group of soldiers can file individual complaints if they are all affected by the superior officer's wrongful action.*

The superior officer whose conduct you are complaining about need not be your immediate CO. He can be the commanding general. But whoever he is, you must have first applied to him for "redress." In every case the complaint must be filed with the next higher authority, and mailing a complaint about a general to the commanding general of the next higher headquarters is sufficient for "filing."

No Army or post regulation may narrow your right to file an Article 138 complaint. Since there is very little legislative history on Congress' intention in enacting the article, just about every Army Regulation or opinion of the Judge Advocate General on the subject is merely an Army-oriented educated guess. Below are some examples of the kinds of complaints that are clearly within the meaning of the article, but the list is by no means exhaustive:

> Improper deprivation of pass or leave privileges; denying, without sufficient cause, a married enlisted member of the command privilege of living off the post and drawing separate rations . . . utilization, without proper authority, of subordinates on personal matters, such as cook, chauffeur, valet, gardener, and the like; requiring subordinates to purchase from personal funds articles of clothing, uniform, or equipment which are authorized but not required by regulations or custom; requiring subordinates to obtain permission to purchase or own motor vehicle; failure to adhere to known command policies with respect to pretrial or posttrial confinement; failure to consider, without justification, a subordinate for promotion although he is eligible and vacancy exists; improper efficiency ratings; imposition of punishment in guise of additional training.[2]

Very significantly, it now appears beyond question that a stockade prisoner may resort to Article 138 to correct conditions of his confinement. (See Chapter Ten, especially the section "The Law of the Stockade," and Note 63.)

THE INSPECTOR GENERAL

The AR governing activities of the Inspector General should be read by every soldier. One paragraph covers the "Rights of Individuals":

All military and civilian personnel on duty with the Department of the Army have the right to register complaints orally or in writing with an inspector general. They should, when practicable, be afforded the opportunity of presenting their individual complaints in person to an inspector general or acting inspector general at least once in each quarter of the year.[3]

The last sentence refers to the IG inspections, which usually contain a complaint period. Needless to say, you can file your complaint when the problem arises, and need not present it in the formal complaint period nor at any particular time of year. The AR goes on to say:

c. Service personnel will be encouraged to discuss their problems or grievances first with their commanding officers . . . However, persons desiring to submit a complaint will not be required to submit to an interview by anyone prior to registering a complaint with an inspector general.[4]

Failure to discuss the matter with your CO first is not a valid ground for the IG to refuse acceptance of your complaint. However, the local office of the IG has the discretion to refuse to "accept" your complaint on the ground that it is "trivial" or "not properly acceptable as a complaint," which presumably means that whatever is being done to you is not unlawful in his opinion.

Inspectors general and acting inspectors general will give careful consideration to all complaints presented to them and will promptly inquire into those accepted . . . An inspector general may decline to act upon a matter he deems trivial in nature, or not properly acceptable as a complaint. In such cases, he will inform the individual accordingly and advise him of other means of recourse.[5]

Because the local IG has the discretion to turn down a complaint, *it is advisable to present it in writing and keep a copy,* preferably a carbon, if you intend to follow up on it. That way, if you subsequently write your congressman, you can attach an exact copy of the complaint you filed, *and it will be harder for them to say they never heard of you, or that you said something different at the time.* Or, if your chosen alternative is not to go through civilian channels, you can send a copy of the rejected complaint to: The Inspector General, ATTENTION: Chief, Assistance and Reviews Branch, HQ, Department of the Army, Washington, D.C., 20315, and request that they review the action of your local IG.

Remember that the people to whom you are submitting your complaint at the IG's office will in all likelihood be career soldiers, and they will not be anxious to root out the kinds of abuses that result from overzealous discipline on the part of commanders. If this is the sort of complaint you are making, it might be best to resort to the Article 138 procedure discussed above, together with a congressional communication. Since the IG is under the control and direction of the installation commander, complaints against the latter are not likely to receive a very sympathetic hearing.[6]

WRITING YOUR CONGRESSMAN

If a matter is worth writing your congressman about (*or anyone else's congressman or senator, for that matter, which you have a perfect right to do*), it should be worth sending a telegram or using registered or certified mail, return receipt requested, which will get quicker attention and possibly better results. No one can stop you from communicating with your congressman in any way, including by telephone, and if they try to, you should include that information in the message you eventually are able to send. Congress has expressed its distrust of military pressure tactics by passing a special law forbidding anyone to interfere with the citizen-soldier's right to seek congressional help or to inform congressmen of Army practices. This right is recognized by AR 600–20:

No person may restrict any member of an armed
force from communication with a Member of
Congress, unless the communication is unlawful
or violates a regulation necessary to the security of
the United States.[7]

*Additionally, it is illegal for anyone to punish or
retaliate against you in any way for your having exercised the right to communicate with a member of
Congress.* You can also write a member of an executive
department or the President, and a letter to the President from the soldier's parent has sometimes been effective. Don't worry about the AR's restrictions on this
right. A complaint would rarely violate "the security of
the United States" and almost never be "unlawful."
What you have to worry about is getting action in time
to redress or prevent a wrong.

Unless the subject matter of your telegram, letter, or
phone call is especially interesting, do not expect any
special interest in the matter. Congressmen receive
many thousands of soldiers' complaints each year, and
the great majority get returned to the post with the
congressman's request for an explanation. On post an
office full of Pfcs and Spec/4s with degrees in English
churns out official responses. *What you must do is
differentiate your complaint from all the rest.* First of
all, the mere fact that you felt the problem was serious
enough so that you spent your money on a telegram will
draw attention to your complaint. Second, congressmen
rarely get all the relevant facts from the soldier, and
even more rarely do they receive any documentation of
the illegal practice complained of; it's up to you to
provide this. Third, they usually do not receive any
follow-up communication from the complainant. If you
follow up your original letter or telegram with eviden-
tiary support of the abuse or threatened abuse, the
congressman can save time by making specific inquiries
of the post commander, including copies of the evidence in his memorandum. Then the command cannot

side-step the congressman's request for an explanation by saying that no complaint was ever filed, or that the original complaint contained different information from the one sent to the congressman. By documenting the complaint as well as you can, you might also give the congressman ammunition enough to trigger an investigation of a pattern of abuses, if that can be established.

Before sending a complaint to Congress, it is important that you be aware that normal procedure in a congressman's office is to photocopy the soldier's letter and return a copy to the local command. *Therefore, don't say anything that you would not repeat to the local authorities directly.* Although a soldier probably could not be court-martialed for intentionally sending erroneous information to his congressman (as he could be for lying to the IG), it is not in your interest to say anything you can't back up either through your personal testimony or otherwise.

RACIAL DISCRIMINATION

It is the policy of the Army to conduct all of its activities in a manner which is free from racial discrimination, and which provides equal opportunity and treatment of all uniformed members irrespective of their race, color, religion, or national origin.[8]

In response to several Civil Rights Acts passed by Congress in the 1960s, the Army has eliminated most *overt* vestiges of racial discrimination at Army facilities. However, it has dragged its feet in the area of off-post implementation of federal policies of nondiscrimination, despite a plethora of ARs on the subject. Commanders are supposed to "govern military police relationships with local authorities to insure that no actual or tacit support is given to community discriminatory practices."[9] Also, "all listings maintained by family housing offices at Army installations or activities of private housing available for sale or rent will include only those units which are available without regard to race, creed or color of prospective tenants referred through installation or activity information media."[10] And in the Army community relations programs—which include recreation programs, community service projects, weapons demonstrations, and furnishing speakers for civic groups—"participation is prohibited unless admission, seating, and all other accommodations and facilities connected with the event or activity are available to all without regard to race, creed, or national origin."[11] Despite these nice pronouncements, off-post conditions for black servicemen are still terrible, and installation commanders in the South have continued to play ball with the local white power structures in many communities.

One of the worst pockets of prejudice is Leesville, Louisiana, near Fort Polk, the Vietnam-oriented infantry base:

> Discrimination against black soldiers and police prejudice against all GIs are sickening realities. On two occasions in which we were personally involved Negro soldiers were refused service at public restaurants and lounges because they were black. On three other occasions soldiers have been robbed and brutally beaten with either the assistance or mysterious nonintervention of the local police.
>
> The Provost Marshal's Office has received other such reports from men assigned to Fort Polk, but nothing has been done. Complaints have also been made through "proper channels" such as Unit Commanders and the Inspector General's Office, but still no action has been taken.[12]

That the problem is still general throughout the South cannot be disputed. Fort Jackson, South Carolina, is but another example, as is illustrated by this letter written in

1969 by the Director of the Office of Federal Programs to the Deputy Assistant Secretary of Defense for Manpower:

> An analysis of the narrative and statistical housing program reports filed by Fort Jackson in South Carolina, has revealed that the base's statistics do not illustrate what we believe to be the true housing situation for Negro servicemen in these areas . . . While clearly there is an increase in the number of open assurances received by the base housing office, these statistics infer *that there has been little integration of housing facilities since our staff visit, at which time we found that the only facilities housing Negroes were trailer courts and slum-type dwellings.* [Italics added.][13]

If you or a member of your family should become a victim of overt racial discrimination in the vicinity of an Army post where you're stationed, there are regulations that create at least the possibility of triggering a legal response by the United States Department of Justice.

Public Facilities, Schools, and Events

AR 600–22 enables the victim of discrimination at hotels, motels, pools, theaters, schools, and other public facilities to file a complaint through Army channels, with the ultimate (though small) possibility that the Justice Department will prosecute the case against the violator.[14] To file a complaint under this AR, you must study it carefully and follow its prescribed steps. *The most important advantage it offers is that the complaint cannot be swept under the rug. After investigation, it must be forwarded to Washington.* If enough complaints were filed near a particular installation, the Justice Department might be persuaded that, in spite of its limited resources and the present Administration's "Southern strategy," a lawsuit is justified in your particular geographical area.

The complainant who requests a suit by the federal government in his behalf (1) must be stationed at the installation where the complaint is filed, (2) must not be on orders to depart the installation, and (3) must be complaining about discrimination occurring within normal commuting distance and during the past sixty days. *The Office of the Staff Judge Advocate should have either a civilian or an Army lawyer who specializes in this area and whose job it is to help you prepare the paper work.* After receiving the complaint, the local commander must investigate the matter and either receive "voluntary assurances" from the offender or forward the complaint and supporting documents to: The Judge Advocate General, ATTENTION: Chief Litigation Division, Department of the Army, Washington, D.C., 20310. This must be done within thirty days from the filing of the complaint.

If the local commanding general should decide that efforts to gain voluntary assurances are likely to be successful he may extend the time up to sixty days more before forwarding the file to Washington. Since the file must be processed further and sent from the Army to the Justice Department for a final decision on whether to seek a permanent injunction in the federal district court having jurisdiction, it will be a long haul. *The best way to assure that the matter will not be forgotten is to file a group complaint, or a series of related complaints, with enough soldiers participating to insure that at least one will be stationed there long enough to prevent the matter from becoming moot.*

Off-Post Housing

Procedures for soldiers and their families to protest discrimination in off-post housing have been set up in AR 600–4.[15] The procedures are similar to those described above for filing a complaint based on off-post discrimination. However, the commander must forward the complaint, report of inquiry, and supporting documents to Washington within *twenty days of the filing of the complaint, and is limited to only ten additional days in which to obtain voluntary assurances* from the persons accused of violating the 1968 Civil Rights Act.

Far more effective is the group complaint which reveals a "pattern or practice of resistance to the full enjoyment" of particular soldiers' rights to equal housing. The Army doesn't like group complaints and forbids them to be used in IG or Article 138 procedures. But this kind they should accept. The paper work is handled differently and *must* be forwarded by the Judge Advocate General to the Justice Department, which can pursue legal relief on the complainants' behalf in federal court.[16] The time period during which the discrimination must have taken place is more liberal under this statute: a complaint may be filed for any discriminatory action which took place during the previous six months. The form on which it is filed, however, is issued by the Department of Housing and Urban Development, Washington, D.C., 20410, to whom you may have to write to obtain one.

A new AR, 600–18, adds to the responsibilities of post commanders to assure equality for Negroes in off-post housing. It permits a commander to forbid *any* military personnel from renting housing from those who discriminate unlawfully. This AR may prove to have teeth, and should be studied carefully.

YOU CAN "SUE" YOUR SERGEANT: ARTICLE 139

Although Article 139 was probably designed primarily to provide a means of compensation to the local bar owner when his place is torn up by a gang of drunken soldiers or sailors, it is by no means limited to that kind of situation. You too can resort to it when your sergeant destroys or confiscates something of yours that he had no right to take or destroy. Article 139 states:

(a) Whenever complaint is made to any commanding officer that willful damage has been done to the property of any person or that his property has been wrongfully taken by members of the armed forces, he may, under such regulations as the Secretary concerned may prescribe, convene a board to investigate the complaint. The board . . . has power to . . . assess the damages sustained against the responsible parties . . .

(b) If the offenders cannot be ascertained, but the organization or detachment to which they belong is known, charges totaling the amount of damages assessed and approved may be made in such proportion as may be considered just upon the individual members thereof who are shown to have been present at the scene at the time the damages complained of were inflicted . . .

AR 27–27 implements Article 139 and provides that an amount up to $250 may be assessed against any one offender and that the amount may be deducted from his pay without the approval of a Staff Judge Advocate (who can authorize higher amounts). What this article does is provide an informal small-claims court within the Army to adjudicate claims of willful damage or destruction or wrongful taking of one person's property by another. For very large amounts the civilian courts are open, but that involves a great deal of time and, of course, legal fees for a local lawyer. In the Army, too, a great deal of time could be consumed and paper work generated by the filing of such a claim, and it is likely that if the case is clear-cut, and you are entitled to compensation from another soldier, the dispute can be settled swiftly (after the filing of the complaint) through voluntary restitution. More important, in a situation like that described in Chapter Two, Basic and Advanced Individual Training, when sergeants looted and pillaged the troops' barracks in search of a "missing bayonet," that kind of behavior can be deterred in the future through the filing of this "civil action" along with the charges under Article 138. It is advisable, in such a situation, to consult with the Legal Assistance Office for help in filing the complaint. It is possible that an Article 139 claim could be turned down on the grounds that the wrongdoers were acting "within the scope of their employment," but then a claim might be supportable under other claims regulations, such as AR 27–29. Check with the claims section of the Staff Judge Advocate's Office.

Article 139(b) also authorizes the assessment of money damages against individuals who could well be innocent of any wrongdoing, but to that extent this section of the law is probably unconstitutional. Deducting an amount from the paycheck of a mere bystander to a riot would amount to an unconstitutional taking of property without due process of law in violation of the Fifth Amendment.

CIVIL ACTIONS IN LOCAL COURTS

Nobody in the military service gives up, by virtue of his status, his right to sue another soldier in a civilian court. If a commander's deprivation of a soldier's rights is so gross that it is characterized by "malice, corruption or cruelty,"[17] the soldier may have a cause of action for money damages in a federal court or any one of the state or lower courts.[18] However, mere errors of judgment will not give rise to an action for damages.[19] The chances of a state court's taking jurisdiction are not very great, and unless you have suffered actual pecuniary damage it will be difficult to recover a judgment. A local lawyer must be consulted to determine one's rights under the law of the state where the lawsuit is contemplated and where service of legal process may be obtained.

There are a number of relatively unexplored areas in the law which directly relate to the civil rights of servicemen. At a recent conclave of lawyers specializing in personal injury cases, Danny R. Jones, a medicolegal expert from California, reported that soldiers may have a right to sue the manufacturers of defective weapons or equipment. He even raised the possibility of suing the Army lawyer who neglects to inform a soldier of his right to sue![20]

For soldiers who have produced an original work of art while in the Army, there may be the possibility of obtaining a copyright in order to prevent others from exploiting it. In one very unusual case, the creators of the statue of a charging infantryman which stands at Fort Dix—it is known as "The Ultimate Weapon"— started a controversy that has found its way to the Supreme Court. With authorization from the Army, the Universal Match Corporation reproduced a picture of the statue on matchbook covers. The sculptors, no longer in the Army, claimed that the corporation had infringed their copyright. The corporation and the Army claimed that the rights to the statue belonged to the Army. So far the Supreme Court has not yet decided which party is correct.[21] But if you have any artistic contribution which the Army has used, you should at least explore the possibility of obtaining a copyright for it by consulting a lawyer knowledgeable in the field.

There are also some situations when a soldier may be permitted to sue the government under the Federal Tort Claims Act to recover damages for negligently caused injuries.[22]

Notes

1. Abraham Nemrow, "Complaints of Wrong under Article 138," 2 *Military Law Review* 43 (1958), p. 50, citing opinion of the Judge Advocate General, JAGA 1955/8275 (20 Oct. 1955).
2. *Ibid.*, p. 54.
3. AR 20–1, Inspections and Investigations, Inspector Gen-

eral Activities and Procedures, para. 3–3 (rev. 22 Aug. 1968).

4. *Ibid.*

5. *Ibid.*, para. 3–7.

6. U.S. Dept. of the Army Field Manual 101–5, paras. 4–27, 4–43 (June 1968).

7. Para. 41(a), implementing 10 USC 1034.

8. AR 600–21, Equal Opportunity and Treatment of Military Personnel, para. 3(a) (rev. 18 May 1965).

9. *Ibid.*, para. 6(f).

10. *Ibid.*, para. 7(b).

11. AR 360–61, Community Relations, para. 2–2(b) (rev. 17 July 1969).

12. "Bias in Leesville," letter to the *New York Times,* Nov. 2, 1969, signed by Sgt. Gregory P. Strattner and eleven other soldiers.

13. Brief for Petitioner, *Levy v. Parker et al.* (Dist. Ct. M.D. Pa.) p. 137, on file with American Civil Liberties Union, New York.

14. AR 600–22, Processing Requests of Military Personnel for Action by the Attorney General under the Civil Rights Act of 1964 (rev. 4 Sept. 1964).

15. AR 600–4, Fair Housing Program of the Department of Defense (rev. 28 April 1969), implementing Titles VIII and IX of the Civil Rights Act of 1968 (42 USC 1982).

16. *Ibid.*, para. 13.

17. *Crozman v. Callahan,* 136 F. Supp. 466, 468 (W.D. Okla. 1955).

18. *Nixon v. Reeves,* 65 Minn. 159, 67 N.W. 989 (1896).

19. *Keppleman v. Upston,* 84 F. Supp. 478 (N.D. Calif. 1949).

20. "Lawyer Stresses GI's Right To Sue," *New York Times,* Dec. 29, 1969, p. 7.

21. *Scherr v. Universal Match Corporation,* 297 F. Supp. 107 (S.D. N.Y. 1967). Petition for writ of certiorari filed by New York attorneys Herbert Kanon and Bernard Olcott on Jan. 8, 1970. (The petition has recently been denied.)

22. *Lee v. U.S.,* 261 F. Supp. 252 (C.D. Calif. 1966); *Schwager v. U.S.,* 279 F. Supp 262 (E.D. Pa. 1968).

8

Orders To Commit War Crimes
and Other Illegalities

"I don't know 'bout you, but I don't want them slanty-eyed fuckers mixin' with my pussies. Men, you got to remember, many men has died, not only in Vietnam, but in World War II, Korea . . .

Ain't that right? So remember . . . duty, honor, country . . . I been in the Army seventeen years and it's a damn fine institution . . . like in civilian life, men, you gonna get out of it what you put in.

But them Chinese—I'll tell you—you line 'em up and in a year you won't a counted all of 'em. But we're sendin' more men over there and there's more of 'em gettin' through.

I don't know, all I know is somethin's got to give over there—you mark my word."
                                        —A Drill Sergeant's Parting Remarks,
                                        Basic Training, March 24, 1967

The only orders you are obliged to obey are lawful ones. Nothing in the UCMJ requires or authorizes punishment for disobedience of an illegal order. *However, all orders are cloaked with a "presumption" of legality, which puts the burden on the recipient to show, at a court-martial, in what respect the order was illegal.* The test set up and followed by the military courts in determining the legality of orders is about as broad as the English language allows:

> All activities which are reasonably necessary to safeguard and protect the morals, discipline and usefulness of the members of a command and are directly connected with the maintenance of good order in the services are subject to the control of the officers upon whom the responsibility of the command rests.[1]

On the other hand, orders can be illegal for many reasons. An order to confess to a crime, for example, would be in violation of your Fifth Amendment and Article 31 rights not to incriminate yourself.[2] An order not to write to your congressman would contravene a federal statute and the implementing Army Regulation, AR 600–20. This chapter discusses orders which may be illegal for various other reasons.

ORDERS TO COMMIT WAR CRIMES

An order to kill a subdued intruder at a South Korean air base has been held to be illegal. In his prosecution for homicide, the soldier who executed the order could not rely on the illegal order as justifying his action in shooting the man.[3] When an order is so "manifestly beyond the scope of the superior officer's authority and the order is so obviously and palpably unlawful as to admit of no reasonable doubt" of its unlawfulness, there is actually a *duty to disobey* it. In determining when such a situation has arisen, general international moral standards are applied.

This rule of law would have been put to a critical test if the trial of the high-ranking Green Berets accused of murdering a captured Vietcong double agent had been permitted to take place. It would have been especially touchy if their defense had been "We did it, but we were under orders from the Central Intelligence Agency, for whom we had done the same kind of thing before and

on whose protection we had come to rely." The law is
clear that, even though government agencies may engage in clandestine assassinations and murder (when
you kill a subdued prisoner, it's murder), there is a legal
and moral duty weighing upon everyone not to engage
in such conduct. Therefore, when an individual's cover
is blown, the government must vindicate itself by right-
eously bringing to justice the individual who carried out
the secret government policy. That way the *government's* cover is not blown. But in the Green Beret case
it is pretty clear that the famous defense counsel hired
by the defendants intended to expose the CIA's most
secret operations and its hypocritical legal and moral
stance along with them. Since the government couldn't
afford to let that happen, the President permitted the
case to be dropped.

Although the Army has clearly failed in its responsibility to instill the basic precepts of international law
and decency in its soldiers, every GI should remember
that when the political chips are down the Army will
begin to enforce them. Something like that is happening
now. After World War II, there emerged from the
Nuremberg war crimes trials the concept of a "new"
crime, genocide, the destruction of an entire people or
race. Recently several military defendants have attempted to establish that the United States is engaged in
the commission of war crimes in Vietnam, in order to
establish the illegality of orders to serve there. When
Dr. Howard Levy was court-martialed for refusing to
teach Green Beret medics, he was convicted, although
he had raised the defense that to teach them would be
aiding and abetting war crimes. His case is still in the
courts.[4] No American court has yet accepted the argument that our war there, or any part of our participation in it, is illegal. It is extremely unlikely that a
court would do so, at least while hostilities are going on.

Which brings us to the Song My (My Lai) massacre.
In March 1968 an American company swept through a

Vietnam village with a reputation as a Vietcong strong-
hold and allegedly slaughtered with small-weapons fire
every living Vietnamese they could find. Although it is
still too soon to judge whether any particular individual
was guilty beyond a reasonable doubt of cold-blooded
murder, we can learn some lessons from the episode.
Since it is not official United States government policy
that its troops should wipe out all civilian Vietnamese
who happen to draw breath in a village that harbors
Vietcong, when soldiers are publicly accused of committing cold-blooded murder, even in war, they will be
prosecuted. Which is another way of saying that if the
U.S. Army doesn't start training its soldiers to stop and
question the legality of questionable orders you had
better learn to do it yourself, as an individual soldier,
because you will likely be held accountable to live and
fight by the moral standards which govern civilized
peoples. Violations of these standards are defined as war
crimes by the Nuremberg Code:

> The crimes hereinafter set out are punishable as
> crimes under international law . . .
>   b)   War crimes:
> Violations of the laws or customs of war which in-
> clude, but are not limited to, murder, ill-treatment
> or deportation to slave-labor or for any other pur-
> pose of civilian population of or in occupied terri-
> tory, murder or ill-treatment of prisoners of war
> or persons on the seas, killing of hostages, plunder
> of public or private property, wanton destruction
> of cities, towns, or villages, or devastation not justi-
> fied by military necessity.
>   c)   Crimes against humanity:
> Murder, extermination, enslavement, deportation,
> and other inhuman acts done against any civilian
> population, or persecutions on political, racial, or
> religious grounds, when such acts are done or such
> persecutions are carried on in execution of or in
> connection with any crime against peace or any
> war crime.[5]

Telford Taylor, U.S. chief counsel at the Nuremberg trials, has recently explored the meaning of the Song My incident against the backdrop of the international law of war:

> The death of an infant in consequence of military operations does not establish that a war crime has been committed. But there must be a reasonable military basis for the act that causes the death, and in this respect the aviator and the infantryman are in different situations. The former is attacking a functioning part of an enemy war machine with a weapon that cannot discriminate. The latter is part of a force occupying conquered territory, and is in a position to discriminate among the inhabitants without shooting babies. Accordingly, the laws of war require that, in dealing with civilians, troops shall take reasonable steps to avoid unnecessary harm to the population.[6]

If the defense of "following orders" should happen to be raised by the defendants in whatever cases grow out of whichever massacres are uncovered, it will be rejected in the same manner as were the excuses of the commandants of the Nazi concentration camps, although such a defense is admissible in mitigation of punishment.[7] Furthermore, the point has been raised that our government's long-standing approval of the delivery of prisoners to the South Vietnamese authorities, who everybody knew were torturing and killing them, soils its hands sufficiently to require an international tribunal to arrive at the most just result.[8]

ORDERS AS PUNISHMENT

If an order is given for the purpose of inflicting punishment and not for the purpose of training, instruction, correcting a defect, or other related military purpose, it is illegal and may be disobeyed. AR 600–20 so indicates in its discussion of how military authority should be exercised:

A private E-1, for example, who is late for formation, appears in improper uniform, or has unclean
equipment may be censured, required to clean his
equipment, or to take extra training or makeup
training in subject(s) directly related to the training deficiency. *Such action is in the nature of instruction, not punishment.* Care will be exercised
at all levels of command to *insure that subordinate
commanders understand and adhere to the principle that training will not be used as punishment.*
[Italics added.][9]

In all probability this type of illegal order is the most
common. *But proving the motive of the officer or NCO
who gives the order is quite another thing. When refusing an illegal order it would be advisable to have some
friendly witnesses and to get the NCO or officer to state
his purpose in giving the order,* if that can be done
without letting him know what you have in mind. An
order to lie down on your back and make sounds like a
dying cockroach is clearly for purposes of harassment
or punishment, and in no way can it be justified. But an
order to go on KP out of one's turn on the duty roster
could be for purposes of punishment, or it could be
simply because of military necessity created by the
sudden illness of the person originally scheduled. In
such a case it would be within a sergeant's discretion to
select you as a replacement. But if he admits (in response to your gentle question) that you have to go on
KP because you didn't shout "Kill" in bayonet training
with enough enthusiasm to suit him, or because he
doesn't like the way you march, or because you went on
sick call that morning, then the order to go on KP is
illegal. The legality depends upon the *motive* of the
person giving the order, and since his motive is presumed to be pure, you have to be able to prove it
wasn't.

Similarly, an order to "drop" for pushups could be
given with the intent of improving your physical condition or for punishment, depending on the circum-

stances. If it is given because someone hasn't done all his exercises properly in a physical training class, an order to "drop" is legal. Incidentally, an officer's non-specific order to "train" or to perform duties to be assigned a soldier by his first sergeant is not a valid order, regardless of the motive behind it.[10] An order must be specific, so as not to impinge too much on a soldier's liberty, say the courts, and an order simply to "train" is too broad.

Any order given for purposes of punishment—not just an order to train as punishment—is illegal.[11] The courts have held that ordering men in pretrial confinement to perform routine details with sentenced prisoners amounts to punishment.[12] And where an airman was ordered to clean up his barracks on a Saturday at 4:00 P.M. (instead of between 7:30 and 10:00 A.M., the normal Saturday clean-up hours), an Air Force Board of Review held that the order was illegal since it was for purposes of punishment.[13] But the evidence was strongly in favor of the defendant there, since the officer testified that he had picked the 4:00 P.M. time "because I felt that to have him report at regular duty hours would be normal and that he should be punished and should be given an odd hour for cleaning." *If the officer had denied this at trial, then it would have been very important to have other witnesses to support the defendant's claim that punishment was the purpose.* It is the rare officer, however, who is sophisticated enough to know that an order given solely for the purpose of punishment is illegal. Nobody has ever told him it is illegal; in his training, nobody has ever seriously tried to instill in him a respect for the rights of his men and the necessity for exercising self-restraint in using the enormous powers he has been given over them.

In a Navy case a sailor who had placed parachutes on the floor in an improper way was given an order to pick them up and walk with them to each shop in the hangar, placing them on the ground and saying in effect: "This is the way to handle and carry parachutes."

He refused to be so ridiculed. The court found that the order had not been given to increase the defendant's skill in handling parachutes, nor to instruct the spectators, but merely as a punishment. A conviction based on such an order could therefore not be upheld.[14]

In another situation a soldier voluntarily returning from a one-day AWOL was ordered to the company guardroom to spend the night. The court there held that the order was for purposes of punishment, *since there was no reasonable necessity for the soldier to be restrained and guarded when he could just as easily have been ordered to bed in his barracks.*[15]

Legislators who hold hearings on the constitutional and other rights of servicemen, and distinguished witnesses who testify at such hearings, never mention these practices because there are so few reported cases. Thus they have the impression that relatively few such incidents occur. The draftee knows, however, that harassments like these are the daily diet in the life of a serviceman. What he has not known before is that they are also illegal. *These cases should be taken, naturally, only as guidelines, since an outcome depends on facts that are different in each case.* If there are any facts at trial which could substantiate a motive other than punishment for an order, it is likely the appellate courts would let a conviction stand. *It is advisable in all doubtful situations to obey the order, protesting politely, and immediately thereafter file an Article 138 complaint against the commanding officer* (or an IG complaint against another person) *to deter the offender from giving oppressive and illegal orders in the future.*

ORDERS FOR THE PURPOSE OF INCREASING PUNISHMENT

Sometimes an officer knows in advance that a soldier will, for some reason, disobey an order to do something. He will then *order* the soldier to do it, just for the purpose of increasing the punishment, first for an act which would have been punishable anyway, and second for the soldier's insistence on doing it. The *Manual for Courts-Martial* prohibits this device:

> Disobedience of an order which has for its sole object the attainment of some private end, or which is given for the sole purpose of increasing the penalty for an offense which it is expected the accused may commit, is not punishable under this Article [90].[16]

The problem with resorting to this ground for a finding of illegality is that it is so narrow and difficult to prove, although in a very few cases a sufficiently sinister intent in giving the orders has been discerned by the courts.[17] For example, a soldier with an urgent family problem may decide that he will have to be absent from his place of duty for a day or two to take care of it. He asks his CO for a special pass and the CO refuses to give him one. The GI then announces that he intends to go AWOL, and the CO gives him a direct order not to. The soldier can be court-martialed for going AWOL, but not for disobedience of the order.[18] Another way of stating this rule is that disobedience of orders that merely duplicate existing obligations is not legally punishable.

ORDERS BASED ON ILLEGAL ADMINISTRATIVE ACTION

When an order is based upon an illegal determination, action, or decision on the part of the Army, the order cannot be enforced. This excuse for not obeying certain kinds of orders is taking on a growing importance in the courts. For instance, when a soldier refuses to embark for Vietnam after his conscientious objector discharge application has been ignored, refused, or turned down arbitrarily, he ought not to be court-martialed for disobeying the order to embark. If he is court-martialed for disobedience of such an order, he may raise the illegality of the underlying determination (i.e., the denial of CO discharge) as a defense.[19] However, when a prisoner who was confined at an illegal location (a provisional guardhouse) left the place of confinement without permission, he was court-martialed for breaking arrest under Article 95. The court upheld the conviction, urging that since the *status* of confinement was legal he had no right to run away, even though the *place* of confinement was illegal.[20]

ORDERS TO OBSERVE NONPENAL REGULATIONS

When a regulation merely sets down broad policy, violation of an order given to "enforce" the regulation cannot be an offense against the UCMJ. For example, when an order was given pursuant to a regulation that soldiers should behave in a manner that would avoid giving the appearance of engaging in a conflict of interest, it was held that the regulation was not intended to affix criminality, but merely to lay down general ethical standards.[21]

Even a very specific regulation, such as the one that advises mail clerks of the cash limits on money orders they sell to other servicemen in Vietnam, cannot be converted into a penal regulation to punish someone whose conduct it is not designed to regulate. It was on this ground that the Court of Military Appeals reversed the conviction of a serviceman who *bought* money orders in amounts above the authorized limits.[22] The regulation was simply not intended to apply to the accused, but to postal clerks and officers.

No advice is being given here to locate the nonpenal regulations solely for the purpose of violating them with impunity. For one thing, ARs don't have labels on them indicating whether or not they may be enforced by the criminal processes. As a practical matter, courts determine these kinds of questions only when they are raised by enterprising defense counsel.

ORDERS TO REFRAIN FROM DOING THINGS THAT ARE BEYOND ONE'S CONTROL

A company commander who believed that a limp exhibited by one of his soldiers had no medical basis gave the soldier an order not to limp. The soldier naturally "disobeyed," since he could not do otherwise, and was court-martialed, as a result of which he was, even more naturally, convicted. The post Staff Judge Advocate had to throw the conviction out, since there had been no crime.[23]

At a naval station the local commander promulgated a regulation which declared: "It shall be an offense for any person . . . to lose his identification card or liberty card." The court held the innocent loss of a card to be an inadequate basis for the creation of a crime.[24] Similarly, an order not to have any automobile accidents while on a weekend pass would not be enforceable criminally, although administrative sanctions might be imposed on "violators" as part of a safety campaign. The rule is that where there is no moral fault based either on negligence or on evil intent, an act or occurrence cannot be converted into a crime.[25]

Notes

1. *U.S. v. Martin,* 1 USCMA 674, 5 CMR 102, 104 (1952).
2. See Chapter Eleven, Military Interrogations and Self-Incrimination.
3. *U.S. v. Kinder,* 14 CMR 742, 773 (1953).
4. *Levy v. Parker,* 2 SSLR 3222 (2 Aug. 1969). Supreme Court Justice Douglas released Dr. Levy on bail a few days

before his sentence was to expire, pending decision by the lower federal courts on his habeas corpus claims.

5. The Nuremberg Principles were adopted by the International Law Commission, upon direction of the United Nations General Assembly. Principle VI, quoted in the text, is substantially the same as its counterpart in the Charter of the International Military Tribunal which was set up to try Nazi war criminals pursuant to the authority of the Treaty of London, 59 Stat. 1544 (1945). See also Department of the Army Field Manual 27–10, *The Law of Land Warfare* (1956), ch. 8, sec. IV, para. 509.

6. Telford Taylor, "Topics: Judgment on My Lai," *New York Times,* Jan. 10, 1970, p. 30.

7. See Field Manual 27–10 (Note 5). It is noteworthy that the defense of "superior orders" was available to American soldiers until 1944, when it was eliminated from the American and British field manuals to help set the stage for the prosecution of Nazi war criminals by international tribunal after the war was over. Alan M. Wilner, "Superior Orders as a Defense to Violations of International Criminal Law," 26 *Maryland Law Review* 127 (1966), pp. 136–137. Coercion or duress might also be available as a defense when the defendant can show he would have suffered "immediate death or serious bodily injury" if he had not committed the act of which he is accused. *MCM,* para. 216(f).

8. See Chapter Four, The Military Mind, Note 26, and accompanying text.

9. AR 600–20, para. 33 (rev. 31 Jan. 1967).

10. *U.S. v. Bratcher,* 19 USCMA 125, 39 CMR 125 (1969).

11. The only exception would be the prescribed written form of order by which Article 15 or court-martial punishment is imposed after lawful conviction.

12. *U.S. v. Bayhand,* 6 USCMA 762, 21 CMR 84 (1956). By creating an exception for "emergencies," the Court of Military Appeals has recently mutilated the *Beyhand* rule, and has made it much more risky for an unsentenced prisoner to refuse to work with sentenced prisoners. See *U.S. v. Phillips,* 18 USCMA 230, 39 CMR 230 (1969).

13. *U.S. v. Robertson,* 17 CMR 684 (1954).

14. *U.S. v. Raneri,* 22 CMR 694 (1956).

15. *U.S. v. McCarthy,* 23 CMR 561 (1957).

16. *MCM,* 1969, para. 169(b).

17. *U.S. v. May,* 1 CMR 704 (1951); *U.S. v. Stock,* 2 CMR 494 (1952).

18. *U.S. v. Granger,* 9 USCMA 719, 26 CMR 499 (1958).

19. *U.S. v. Sigmon*, 1 SSLR 3054, CM 416366 (Army) (1969); *U.S. v. Noyd*, 2 SSLR 3218 (1969).
20. *U.S. v. Hangsleben*, 22 CMR 503 (1956).
21. *U.S. v. Henderson*, 36 CMR 854 (1965).
22. *U.S. v. Baker*, 18 USCMA 504, 40 CMR 216 (1969). See also *U.S. v. Causey*, 18 USCMA 282, 39 CMR 282 (1969).
23. Personal interview.
24. *U.S. v. Flanagan*, 9 CMR 574 (1953).
25. As an outgrowth of that common-sense rule, *MCM*, para. 216(g), authorizes physical or financial inability as a defense.

9

The Framework
of Military Law

A court-martial is not yet an independent instrument
of justice but remains to a significant degree a
specialized part of the overall mechanism by which
military discipline is preserved.

> —JUSTICE WILLIAM O. DOUGLAS,
> *O'Callahan v. Parker*

In himself man is essentially a beast, only he butters
it over like a slice of bread with a little decorum.
The army is based on that; one man must always have
power over the other. The mischief is merely that each
one has much too much power. A non-com can tor-
ment a private, a lieutenant a non-com, a captain a
lieutenant, until he goes mad.

> —ERICH MARIA REMARQUE,
> *All Quiet on the Western Front*

SOURCES OF MILITARY LAW

The Constitution

Military laws, regulations, directives, or orders can be
unwise, illogical, inhumane, counterproductive, or even
silly, and the soldier must obey them. But because ours

213

is a constitutional government, the Army's power to be any of these things has its limits.

The highest temporal law in our country is the United States Constitution. *It applies to the military establishment.* If any congressional statute, Army Regulation, or sergeant's order should conflict with any right you are given by the Constitution as it is interpreted by the courts, the Constitution prevails and you cannot legally be punished for exercising the right. This illustrates the fundamental concept of any legal system: If any rule or order by a lower authority contradicts a law, rule, or order of a higher authority, it is invalid and should not be enforced. Of course, every attempt is made by courts to reconcile apparently inconsistent rules, and this creates a lot of leeway for enforcing a great many of them.

Except for people who work with the military overseas in a declared war, civilians do not, in the absence of an emergency, come under the jurisdiction of military law. But when there is a national or local emergency, the chief executive may declare martial law, under which—depending on the exigencies of the situation—some or all constitutional guarantees may be suspended, and under which some or all of the powers of government may be exercised by the military. In such a situation civilians may be tried by military courts until the emergency is over. America has not yet experienced martial law on a national scale, although it has been proclaimed at various times and places.

The power to draft you into the Army is grounded in the Constitution's grant to Congress of the authority to "raise and support Armies," although even the conscription power has become the target of ever more vigorous legal challenge.[1] The same section of the Constitution, Article I, section 8, grants Congress the power to "make Rules for the Government and Regulation of the land and naval forces," which is the legal basis for subjecting soldiers to a separate system of law that is benignly called "military justice." Pursuant to this authority, the Uniform Code of Military Justice was enacted. By virtue of this grant and other specific exemptions in the Constitution, certain rights which are available in civilian criminal cases, such as the right to a jury trial, do not have to be provided to soldiers on active duty.

But even this grant of power over the lives of soldiers is restricted. The Supreme Court has recently held that the military's criminal jurisdiction over servicemen is limited to those kinds of activities which are "service-connected." In *O'Callahan v. Parker,*[2] a landmark case decided in 1969, an Army sergeant filed a petition for a writ of habeas corpus in an attempt to get out of a federal penitentiary where he was confined after court-martial conviction of housebreaking, attempted rape, and assault with intent to rape. The offense had been committed upon a civilian girl in a Honolulu hotel while the sergeant was on leave during peacetime. The Court held that the accused's acts lacked a sufficient relationship to any legitimate interest of the Army's to justify taking away his constitutional right to be tried in a civilian court by a civilian jury and ordered that he be released. As a result of this decision, the courts will have to decide on a case-to-case basis what kinds of actions bear a sufficient relationship to military discipline to give the military courts jurisdiction. *The practical result is that many more servicemen will now be tried in civilian courts for actions which were formerly handled by military courts. Also, the military police will have less power off post over the activities of GIs.* Practically speaking, however, although freedom has been expanded for the citizen-soldier, many GIs who commit civilian-type crimes will be worse off in civilian courts in some sections of the country than they would be in military courts.

The *O'Callahan* case has thrown the military establishment into considerable panic—and with some justification, since no one knows any more what the limits are of its power to punish. Defense Secretary Melvin Laird complained that the decision "deals a cruel blow to law enforcement in the armed forces" and asked the Justice

Department to seek a rehearing, which the Justice Department decided would be a fruitless gesture—at least until President Nixon has had a chance to fill Supreme Court vacancies with his own men.[3] Almost immediately after the *O'Callahan* decision, high-ranking Pentagon officials began making mathematical "calculations" of the number of additional casualties the presumably discipline-destroying decision would supposedly cause in "the next war."[4]

The political meaning of the *O'Callahan* decision was much less murky than its legal ramifications. It has been taken as an expression of profound distrust by the Supreme Court of the military's ability to dispense justice. Without declaring the Vietnam war to be an illegal action on the part of the United States government, which several litigants had previously urged the Court to do,[5] a more politically palatable blow was struck at the warmakers' power. Eventually lawbooks, Army Regulations, and the UCMJ itself will have to be rewritten once the factors relevant to "service connection" are known. The Court listed some examples of crimes which, although committed off post, would clearly come within the military's jurisdiction, such as "plundering the civil population, or abusing its women while on duty" and "desertions, assaults on and thefts from other soldiers, stealing government property." But the list is not exhaustive, and the mere fact that an offense takes place off post or on post may not be determinative of jurisdiction.

The early decisions of the Court of Military Appeals under the *O'Callahan* doctrine seem to presage a long period of groping for jurisdictional standards. In a later case involving sex offenses the Court held that the military had no jurisdiction to try a soldier for committing rape and sodomy on civilian victims in a private car, off post, while not in uniform, and where the only visible connection between the assailant and his military status was the bumper sticker on his automobile.[6] In another recent case the Court held there was no military jurisdiction when the offense was carnal knowledge of the fourteen-year-old daughter of another serviceman and the act took place off post. The fact that the victim was related to another serviceman and that she had made prior arrangements on post to meet the accused later were not considered sufficient to create a "service connection."[7]

In the area of drug offenses the Court has held that the use of marijuana on or off post could have "disastrous effects" on the health, morale, and fitness for duty of soldiers, and therefore its possession or use is always service-connected, and the military courts are empowered to enforce the military's drug regulations.[8] Defense counsel could conceivably attempt to disprove any disastrous effects from its use through scientific proof, and thus destroy any basis for jurisdiction, but it will be a long time before that tack is successful. The Court has also held that the importation of marijuana into the United States from a foreign country has no special military significance and cannot be tried by court-martial. Therefore it is still conceivable that possession of marijuana while on leave and away from a military base or soldiers would be held to have no service connection. At least one federal judge has been so persuaded.[9] The Court has indicated it will probably treat all illegal drugs alike for purposes of conferring jurisdiction. It held the unlawful delivery of barbiturates to another serviceman off post to be service-connected.[10] It is possible that military jurisdiction would have been upheld even if the delivery had been to a civilian. But it is clear that any time a serviceman is victimized by an off-post crime the courts will have little trouble in finding a service connection.[11]

A military court no longer has jurisdiction over a soldier for murdering a civilian off post[12] or for carrying a concealed weapon off post.[13] A larceny, burglary, or robbery committed by a soldier off base upon a civilian victim is not service-connected.[14] And the fact that a soldier was AWOL and wore his uniform when he committed a civilian offense does not mean that military courts automatically have jurisdiction over the crime.[15]

But when the military status is relied upon by the victim, as when a soldier in uniform takes a car from a used-car lot for a test ride and never returns, the Court will find that military jurisdiction exists if the owner's *motive* for giving the soldier the automobile was his reliance on the soldier's military status.[16] To rule otherwise, the Court has said, would undermine public confidence in the armed forces! Even when the serviceman is not wearing his uniform but *merely states he is in the military* and the victim (such as the recipient of a soldier's forged check) *relies* on that statement in the course of becoming the victim, the Court will uphold military jurisdiction.[17]

If any general rules have emerged from these cases, they would seem to be the following:

1) Just about any act done on post will confer military jurisdiction over the soldier.

2) An act off post involving or victimizing another serviceman will confer military jurisdiction.

3) An act victimizing a civilian will be deemed service-connected if the soldier's status as a soldier played a role in the civilian's "decision" to become a victim.

4) In the case of traditional crimes committed upon civilians off post, the mere fact that the victims are military dependents will not confer military jurisdiction.

Future cases decided by the Court of Military Appeals or by the federal courts upon habeas corpus petitions could either expand upon or undermine the rules already established as guidelines. The Court of Military Appeals has already held that *outside the United States* soldiers are subject to military jurisdiction for *all* criminal offenses; that is, *O'Callahan* has no application outside the United States.

Uniform Code of Military Justice

The prime statutory authority for enforcement of military discipline is the Uniform Code of Military Justice, which governs the conduct of all *active-duty* servicemen, and possibly some ex-servicemen.[18] It lists and defines the crimes against military law, including such military-type offenses as willful disobedience of a superior officer's order and such traditional civilian-type offenses as larceny and murder. The UCMJ is also a comprehensive procedural code, covering the preparing of charges, convening of courts-martial, conduct of trials, means for review and appeal of convictions and sentences, and informal nonjudicial punishments. It gives the President of the United States the discretion to set maximum penalties for most offenses; these penalties appear in the *Manual for Courts-Martial*. For the most part, military law in the United States is today concerned with the operation and interpretation of the UCMJ, which first went into effect in 1951.

The Code's passage was supposed to herald the birth of justice in the American military. Although a parade of "experts" have praised it as being overwhelmingly successful before congressional committees, the American draftee knows better. After World War II there was a torrent of criticism of the old system's grotesque inequities. This torrent lasted for years, but was channeled into a number of boards and special commissions appointed by the armed services to study military justice in relation to its social system. *Eventually the UCMJ was enacted, a compromise between those who wanted to preserve for soldiers the rights of citizens and those who wanted to keep military courts what they were— conviction mills that served only the military commanders.*[19] A great many procedural rights were guaranteed to servicemen for the first time, *but commanders retained control of the courts, which frequently meant control of the outcome of military trials.* The irony of the *O'Callahan* decision is that if the military had been less successful in keeping control of its courts in the UCMJ compromise, the Supreme Court might not have felt the need as late as 1969 to lop off a portion of military jurisdiction and give it back to civilians. And yet that's exactly what it did.

Army Regulations and DOD Directives

Once, as a joke, someone wrote a regulation on how to tie a shoelace.[20] It was published in a service journal. Suffice it to say that the Army has regulated many things and many people—from the arrangement of toothbrushes on privates' bunks to the cross-country transport of nerve gas and deadly germs. Since all Army Regulations are treated with equal solemnity, the Chief of Staff promulgates them. Together with the *Manual for Courts-Martial,* ARs implement the UCMJ, many other federal statutes, and the multitude of Army policies and practices. The other services have their own regulations, but in many respects they parallel the Army's. With the exception of orders from immediate superiors in the chain of command, most of your dealings with "The Law" in the Army will be in connection with ARs. They are to be found at the post personnel office, the Staff Judge Advocate's Office, and sometimes the library.

Army Regulations are public information and you have a right to read them for your own purposes, which are to be defined by you and no one else.

As custodians of Army Regulations, some sergeants and warrant officers have an odd regard for them, a certain wary possessiveness. They feel that The Law, as embodied in ARs, is properly in the possession of people like them, to be protected from the lower-ranking troops —as if it were theirs to dispense. As one of the "lower four" grades of enlisted men, your function is more simple. It is to *receive* the law in receptacles and doses selected by them. Now, this is too narrow a view of the law. In fact it is legally insupportable. *They know this, and if you insist on the right to check out an AR for yourself, they cannot deny you that right indefinitely.*

The ARs have a subject index (AR 310–1) which will help you to find what you want. The only regulations that might prevail over ARs are Department of Defense (DOD) directives and letters, which apply to all services. One problem in determining what the law is on a problem in a dynamic area (such as conscientious objector discharge applications) is that AR revisions may become obsolete as quickly as they are distributed to local commands. Sometimes a DOD directive supersedes an AR but the local command doesn't find out for several months, or if it does find out it doesn't tell anybody; nor does it assure that the directive is filed where the general military public can read it. One of the few fully up-to-date libraries of Army Regulations in the world is in the Pentagon. You can go there and read them, or almost anything else in the library. To obtain by mail a copy of any unclassified AR, write to:

AG Publications Center, USA
2800 Eastern Blvd.
Baltimore, Maryland 21220

Any citizen, including a soldier, has a right to receive free one copy of each of the ARs he wants.[21] A second copy of any AR will cost a minimal fee.

Although most ARs have the force of law and must be obeyed, others are merely intended to lay down broad policies and not to be penal in effect. Therefore, in some cases, although an AR is not followed by a particular person, he cannot be court-martialed for failure to obey that particular general regulation.[22]

Army area commanders and installation commanders can also issue regulations. They must, however, be consistent with the Army Regulations and the UCMJ.

Most frequently, the way it is discovered that a particular post regulation is invalid is through a court reversal of a conviction for disobedience of an order based on the invalid regulation. There are safer ways of testing the legality of regulations, but none so certain.

Manual for Courts-Martial

The *Manual for Courts-Martial* is promulgated by the President pursuant to authority granted by Congress. The 1969 edition incorporates important changes made by the Military Justice Act of 1968 and serves as a fairly up-to-date guide for all branches of the armed forces. It expands upon and illuminates the provisions of the UCMJ and is the most important source book for military commanders, military lawyers (Judge Advocates or "JAGs"), military judges, investigating officers, and courts. In it are reproduced the Constitution, the UCMJ, other federal statutes relating to servicemen, and most of the forms used in connection with courts-martial and nonjudicial punishment.

The *Manual* is also the handiest source for learning what acts are considered crimes in the military system. It lists the specifications (specific charges) of Article 134, the general article, which makes criminal "all disorders and neglects to the prejudice of good order and discipline in the armed forces" and "all conduct of a nature to bring discredit upon the armed forces."

If a criminal statute in any state in the country were defined so vaguely, the courts would probably declare it unconstitutional. But the general article (together with Article 133, which makes illegal "conduct unbecoming an officer and gentleman") has been upheld by the Court of Military Appeals on the theory that the *specifications* must allege acts which all members of the armed forces should know are wrong. However, the *O'Callahan* decision cast doubt upon the article's validity and it is possible that the older Supreme Court decisions might be overruled in the near future. Sample offenses under Article 134 are found in the *Manual*, Appendix 6(c): failure to keep a promise to pay a debt, wrongfully possessing or transferring marijuana, breaking restriction, being drunk and disorderly, passing a worthless check. There are some pretty quaint ones too: abusing a public animal and gambling with a subordinate.

The *Manual*'s list is not exhaustive, and *the soldier can be tried for unlisted offenses*. From time to time some of its specifications come under constitutional attack, especially those which infringe on the right to free speech.[23]

Standing Operating Procedures

Many brigades, battalions, and companies have standing operating procedures which are publicized by posting on company bulletin boards or by announcement at company formations. SOPs do not in and of themselves have the force of law, but if a direct order is given to follow a particular SOP, and the SOP is not in conflict with any higher regulation, then that order must be obeyed. It is a crime under Article 92 if a soldier, "having knowledge of any . . . lawful order issued by a member of the armed forces, which it is his duty to obey, fails to obey the order." It must be shown that the soldier had *actual knowledge* of the order. This can be proven by circumstantial evidence, which "includes evidence that the order was generally known in the command, that it had been posted at such a time and place that the accused would be likely to have read it, and similar circumstances tending to prove the knowledge."[24]

Court Cases and Published Opinions

With this complicated and occasionally conflicting mass of "Law," who decides what it all means? For the most part, it is the authorities who administer the system on its lowest levels who have traditionally taken advantage of unsophisticated GIs and denied them effective review.

When a court-martial conviction is appealed, the appellate courts are sometimes required to make decisions on claims of defendants that certain orders, rules, regulations, or statutes are illegal. *When such a decision is made, it affects not only the individual soldier in his case but—in theory, at least—all authorities under the court's jurisdiction, who are bound to administer the law as it has been interpreted.* Keeping up to date with the courts' decisions is made possible by the publication of judges' opinions which give reasons for particular decisions. At the conduct of future trials, lawyers for the government and the accused cite these published opinions as authority for their respective views. The trial courts are supposed to be bound by the law as stated in higher court opinions.

Researching cases to determine the current state of the law on any precise issue is one of the skills a lawyer is trained to perform. It is virtually impossible for the layman to do without becoming enmeshed in confusion. Lawyers are also much more cautious and rely less on a court opinion in any particular case as a guide for possible decisions in future cases. *They know that a small fact can change the expected result.* These obvious conclusions underscore the idiocy of the Army's serious contention for years that nonlegally trained defense counsel at special courts-martial could do an adequate job. Nonlegally trained counsel were all the Army provided in tens of thousands of special courts-martial until August 1, 1969.

Cases are located by lawyers through a system of citation. For example, the citation "18 CMR 187 (1955)" means that the court's opinion in the case cited can be found in Volume 18 of the Court-Martial Reports, beginning at page 187, and the case was decided in the year 1955.

ARTICLE 15:
NONJUDICIAL PUNISHMENT

The most frequently used weapon in the Army's disciplinary arsenal is Article 15 of the UCMJ. *It authorizes any commanding officer, no matter how small his unit, to impose punishment on the men in his command without having to prove his case before a court-martial.* The company commander cannot delegate his authority. His powers are considerable; in some instances punishments imposable under Article 15 may exceed those of a summary court-martial. However, if an individual has ceased to be within the command of his old unit—that is, he has signed out—the old CO cannot impose Article 15 punishment on him.

The soldier usually has forty-eight hours to decide whether to accept an Article 15. If he does accept it, a commanding officer of less than field grade (major or higher) can legally impose a maximum punishment of seven days' forfeiture of pay, reduction in rank one grade, extra duties up to fourteen days, restriction up to fourteen days, and correctional custody up to seven days. If a field-grade officer imposes the Article 15, punishments can be more severe, depending on the rank of the officer. However, an Article 15 can be given a soldier with only a "reprimand" as punishment, the infraction being listed on the soldier's record.

After acceptance of an Article 15, the accused can "appeal" to the next higher authority, who in some cases may, and in others must, forward the appeal to a Judge Advocate for his recommendation, but he is not required to follow the lawyer's advice. *Always consider an appeal. The infraction for which an Article 15 is given must be an offense against the UCMJ! Always check with the JAG Office to make sure the Article 15 you're getting is not completely lawless.*

Nobody should be held beyond his scheduled date for discharge from active duty (ETS) for the purpose of completing any unexecuted portion of punishment imposed under Article 15.[25] However, if an offense is serious enough, a "flagging action" can be effected to hold the soldier for court-martial. He may also be held to complete any sentence adjudged by a court-martial.

THE COURTS

All military trial courts are what lawyers call *ad hoc* courts. They are created solely for the function of trying certain individuals on specific charges brought by the commander with power to convene them. This commander is called the "convening authority." *Convening authorities still retain—collectively—more power to control and influence the outcome of military trials than any other identifiable group in the military system.* They convene the courts and select the officers to serve on them. If the accused exercises his right to have one-third of the officers replaced by enlisted men, the convening authority selects them too. They are almost invariably senior NCOs. The personnel who participate in the trial—with the exception of the military judge—are usually *his* subordinates in *his* command. He has the power to throw out findings of guilty and reduce sentences resulting from courts-martial he has convened. Knowledge of this is frequently reflected by officers who hand out ridiculously high sentences in the belief that the convening authority should be given a free hand to do what he thinks is best.

As an *ad hoc* court, a court-martial exists for as long as may be authorized in the appointing orders. The members of the court are named in the appointing orders and perform the equivalent function of a civilian jury, while the military judge performs the functions of the civilian judge, although he is not nearly as powerful. An attempt was made in the Military Justice Act of 1968 to upgrade the authority of the military judge (formerly the "law officer") so that his authority would be like that of a federal district court judge, but it remains to be seen whether the military judges will aggressively assert their new power over courts-martial. One step in the right direction after the passage of the 1968 law was the use of judicial robes by military judges. In the military this can be of profound importance, since the presidents of general courts-martial are frequently of higher rank than most military judges and so not disposed to take instructions on the law from them, regardless of the fact that the presidents of courts are not legally trained.[26] Military judges do not write opinions and thus are not a source of law except in the trials in which they make their rulings. It has been ventured that this too may change, and that a body of decisional law may be built up by military judges over a long period of time. The military judge cannot, however, become as powerful as the federal district court judge, since he has no permanent assignment and there is no "courthouse" from which he can issue emergency orders and writs, which he has no authority to do in any event.[27]

Only a court-martial can adjudge one of the two punitive discharges, the bad conduct discharge (BCD) and the dishonorable discharge (DD). (The other discharges—undesirable, general, and honorable—are discussed in Chapter Thirteen, Administrative Discharges.)

Summary Courts-Martial

Summary courts-martial still exist solely to make the rest of military justice look just. In the opinion of practically everybody but the Army, they should have been abolished by the Military Justice Act of 1968.[28] As the lowest-level military court, the summary court consists of one commissioned officer who serves as judge, jury, prosecutor, defense counsel, and court reporter. The lawyerless special court-martial prior to August 1, 1969, had a few defenders, but no one even pretends the summary court is anything but a kangaroo court. Before the latest changes in the UCMJ, an enlisted man who wanted to refuse acceptance of an

Article 15 could elect trial by the summary court-martial. Upon conviction, the appeal was only to the convening authority and the Staff Judge Advocate, but since the charge sheet was all the record consisted of there was no way of knowing what actually had happened at the "trial." *This is still what happens, except that a soldier can turn down trial by a summary court-martial and elect trial by either general or special court-martial* (most likely the latter). This increases his chances of winning an acquittal because he is represented by a lawyer, but it also increases the potential punishment tremendously. The maximum punishment a summary court can impose is one month's confinement, two months' restriction, hard labor for forty-five days, and forfeiture of two-thirds of a month's pay. *Consultation with counsel is essential before deciding whether to accept trial by summary court or to demand a special court.*

Special Courts-Martial

As intermediate military courts, special courts-martial can try the same crimes which are tried by general courts-martial, but they are used for less serious offenses. The greatest sentence that a special court-martial can assess is six months' imprisonment, forfeiture of two-thirds pay per month for six months, and reduction to the lowest enlisted grade. A bad conduct discharge can be given, but it would be necessary to detail a military judge and a court reporter (who prepares a verbatim transcript) to the trial. The Army has not used special courts for bad conduct discharges until very recently.

The court is appointed in the same manner as a general court-martial, through appointing orders of the convening authority. However, the convening authority of a special court-martial is usually the commander of a battalion, brigade, or regiment while the convening authority of a general court-martial is usually the commander of a post, corps, or Army headquarters. Three officers or more compose the court, and the highest ranking is the president. *Even though he is a layman, he makes the rulings on admissibility of evidence and on motions* (unless a military judge has been detailed). No verbatim transcript is made, but notes are taken by a *clerk provided by the convening authority,* and these are incorporated into the record of trial. The clerk is not sworn to summarize fairly the testimony of the trial in the record, although the record is the only possible realistic basis for review.

Effective August 1, 1969, the convening authority, in his discretion, may detail a military judge to preside at the trial if he believes the issues are likely to be complicated. (Most court-martial issues are very simple to convening authorities; otherwise they wouldn't have convened the court-martial.) The accused can then request that the military judge try the case alone, and if the judge goes along with this idea the court is dismissed. *This could turn out to be an extremely valuable right when the defense has strong legal arguments. It is available at general courts-martial as well.* The military judge will make findings of fact as well as rulings of law, as a civilian judge does when he hears a case without a jury.

Also effective August 1, 1969, counsel must be legally qualified and members of the bar. Prior to that date they merely had to be commissioned officers which occasionally resulted in the anomalous situation of a college dropout (but OCS graduate) lieutenant defending, and not too effectively at that, a college graduate who happened to be a private. The paper right to have one-third of the court replaced by enlisted men (selected by the convening authority) exists at special courts too. Unless a bad conduct discharge is adjudged, which almost never happens at a special court, there are no appeal rights beyond review by Army authorities. The Staff Judge Advocate of the supervising general court-martial jurisdiction has one of his JAG captains review the record—after the convening authority has completed his review—and unless there is something terribly wrong with the record the conviction will be affirmed at that level.[29]

Even with the retention of limited review, the special-court system should now be a vast improvement over the old one, which was an openly lawless farce.

The Army used to prepare its infantry, artillery, armor, and miscellaneous branch lieutenants for their courtroom tasks by giving them a few hours of lectures on military justice in Officers' Candidate School. They were usually commanders of line companies and pre-occupied with their other duties and problems when they found themselves on orders as appointed defense counsel.

The untrained defense counsel would go to the Staff Judge Advocate's Office and consult with a JAG captain who would try to tell him how to defend the case (while another JAG captain would be telling the trial counsel how to try *his* case). Five minutes after leaving the JAG Office he'd have forgotten most of what the JAG captain had told him. He would feel no need or find no time for investigation before trial, preparation of witnesses, or research of the law applicable to the case. Sometimes he would pursue a few lines of inquiry in the library, or look something up in the Manual for Courts-Martial, or, if he was very ambitious, read a few cases in the Court-Martial Reports and bring them into the courtroom to read to the court. No one in the room had the slightest idea how these cases were relevant to the case at hand.

No lawyer was required to be present in the court-room as law officer or judge, as court or jury, as trial or defense counsel. Sometimes the only lawyer in the court happened to be the legal clerk, a draftee who worked for the convening authority and whose functions consisted of distributing paper and pencils and keeping the courtroom neat. Most career military lawyers were comfortable with this arrangement.

Then the federal courts began to entertain petitions

for writs of habeas corpus from soldiers who had been denied the right to a lawyer's assistance, and one court declared the Army's deprivation of qualified counsel and substitution of untrained officers unconstitutional. It amounted, in the court's opinion, to a denial of the Sixth Amendment's guarantee of the right to "have the Assistance of Counsel" for one's defense.[30] The military became apprehensive about the validity of their special court-martial convictions and finally gave their reluctant approval to the change requiring lawyers at all special courts.[31] This had to be done because the Army holds about nineteen times as many special courts as general courts each year, and it could no longer take the risk that those convictions might be invalid.[32]

General Courts-Martial

The general court-martial is the highest court for the trial of criminal cases in the military. It can adjudge the most severe penalties, including death. The general court-martial must consist of at least five members and a military judge. Each side has one peremptory challenge, which means a member of the court can be relieved of his duties by verbal challenge and the challenger doesn't have to give a reason. Counsel must be qualified lawyers, and a verbatim transcript must be prepared of the entire proceedings. Like other courts-martial, it takes place in a military atmosphere, where all military witnesses must salute the president of the court both before and after taking the witness stand.

Because the general court-martial is supposed to be convened only for the most serious charges, Article 32 of the UCMJ requires that a preliminary investigation be held before an officer who must decide whether there is sufficient evidence to justify referring a particular case to trial. The investigative hearing is called the Article 32 hearing, and the officer is the Article 32 officer. At this hearing the accused has an opportunity to be represented by a lawyer, to get a preview of the prosecution's case against him, and to cross-examine any government witnesses. He may also offer witnesses of his own in an attempt to convince the Article 32 officer to recommend that the charges be dropped. But since this rarely happens, and in any event the convening authority who appoints the Article 32 officer can disregard his findings and recommendations and convene a general court anyway, this is not a good defense tactic. Although the constitutional protection against double jeopardy applies to the military,[33] a new Article 32 hearing can be held if the convening authority is displeased with the results of the first one. That is because the hearing is not a trial but merely a proceeding designed to aid the convening authority in deciding which cases should be referred to a general court.

Courts of Military Review

Courts of Military Review (formerly called Boards of Review) are the first-level appellate courts in the military system. Their decisions on the law are binding on all trial courts within their branch of service. They are set up and supervised by the Judge Advocate General of each service, and he determines the number of "panels" necessary to handle the case load. Each panel is composed of at least three military judges (which means that *these courts are comprised entirely of career military or civilian civil service lawyers*). Civilians *may* be appointed to sit on these courts as judges, but the Army has not seen fit to exercise its option. (The Navy has, but it generally picks retired Navy officers.)

Any case decided by a special court-martial in which the sentence includes a bad conduct discharge and any general court-martial in which the sentence is a punitive discharge or a year or more of imprisonment must be reviewed by a Court of Military Review.[34] The Courts of Military Review examine about seven per cent of all military cases.[35] Thus the great bulk of courts-martial are reviewed in the commands where they originate, an arrangement that military commanders have absolutely no quarrel with.

U.S. Court of Military Appeals (COMA)

The United States Court of Military Appeals is directly responsible for the administration of military justice. *As an appellate court, it rules on approximately one per cent of all courts-martial tried in all branches of the military.*[36] In the typical general court-martial, there is very little possibility that the case will ever be reviewed by the Court of Military Appeals. It virtually never reviews Army special court or summary court-martial convictions from any branch of service.[37]

Since so few cases are ever reviewed by the only civilian-manned court in the system, one cannot look only at the noble pronouncements of the Court of Military Appeals in ascertaining the true nature of military justice. A view from the system's underside is far more instructive in learning how it works, but the Court of Military Appeals and Congress have yet to discover that.

COMA consists of three civilian judges, appointed by the President for fifteen-year terms. Except in cases involving generals or death sentences, or those certified by the Judge Advocate General to the Court for review, the Court of Military Appeals need review only those cases involving approved punitive discharges or confinement of one year or more that have been reviewed first by the lower appellate courts (Courts of Military Review) on petition of the accused and a showing of "good cause."[38] The Court has also stated recently that it has the power to grant "extraordinary writs," like the writ of habeas corpus, but the occasions on which it has chosen to exercise this power can be counted on one's fingers.[39]

The highest court in the land, the Supreme Court of the United States, does not directly review any military cases. But it has the last say on all federal and constitutional matters, including cases decided by military courts-martial. There is no congressional authority for a case to be appealed from COMA directly to the Supreme Court. Only after all a soldier's military remedies have been exhausted can he hope for review by the federal courts through the filing of a habeas corpus petition. Unfortunately, the Supreme Court has not settled the question of whether military convictions can be reviewed in federal courts, and the lower federal courts are divided. In any event, if a lower federal court refuses to review a military conviction by way of habeas corpus, an appeal may be taken to the Supreme Court, which makes its rulings on matters of military law in the indirect manner of reviewing decisions of the lower federal courts on soldiers' habeas corpus petitions.

Needless to say, it is only in the rarest of circumstances that a soldier receives a hearing in the Supreme Court of the United States, and then only after he has completely traveled the routes provided by two separate court systems.

THE JUDGE ADVOCATE GENERAL

The Judge Advocate General of the Army is not a court, but the Army's chief legal adviser who performs some judicial and administrative functions. Every general court-martial conviction in which there is a sentence of less than one year at hard labor and no discharge is "examined" in the office of the Judge Advocate General in Washington, even after review by lower authorities in the field—the convening authority and his Staff Judge Advocate. The Judge Advocate General has the power to vacate or modify the sentence and findings in any case he reviews for such reasons as newly discovered evidence, fraud on the court, or error prejudicial to the substantial rights of the accused.[40] The Judge Advocate General can refer any case he reviews to a Court of Military Review or certify certain cases to the Court of Military Appeals. Additionally, within two years after the discovery of new evidence or fraud on the court, the accused may petition the Judge Advocate

General for a new trial, but if he has an appeal pending in a military court the petition will be referred to the court.[41]

The Staff Judge Advocate is legal adviser to the general court-martial convening authority. He provides and often selects trial and defense counsel for courts-martial from a pool of JAG officers on his staff. These "JAGs" are typically civilian-minded lawyers right out of law school who are doing a four- or five-year hitch in lieu of the draft.

The Defense Appellate Division of the U.S. Army Judiciary is assigned the job of preparing and arguing before the Courts of Military Review and COMA the appeals of soldiers convicted by general courts-martial who are given prison sentences of one year or more or discharges less than honorable. Appointed defense counsel are stationed in Washington and are not the same people who defend soldiers at the trial stage. In most cases the accused and his appellate counsel communicate by mail or telephone.

FEDERAL COURTS AND
HABEAS CORPUS

When all else has failed within the military system, federal courts occasionally come to the rescue. At the pinnacle of the federal court system is the Supreme Court, which hears appeals and petitions from many different kinds of courts in the state and federal systems. Right below the Supreme Court in the federal system are the Courts of Appeal. Each covers a specified geographical area and reviews the decisions of the federal district courts within its jurisdiction. Each state must have at least one federal district court. The New York City area alone has two federal districts and many dozens of judges to handle its federal legal business.

When a soldier becomes the victim of illegal detention by the Army, either in a court-martial proceeding or through administrative action, he can file a petition for a writ of habeas corpus in the appropriate federal district court and ask to be relieved of the unlawful custody, whether it is by the commander of a stockade or by his unit commander who is keeping him in the Army. If the judge thinks the detention of the petitioner is illegal, he can order the custodian to release him. But the judge must be convinced either that the military has no jurisdiction at all over the petitioner or, in some situations, that he is being confined because of a denial by military authorities of a constitutional right.[42]

Other extraordinary remedies, such as mandamus, declaratory judgment and injunction, or suits based on diversity of citizenship, may be used to invoke federal court jurisdiction. These remedies may be used to invoke federal court review of military *administrative* determinations involving clear denials of constitutional rights, failure to follow regulations, or extreme arbitrariness.[43] *But whether a federal court may review a court-martial conviction on grounds other than jurisdiction is still a matter of dispute among the federal courts.*

The writ of habeas corpus is one of the greatest creations for the preservation of liberty; it has a long history in England and America and it is still effective. Most petitions are denied, but the judge often holds a hearing. Judges have traditionally avoided any interference with the operation of the military, but in recent years inroads have been made into the exclusive domain of military arbitrariness, and the cause of civilian review has inched ahead. Whether you are successful in obtaining civilian review at the district court level of an administrative or judicial action in the Army will depend very much on the section of the country where you happen to be stationed. *Also important is the individual judge you happen to select and the expertise of your civilian lawyer in this field.* No appreciable success can even be hoped for unless you obtain one, either through one of the groups listed in Appendix B or by your own resources.

Military defense counsel are not authorized to resort to legal processes outside the military system, even if they believe their client's best interests would be served thereby. They are authorized to assist you in finding a civilian lawyer, but this might have to be done without letting their boss know, since his displeasure could be costly for them.

Notes

1. In June 1969, in the federal district court for the Southern District of New York, a motion was made to dismiss an indictment against David Zimmerman for refusing to submit to induction. In a memorandum of law prepared by New York Civil Liberties Union attorneys it was argued that the Founding Fathers never intended to authorize conscription but merely the raising of a volunteer army. The memorandum has been published as an article. See Leon Friedman, "Conscription and the Constitution: The Original Understanding," 67 *Michigan Law Review* 1493 (1969).
2. 395 U.S. 258, 2 SSLR 3068 (1969).
3. "Justice Won't Ask Rehearing," *Army Times,* July 16, 1969, p. 2.
4. Personal interview.
5. In *Mora v. McNamara,* 389 U.S. 934 (1967), three soldiers (who came to be known as the Fort Hood Three) attempted to thwart their Vietnam shipping orders by asking the courts to label the war and any orders to participate in it unconstitutional. The Supreme Court refused to hear the case by denying a petition for a writ of certiorari. Justices Douglas and Stewart dissented.
6. *U.S. v. Borys,* 18 USCMA 545, 40 CMR 257 (1969). See also *U.S. v. Shockley,* 18 USCMA 610, 40 CMR 322 (1969).
7. *U.S. v. Henderson,* 18 USCMA 601, 40 CMR 313 (1969).
8. *U.S. v. Beeker,* 18 USCMA 563, 40 CMR 275 (1969).
9. *Moylan v. Laird,* Civ. Act. No. 4179 (D.C. R.I. 20 Oct. 1969).
10. *U.S. v. Rose,* 19 USCMA 3, 41 CMR 3 (1969).

11. *U.S. v. Rego,* 19 USCMA 9, 41 CMR 9 (1969) (larceny and housebreaking); *U.S. v. Cook,* 19 USCMA 13, 41 CMR 13 (1969) (theft).

12. *U.S. v. Armstrong,* 19 USCMA 5, 41 CMR 3 (1969).

13. *U.S. v. Castro,* 18 USCMA 598, 40 CMR 310 (1969).

14. *U.S. v. Cochran,* 18 USCMA 588, 40 CMR 300 (1969); *U.S. v. Chandler,* 18 USCMA 593, 40 CMR 305 (1969); *U.S. v. Prather,* 18 USCMA 560, 40 CMR 272 (1969).

15. *U.S. v. Armes,* 19 USCMA 15, 41 CMR 15 (1969).

16. *U.S. v. Peak,* 19 USCMA 19, 41 CMR 19 (1969). In a subsequent case the Court said that where "military rank is the moving force" in victimizing a civilian, the military can prosecute. *U.S. v. Fryman,* 19 USCMA 71, 41 USCMA 71 (1969).

17. *U.S. v. Morrisseau,* 19 USCMA 17, 41 CMR 17 (1969). But where the military status has no bearing at all on a victim's decision to cash a soldier's bad check, no jurisdiction will be conferred: *U.S. v. Williams,* 18 USCMA 605, 40 CMR 317 (1969).

18. See Joseph W. Bishop, Jr., "Court-Martial Jurisdiction over Military-Civilian Hybrids: Retired Regulars, Reservists, and Discharged Prisoners," 112 *University of Pennsylvania Law Review* 317 (1964).

19. E. Morgan, "The Background of the Uniform Code of Military Justice," 28 *Military Law Review* 17 (1965); and 6 *Vanderbilt Law Review* 169 (1953).

20. James K. Gaynor, "The Military and the Law," 18 *Cleveland State Law Review* 485 (1969), p. 486.

21. Air Force Regulations are indexed in AF Reg. 0–2, Numerical Index of Standard Air Force Publications. *Counterdraft,* Jan.–Feb. 1970, vol. 2, no. 7, p. 13, says:

> Counselors advising Naval personnel should obtain a copy of Title 32, Code of Federal Regulations, Chapter VI, dealing with the U.S. Navy and U.S. Marine Corps, from the U.S. Government Printing Office, Washington, D.C., for a cost of $3.50. Many important Naval and Marine Corps regulations are printed in this volume . . . an index to Marine Corps directives and bulletins may be found in Marine Corps Bulletin 5215, dated Oct. 6, 1969. The title of this document is "Numerical Check List of Effective Directives Issued as of 30 Sept. 1969."

22. See "Orders To Observe Nonpenal Regulations," Chapter Eight, Orders To Commit War Crimes and Other Illegalities.

23. See "Criticism of American Society, the Military System, and the War," Chapter Five, The Soldier's First Amendment Rights.

24. *MCM,* para. 171(b).

25. AR 27–10, Military Justice, para. 3–19 (rev. 26 Nov. 1968). If this is done, see Chapter Seven, How To File a Complaint or Bring Charges.

26. In *U.S. v. Caldwell,* 11 USCMA 257, 29 CMR 73 (1960), the president of the court openly refused to follow the law officer's procedure.

27. The Court of Military Appeals may have impliedly recognized the new military judges' power to grant extraordinary writs in denying a soldier's application for a writ of habeas corpus. *In re Strickland,* Misc. Docket 68–48 (COMA, 24 Sept. 1969).

28. Dozens of witnesses urged the summary court's abolition in the 1966 Joint Hearings held by the Senate Judiciary Committee's Subcommittee on Constitutional Rights and a Special Subcommittee of the Senate Armed Services Committee, 89th Congress, 2nd Session.

29. Article 69 gives the Judge Advocate General authority to vacate or modify, in whole or in part, any court-martial conviction on the ground of "newly discovered evidence, fraud on the court, lack of jurisdiction over the accused or the offense, or error prejudicial to the substantial rights of the accused."

30. *In re Stapley,* 246 F. Supp. 316 (D. Utah 1965).

31. There is a very limited exception: where counsel cannot be provided because of "physical conditions" or "military exigencies," which fact must be certified and justified by the convening authority. For the time being, at least, the limitation has been rendered academic in continental United States, where counsel must be provided in every special court-martial, according to a recent Department of Defense directive. See Senate Report #1601, 90th Congress, 2nd Session, Sept. 24, 1968, p. 8, and Public Law #90–632, 90th Congress, H.R. 15971, enacted Oct. 24, 1968.

32. In fiscal 1968, special courts-martial in the Army numbered over 43,700, while only slightly over 2,300 general courts were held. Ann. Report of the Judge Advocate General of the Army, 1968.

33. *Grafton v. U.S.,* 206 U.S. 333 (1907).

34. Article 66. Also, under Article 69 cases can be referred by the JAG.

35. Ann. Report of U.S. COMA and the Judge Advocates General of the Armed Forces, 1968, p. 5.
36. *Ibid.*
37. *Applic. of Snyder,* 18 USCMA 480, 40 CMR 192 (1969). COMA will not review a special court-martial conviction where no bad conduct discharge was awarded, except where trial court lacked jurisdiction.
38. Article 67.
39. Edward F. Sherman, "Judicial Review of Military Determination and the Exhaustion of Remedies Requirement," 55 *Virginia Law Review* 483 (1969), p. 532, ftnt. 228.
40. Article 69.
41. Article 73.
42. *Burns v. Wilson,* 346 U.S. 137 (1953).
43. Sherman, *op. cit.* (Note 39). The procedural steps necessary to obtain review of an administrative discharge are discussed in Chapter Thirteen, Administrative Discharges.

10

Courts-Martial in Action: The Military Mind in Wonderland

The first thing we do, let's kill all the lawyers.
— SHAKESPEARE, *Henry VI*

"What do you know about this business?" the King said to Alice.

"Nothing," said Alice.

"Nothing *whatever?*" persisted the King.

"Nothing whatever," said Alice.

"That's very important," the King said, turning to the jury.

". . . Let the jury consider their verdict," the King said for about the twentieth time that day.

"No, no!" said the Queen. "Sentence first—verdict afterwards."
— LEWIS CARROLL, *Alice in Wonderland*

In spite of the radical structural changes imposed on military courts by the UCMJ of 1951, the old philosophy has managed to persist. Officers serving on military courts still impose authoritarian values through the charade of a semidemocratic form. The product is a bizarre mixture of paternalism, pettiness, caprice, confusion, and sham.

Originally, American military courts were considered agents of the executive branch of government, and as such were under no legal obligation to dispense anything but discipline.[1] They were treated as advisory boards for the commander, who, if displeased with a particular defendant's acquittal, had the power to send the case back to the court for the purpose of having them find the man guilty.[2] As a result of forced contact with the military through participation in two world wars, civilians found out what was going on and became outraged. To make the system a little more fair, some features of the traditional Anglo-American adversarial system were transplanted onto the military. Instead of having one person play the roles of accuser, prosecutor, judge, jury, adviser to the accused, and dispenser of clemency, these functions were partly separated. In theory, each participant now has something approaching a single loyalty. It is the philosophy of our criminal law in civilian jurisdictions that if you select a prosecutor and a defense attorney and let them slug it out according to agreed-on rules at a trial before an impartial judge and jury, the result will be as close to justice as could be expected in any human system. Unfortunately, the military convinced Congress to sacrifice the possibility of a truly just system to the needs of "discipline," and we are left with a structure in which the loyalties and roles of the players are still all mixed up.

THE MILITARY MIND VS.
THE LAWYERS

In reviewing one of the earliest American courts-martial on record, a general expressed his opposition to the role of lawyers as defense counsel:

Shall Counsel be admitted on behalf of a Prisoner to appear before a general Court Martial, to interrogate, to except, to plead, to teaze, perplex &

embarrass by legal subtleties & abstract sophistical
Distinctions?

However various the opinions of professional
men on this Question, the honor of the Army & the
interests of the service forbid it . . .[3]

The Army didn't trust lawyers then and it doesn't
trust them now. In discussing a proposal in the 1966
congressional hearings to extend the subpoena power of
investigating officers, General Kenneth J. Hodson (who
is now Judge Advocate General) noted the Army's
opposition unless some limit were put on it. He was
afraid the investigating officer might be "harassed to
death with respect to a lot of unusual requests for
witnesses" by defense counsel.[4] Air Force General R.
W. Manss was also worried about the defense counsel's
ability to drag out the proceedings. "They can try to
muddy the waters as much as possible," he remarked.
Naval line officers exhibited the same distrust of a
lawyer's loyalty to his client by opposing the establishment of a separate JAG corps in the Navy.[5] The military's attitude toward law and lawyers could be detected
in their denial of proficiency pay for lawyers until very
recently, while authorizing it for doctors. It could be
inferred from their maintenance of the most meager
facilities for use as courtrooms.[6] It could be seen in
their military justice training films emphasizing obedience over soldiers' rights.[7] These are manifestations of
the military's frustrated wish to neutralize the most
chronic type of "continual complainer."[8]

Given this hostility toward lawyers, part of which is
explainable as inherent in the nature of the differences
between the military and legal professions, the Army
nevertheless has a fondness for courts-martial. The Military Mind would prefer to have a trial and would be
greatly disappointed if there were none at all. The trial
lends an aura of dignity to the occasion of military
discipline, which in its absence would become routin-

ized and uninspiring. Like a religious ritual, the trial provides an occasion for the reinforcement of military values and the glorification of symbols of power and belief.

Legal procedures and the presence of lawyers adversely affect the two most valued features of traditional courts-martial: *speed* and *certainty*. Many old-timers felt that the involved procedures required by the UCMJ would break down in wartime, but the Army's ability to function under the UCMJ in Vietnam seems to have contradicted that judgment.

While the Army respects law as a tool for social control, it shows undisguised contempt for the lawyer in his traditional role as the defender of the individual against arbitrary authority. Reflecting this dichotomy, the Army could simultaneously embrace the old special court-martial for its ceremonial values and argue in Congress for the preservation of its farcical, lawyerless identity. The Army can promote periodic articles of self-congratulation in legal journals in which it takes the credit for reforms favoring the accused while concealing the existence of its reform-delaying tactics.[9] The military establishment could and did oppose administrative discharge reforms in principle while cynically creating them by regulation in an effort to discourage congressional action. One congressional witness called its crass use of such a device "an insult to this committee."[10]

Even more incredibly, no one had the stomach at the 1966 hearings to remind the committee of the Army's earlier attempt to undermine reforms instituted by the UCMJ and to torpedo the authority of the Court of Military Appeals. In a 1960 report to the Secretary of the Army known as the Powell Report, a committee of Army generals made recommendations which, if carried out, would have reversed a number of the more "liberal" decisions of the Court of Military Appeals and returned military law almost to the level of the good old days before the UCMJ. The generals found that "trials

by general courts-martial are slow and cumbersome"
and that the UCMJ "is inadequate to support good
order and discipline under present conditions because
constant changes in definitions of offenses and modes of
proof make court-martial results uncertain."[11] When
these statements are compared with the ones presented
for public consumption in such organs as the *American
Bar Association Journal,* the disparity between the
Army's public and private assessments of the role of law
can be seen.[12]

SOLIDARITY: THE MILITARY MIND IN COURT

One of the aims of a criminal defense lawyer is to
obtain a jury that represents the broadest cross-section
of the community, no matter what the community
happens to be. This is done because the traditional
wisdom of defense counsel has taught them that people
who are all alike tend to reinforce each other's prejudices and biases and become "hanging juries." By civilian standards, practically all military "juries" are hanging ones. They do not represent a cross-section of either
the American or the military community. They contain
no draftees and no privates. Their biases and prejudices
reinforce one another, and there is very little room for
the kind of clash that occurs in the jury rooms of
American cities. The members' entire life style is designed to build solidarity and foster sameness. Their
cohesiveness is cemented by a common commitment to
the military code of honor and caste system. Since the
social code of the field-grade officer encourages him to
associate primarily with his fellow officers of similar
rank, the top officers at any installation do not remain
strangers for long. This fact of life in the officers' corps
comes in handy when the commanding general of an
installation selects his men to serve on any general court-

martial. He need not know them personally because it is his job to know what they are like from the reports of others.

The composition of the court in the case of Dr. Howard Levy (on trial for refusing to give medical training to Special Forces aidmen on the grounds that they were committing war crimes in Vietnam) illustrates the commander's power to create a cohesive court. Eight of the ten officers were southerners, five from South Carolina where the trial took place. Their average length of service in the Army was 19.3 years. Levy was a two-year short-timer. There were no non-career people on the court, and no medical personnel who might have been sympathetic to the ethical problems of an Army doctor.[13]

When a court is assembled, both counsel have a right to *voir dire* the court, to question its members on their attitudes toward the law, the offense charged, the defendant himself, and other matters. Because of the military setting, it is not traditional to question for very long, especially since the majority of officers on the court are of higher rank than the military counsel and it would be unwise to embarrass them. So the questioning of the members of the military "jury" is, as might well be expected, less fruitful than in civilian courts from the point of view of exposing information, attitudes, biases, preconceptions, and personal animosities of those whom the law requires to be absolutely objective. Only rarely does a court member actually get caught saying, "Anyone sent up here for trial must be guilty of something."[14]

One military lawyer suggests that what underlies this deviation from the normal experience in jury selection is the notion of an officer's honor. Since an officer never lies, it is greatly resented by higher-ranking members of courts-martial when their commitment to certain rules of law is politely tested by defense counsel upon the *voir dire*. It is to be *assumed* that the officer will do his duty and take his instruction from the military judge, even if all human experience shows that officers are reluctant to do just that.

> . . . the old attitude hangs on and from time to time there is a case where attempted examination of the court provokes an outburst from a "traditionalist" that he resents his word being questioned. Undoubtedly some counsel, particularly those junior in rank, are deterred from at least some examination because of this . . .
>
> . . . personal experience of the writer, his discussion with other military counsel and law officers, and a study of the relatively few cases reaching appellate level compel the conclusion that by and large, there is either no *voir dire,* or, if an examination is conducted, it tends to be very perfunctory in nature.[15]

The notion of an officer's honor carries over even to his evaluation of witnesses. On *voir dire* during one of the Fort Dix Stockade riot cases, a West Point major stated that if all other factors were equal he would always take the word of an officer over that of an enlisted man.[16] He thus gave utterance to a prejudice that many observers know pervades the officers' corps and that inevitably prevents a fair trial.

The convening authority is usually as interested in obtaining convictions as a civilian district attorney. Officers selected by the convening authority to serve on military courts are necessarily past, present, or potential prosecutors. They sympathize with a commander's frustration in being forced to wait so long before he can punish someone he is convinced merits punishment. The older ones recall the good old days when military punishment was certain, swift, and businesslike.[17]

In military-type offenses, which go to the core of an officer's identity, the chances of a biased verdict are escalated. No one would consider it fair for a civilian to be tried on charges of disrespect toward or assault upon a police officer before a jury composed of cops, or even before a jury of people who closely identify with cops, such as firemen. We know it is asking too much for a person to put himself in an objective position when the nature of the offense is too close to home. So insurance adjusters are excused from negligence cases and policemen from criminal cases. This is impossible in a military court because you cannot easily find a juror who is objective by civilian standards. Many defense counsel feel that it is easier to win a murder, rape, or larceny case in the military than one involving disrespect or disobedience. The latter type of case involves military discipline, and courts in the Army uphold discipline as the foremost value, even over fairness. They fail to understand that in a conscripted Army lacking fairness discipline will eventually crumble. In justifying their court system, military officers have asked to be treated as a special breed of men, capable of putting aside those biases which affect all men and which civilian legal systems try to neutralize. Yet they have demonstrated—sometimes with a vengeance—that they are not superhuman.

In this atmosphere "rules of law" are practically reversed. The defendant is likely to be *in fact* presumed guilty until he proves himself innocent. The accused must endeavor *in fact* to prove himself innocent beyond a reasonable doubt, although the prosecution is burdened by law with the duty to prove him guilty beyond a reasonable doubt. More than a few high-ranking officers on general courts-martial have had the poverty of discretion to urge upon junior officers that the convening authority has already determined guilt, that he would not have referred the case for court-martial if the accused was not in fact guilty, and that the court's real function is to determine *how* guilty and to adjudge a punishment.[18] The percentage of career officers, full of faith in the goodness of their brethren, who adhere to this view is impossible to measure, but so long as the system remains as it is, it will continue to be cause for profound distrust.

ENLISTED MEN ON COURTS:
A REFORM TURNED SHAM

Trial by officers as superiors, of their troops as inferiors, is a traditional feature of armies under monarchies. This caste system made a kind of sense because officers were drawn from the upper classes and soldiers from the lowest levels of the humble classes.[19] Almost all the trappings of this predemocratic system survive in the American Army and are cherished by lifers. Any modifications—such as the meager right of a soldier to have enlisted men replace one-third of the officers appointed to hear his case—have been the direct result of civilian pressure. For the first time in American history, Congress in the UCMJ required the military to replace one-third of the officers on a court-martial panel with enlisted men if an accused enlisted man requested this in writing. Unchecked by anyone, convening authorities have subverted what was supposed to have been a revolutionary reform, turning it into a gimmick to reinforce the caste system. Only senior NCOs are appointed to serve on military courts, and of this group almost always the very top grades. The three highest grades of enlisted men accounted for over eighty-nine per cent of the enlisted men who served on Army courts-martial in the period between 1959 and 1962.[20] It might even be safe to assert that no private has ever sat on an American court-martial. So long as it can be shown that the statutory factors of "age, education, training, experience, length of service, and judicial temperament" (sic!) as listed in Article 25(d) were considered, the exclusion of lower-grade enlisted members cannot be relied upon as a ground for reversing a conviction. In an important case the Court of Military Appeals upheld a system of selection that obviously discriminated against lower-grade personnel throughout the Army. Yet the Court said that the deliberate exclusion of low-ranking soldiers *who were otherwise quali-*

fied would be illegal.[21] The obvious fact staring the
Court in the face, that many thousands of privates are
infinitely better trained to weigh evidence in a rational
fashion than the average high-ranking NCO, seemed to
be ignored. On the other hand, the fact that limited
"experience, length of service, and judicial temperament" of lieutenants did not prevent *them* from being
appointed to courts-martial with great regularity was
ignored. Yet the low-ranking enlisted man's lack of
those same qualifications appeared to be the convening
authority's only ostensible excuse for excluding them
from his courts.

Because only high-ranking NCOs are utilized on
courts-martial when the soldier requests replacement of
officers by enlisted men, defense counsel do not take
very seriously their duty to advise clients of their option.
They invariably recommend, and the soldier invariably
agrees, that there is no advantage to be gained. This is
unfortunate because, if defense counsel kept up the
pressure, the Court of Military Appeals might be forced
to recognize that the Army's convening authorities have
always violated the mandate of Article 25.

The Army has argued that placing NCOs on courts-
martial has resulted in higher acquittal rates than for all-
officer courts and that the soldier therefore does have a
better chance when he exercises his option. But it is
questionable whether the Army's statistics prove its
point. It is not known what the *rank* was of the defendants who requested enlisted members. *It is possible
that these defendants were NCOs themselves.* And it is
known that the majority of enlisted-member courts-
martial involve nonmilitary offenses, where discipline is
not directly in issue. It is known that as a court member
the NCO is especially tolerant of offenses involving
financial problems, domestic situations, drunkenness,
and sexual misbehavior—the kinds of indulgences that
get NCOs themselves in trouble and for which they are
court-martialed.[22] NCOs on courts feel some sympathy
for NCOs charged with such offenses. Abuse of a

trainee by a drill instructor can also be expected to strike a sympathetic chord in an NCO court member, who can easily identify with the defendant (who was unfortunate enough to get caught).

In this way a double standard of judgment is built into the system. While the trainee or draftee can expect to be dealt with at least as severely by a court with NCOs on it as by an all-officer court, the system provides a possible escape hatch for the NCO who is accused of doing what NCOs consider part of their job— breaking down trainees into disciplined robots by methods that NCOs have always used.

SELECTIVE ENFORCEMENT OF MILITARY LAW

Given the traditions, values, mores, powers, and prerogatives of the people who run the system, it is not astonishing that the UCMJ is manipulated to preserve the military's traditions, values, prerogatives, and powers. In sum, the draftee, the short-timer, and the nonconformist get shafted.

This phenomenon is not a unique feature of the military caste system: it has its analogies in civilian life. It's just that the controls provided by the courts and elected officials in civilian life are somewhat more effective in assuring equal enforcement of the law than in a military context. (The glaring exception is the use of the criminal law in the South to preserve a racial caste system.[23]) But generally it is at least possible for the president of a major stock exchange to be indicted for a sophisticated form of theft, for corporate executives to be convicted of fixing prices illegally, and for a few judges to go to jail for fixing cases. *However, since equal enforcement of the law is completely foreign to military values, it is not surprising that no military commander has ever been prosecuted for influencing or attempting to influence the decision of a court-martial, although some generals and Staff Judge Advocates have been caught red-handed.*[24]

It was contemplated that Article 98 of the UCMJ[25] would provide the machinery for making convening authorities subject to criminal punishment for the grosser exhibitions of command influence, but it has never been invoked by one general to punish another. A reprimand and early relief of command is the most severe penalty that has befallen the worst offenders. More typically, the "punishment" consists of a slap on the wrist and a reversal of a conviction by the Court of Military Appeals a year or two later—and possibly a military promotion in the meantime.

The offense of command influence could well be the only one that is "never committed." Almost "never committed" are the offenses of unlawful detention,[26] making false official statements,[27] and cruelty and maltreatment.[28] It is strange that in a system that churns out over 50,000 courts-martial a year so few NCOs or officers are ever tried for these offenses.

When an officer commits some offense for which an enlisted man would be tried by court-martial, it is the Army's policy to give him an opportunity to resign. This type of "punishment" is considered to be such a grave rebuke to the officer's sense of honor that the authorities truly think of it as worse than a court-martial conviction. This viewpoint may have some validity for a career officer, but it nevertheless represents a special privilege not available to enlisted men, most of whom would not mind having their "honor" sullied so painlessly instead of undergoing court-martial.

It is not just the officers who, by virtue of military preoccupation with the preservation of discipline, benefit from the selective enforcement of military law. NCOs also get away with violations of the UCMJ when the offenses are committed upon trainees or lower-ranking EMs in their command. A sergeant has to be a rather persistent violator of the regulations against brutalizing troops before he is court-martialed by higher authorities on their own initiative. Training NCOs who make illegal threats[29] or use provoking gestures[30] against trainees as a matter of everyday practice are never court-martialed for what *they* say. But one disrespectful slip from the mouth of an exasperated trainee could end in a federal conviction.

War hawks in Vietnam can call their civilian and military commanders a variety of unappetizing epithets for not dropping nuclear bombs on Hanoi and China, and no one even suggests prosecuting these military Strangeloves for disloyal statements under Article 134. When innocuous privates, on the other hand, try to persuade their colleagues that bombing peasants may be an immoral and stupid thing for their country to be doing, they are given dishonorable discharges and jail sentences in Leavenworth.[31] This selective and short-sighted persecution of dissenters can only awaken other soldiers to question the powers of their persecutors and the legitimacy of their laws.

THE CONVENING AUTHORITY PICKS THE PLAYERS

In the post–World War II battle between military and civilian forces, retention of control over courts-martial was the military's most significant victory. When a commander's investigative agencies (such as the MPs or the CID) have determined to his satisfaction that a crime has been committed, the convening authority can appoint a court-martial and assign its members, including the trial (prosecution) and defense counsel. Only the judge is detailed by a separate authority, the U.S. Army Judiciary. However, in the case of a special court-martial, the convening authority, at his option, can detail a judge advocate from his command to act as military judge. If, after the court has sat on a case, the convening authority does not like the outcome, he doesn't have to refer any more cases to it; it is in effect disbanded. The convening authority can simply convene a different court, picking its members with more care for their attitudes and opinions, and refer all future cases to it.

Sometimes a convening authority selects a court to try a particular case or series of cases. For example, the officers who served on the court that heard the original Presidio Stockade mutiny charges showed all the signs of having been hand-picked. They were almost all Vietnam veterans, selected to try soldiers who had made a peaceful sitdown demonstration in October of 1968 to dramatize horrible stockade conditions and treatment, particularly the wanton killing of a suicidal prisoner by a guard.[32] That court-martial selection was too successful for the general who convened the court, because the resulting sentences of fourteen and sixteen years so outraged the public, including some congressmen, that the Army was obliged to reduce the sentences to two years with unusual speed. The power of jury selection is extraordinary by civilian standards and is justified on the ground of military necessity—that the convening authority should have a free hand in deciding who in his command is not too "busy" with military duties to take time off to sit on a military court. If a district attorney had equivalent power, he could dismiss a jury panel selected by the jury commissioner and pick the jurors himself. Of course, the military fosters the fiction that the convening authority is "impartial" and not at all like a district attorney. But only the Congress and the Court of Military Appeals actually seem to believe that.

Before the most recent amendment to the UCMJ, once a convening authority had selected a court he could legally lecture its members and tell them how serious he deemed certain offenses to be. But he could not "unfairly" impinge on the independent judicial functions of the court-martial in any particular case. The Military Justice Act of 1968 forbids all instructions to court members except through general instructions at service schools or by military judges during trial. The change was designed to reduce the instances of "command influence" by convening authorities on their courts and to prevent them from undermining the integrity of their judgments.

In the most notorious "case" of command influence to erupt before the 1968 changes in the UCMJ—a scandal involving unlawful influence over at least ninety-three cases by the commanding general of Fort Leonard Wood, Missouri, in 1967—the appellate military courts were so thunderstruck that they did not know what to do. It appeared that the Leonard Wood commander had been dissatisfied with the actions of some of his military judges in general court-martial cases as well as the outcome of some of the cases. The general's dissatisfaction had been made known throughout the command. To inform all participants in future courts-martial who was boss of his courts, he had the courtroom reconstructed so that the president of the court was seated higher than the law officer. And to demean the role of the military judge further, the general directed that all subsequent general court-martial appointing orders, contrary to Army-wide precedent, no longer list the name of the military judge at the top of the list of court members, but at the bottom.

Lieutenants and warrant officers were suddenly no longer selected for service on courts-martial, thus making room for more field-grade officers. As a result of the general's campaign the length of sentences rose dramatically, which encouraged defendants to seek guilty pleas and pretrial agreements limiting their maximum sentences. The general was pleased until a disgruntled Judge Advocate reserve officer saw to it that appellate defense counsel in Washington received enough information to raise the issue of command influence on appeal in some of the cases, thus tainting the remainder of the convictions to come out of that command. One Board of Review found illegal command influence in some cases; a second Board of Review failed to find it in others. The Judge Advocate General manipulated the

Board of Review dockets by sending the subsequent Leonard Wood cases to the second board instead of the less "cooperative" one—but the Court of Military Appeals resolved the matter by directing that all the cases be returned to a different convening authority for further hearings on command influence.

These extraordinary hearings were held at Fort Sheridan, Illinois, Fifth Army Headquarters, to determine whether the convictions had been obtained illegally. The results were inconclusive, but the military themselves ended up either reversing or adjusting downward ninety-three general court-martial convictions.

The Army would like the Fort Leonard Wood episode to stay buried, but it is unlikely to receive complete cooperation from the military lawyers who were sufficiently repelled by the existing system to lose all their faith in its legitimacy.[33]

Actually, very few commanders feel they have to engage in *overt* influence on their courts.[34] With growing sophistication, they have come to realize they don't have to tell the courts what to do in every case. The section of the UCMJ which governs selection of court members has been taken by some convening authorities as full authorization to choose only those officers who have an unqualified commitment to the military code of "honor" which is so vigilantly enforced by the court-martial system. Article 25(d) says:

> When convening a court-martial, the convening authority shall detail as members thereof such members of the armed forces as, in his opinion, are best qualified for the duty by reasons of age, education, training, experience, length of service, and judicial temperament.

Under this section officers can be excluded who are known to question established ways of doing things, or who have off-beat ideas, or who are known to sympathize with the plight of enlisted men to an unusual degree, or who are personally ill at ease in the Army's caste society. Such blatant discrimination in the selection process is not tolerated by civilian courts.[35] Article 25 is also the vehicle for keeping qualified rank-and-file enlisted men, including all draftees, off the courts, even though they are clearly eligible to serve.

Technically, the convening authority is not allowed to be the "accuser" under the UCMJ.[36] The test of whether a convening authority is the accuser is whether he "was so closely connected to the offense that a reasonable person would conclude that he had a personal interest in the matter."[37] In one case the Court of Military Appeals held that where the convening authority's home had been burglarized by the accused there was too personal an interest in the case on the convening authority's part. Someone else should have convened the court-martial because the convening authority is supposed to act in an impartial, judicial capacity in reviewing the sentence and findings after trial and conviction. This is one of the cases that reveals just how regrettably unrealistic the Court of Military Appeals has been. The truly disinterested convening authority would be thought by his peers to be a lousy commander.

Most unimpartially, a convening authority must pass judgment on the seriousness of an offense in the very process of deciding what kind of court-martial to refer it to. By merely selecting a general court over a special he has told the court members something. As one military law authority has pointed out, the commander has "tipped his hand."[38] And the members of a military court know how to read it.

Together with the discretion to convene courts-martial in the first place, a convening authority's duty to review the sentence and findings of the court before execution of sentence is a source of enormous power. If a state or federal district attorney had equivalent power, he could decide when an accused should be brought to trial; he could select the lawyers in his office who would prosecute and defend him; he could pick the jury to hear the case; he could review the jury's verdict and the judge's sentence as though he were an appellate court, reducing or throwing out any sentence or charge on which he had second thoughts. And he would have the security of knowing that the members of the jury were *aware* of his broad clemency powers, since they too were in a position of, and thought like, district attorneys most of the time.

Military law gives the convening authority all these powers. He can suspend a sentence of ten years in jail and send the man back to duty the next day. If he decides there was insufficient evidence upon which a finding of guilty beyond a reasonable doubt could have been made, he can set aside findings of guilty and dismiss the charges. (Of course, it is clear that a convening authority would be reluctant to use this power, since he was the one who referred the case to trial in the first place.) In actual practice convening authorities usually defer to their Staff Judge Advocates to conduct the posttrial review and to pass on the legal sufficiency of the evidence to sustain a conviction.

Because overt attempts to influence courts are very hard to prove, the Army maintains that command influence as a problem has been licked. Because they see so few cases in which it can be documented by defense counsel, even the Court of Military Appeals believes the problem has been "substantially eliminated."[39] Although many lawyers believe command influence is punishable under Articles 37 and 98 of the UCMJ, no prosecutions for the offense have ever been brought against any convening authority. Recognizing that the system has been unwilling to punish those who are a little overzealous in upholding its authoritarian values, a witness at the 1966 congressional hearings suggested that unlawful command influence be made a federal offense and the commander tried in a federal rather than a military court.[40] The problem was pooh-poohed by a united front of impressive officers, and the military had too many friends in Congress for that idea to be taken seriously. General Hodson made a typical response to a committee inquiry about whether it is possible to avoid command influence when the court is selected by the person convening the court:

> Oh, yes, I firmly believe this. Our experience . . . leads me to the conclusion that the courts-martial selected by the convening authority are not subjected to command influence in any particular . . . Of course, there have been two or three command influence cases . . . but generally speaking, those are very rare exceptions. Generally speaking, I do not think there is any doubt about it.[41]

That was good enough for Congress.

THE "LAWLESS ROLE" OF THE STAFF JUDGE ADVOCATE

The Staff Judge Advocate (SJA) is primarily the commanding general's legal adviser and overall administrator of a major installation's legal affairs. With respect to courts-martial, the Staff Judge Advocate is supposed to act as nonpartisan administrator of the system, like the clerk's office of a federal court. In practice, he is the prosecutor's man. (The real prosecutor, remember, is the convening authority, who is supposed to be as impartial as a judicial officer.) An SJA must be careful to tread a tricky tightrope, since he must fulfill with equal fidelity his role of adviser to the convening authority and nonpartisan administrator of the system. It is an impossible job.

The difficulty was recognized in a Court of Military Appeals case when Judge Homer Ferguson wrote, in a stinging dissenting opinion, of the "essentially lawless role" of the Army SJA:

> We simply must face up to the facts in the administration of military law. Staff Judge Advocates act and behave in case after case as if they were attorneys for the United States, with their sole ob-

jective being the production of a legally sustainable conviction and adequate sentence.[42]

An SJA can perform many services for the convening authority without sacrificing his "impartiality" to the extent of disqualifying himself from conducting the posttrial review of a case:

1) He can help the convening authority prepare charges.

2) He can help secure witnesses for the prosecution.

3) He can make deals with prosecution witnesses on behalf of the convening authority to obtain testimony against other men on trial.[43]

4) He can provide a trial memorandum for the use of trial counsel, in which possible defenses are analyzed and suggestions are made which trial counsel can follow to overcome these defenses. Even this does not sacrifice the SJA's "impartiality," according to the highest appellate court.[44]

5) The prosecuting counsel has the discretion to issue subpoenas for all prospective witnesses. If he or the SJA does not feel that a particular witness requested by the defense should be subpoenaed, the defense must convince the officer who convened the court-martial that the witness is necessary to the defense and that the request is reasonable. Otherwise the defense can't have the witness produced if he happens to have been assigned elsewhere.[45]

Additionally, the SJA is obligated to remain in constant contact with the military police, the CID, and, when appropriate, other investigative agencies, such as the Federal Bureau of Investigation. Field manuals for both the Provost Marshal (head of the military police) and the Staff Judge Advocate exhort the respective departments to work at improving their liaison.[46] Any civilian police department would similarly have to cooperate with the district attorney's office.

To bolster the image of impartiality, the SJA must be careful not to appear *too* helpful to the prosecution. He cannot get *too* closely involved in an investigation prior to trial. If he does he is supposed to let another legal office, presumably at the next higher command, conduct the posttrial review of the record of trial. Attempts by the Court of Military Appeals to distinguish between what an SJA can do and what he should not do have failed to clarify for military lawyers the proper limits of their actions. Given the fact that the SJA, like the convening authority, has been directed by law to perform conflicting roles, this is not surprising.

The fiction is nevertheless maintained that the "prosecution" in any given case is the trial counsel and that his superiors are interested only in letting the chips fall where they may—in justice. But the trial counsel, being a civilian at heart, desires a conviction more often as a matter of personal accomplishment than out of a fear that discipline in the Army will crumble if he should lose. Preserving the SJA's image as the impartial administrator of the system facilitates another fiction: that the Army defense counsel can be and is as free as the civilian lawyer in zealous representation of a client, even though he is under the command of the SJA.

SPECIAL PROBLEMS OF THE ARMY DEFENSE COUNSEL

Although they are by and large inexperienced when they enter the Army, JAG captains serving as defense counsel sometimes give strong representation. But they too are in the Army, and more than a few are reluctant to raise issues that might embarrass the convening authority, particularly when the rationalization is available that a tactic would not work anyway. The defense counsel's boss is the SJA, whose superior in turn is the commanding general. Defense counsel's office is usually a few steps from the SJA's and right next to trial counsel's. No lawyers trained in advocacy should let friendship interfere with fidelity to their clients, but the Army lawyer has to be concerned about more than offending his friend the trial counsel. He must think about the consequences of offending his boss or his boss's boss, the general. The SJA has the discretion to assign his JAG captains to the various jobs in a post legal office, which range from very dull to reasonably interesting. A particular JAG officer can be deemed "qualified" to fill an extremely dreary slot for an extended period of time. The SJA approves and disapproves leaves, early rotations to the States for overseas personnel, and transfers to other units. He can affect a JAG captain's employment career in the Army through bad or (even more destructive) subtly lukewarm efficiency reports.[47] He can do this without making specific reference to the officer's conduct as defense counsel, which has been prohibited by recent changes in the UCMJ.

The legislative history behind the change forbidding the evaluation of conduct as defense counsel as a basis for efficiency reports illuminates the Army's continuing reluctance to create the conditions for a truly partisan defense counsel. During the first fifteen years of the UCMJ several cases were reviewed by the Court of Military Appeals in which extremely bad efficiency reports had been written by SJAs on defense counsel whose sole sins had been zealous defense of their clients. Although the Court reversed the convictions and condemned the Staff Judge Advocates, these career Army lawyers were never punished in any way by higher authority.[48] Yet the armed forces argued that defense counsel should not be "deprived" of the opportunity to have their performance rated! In the words of General Hodson, it would "be unfair to the counsel."[49] This justification for the direct exercise of command pressure was felt by Congress to be an inadequate basis for preserving the SJA's right to evaluate a defense counsel's performance, and the prohibition became part of the 1968 patchwork reform.

The Army's attempt to keep its powers over the

activities of defense counsel reflects the philosophy of at least a substantial number of SJAs: The Army defense counsel's role is to "protect the rights of the accused" but otherwise not to engage in any activity that would reflect badly on the Army or the command.[50] The Army defense counsel is regarded by these career military lawyers as a "team player" who should be as concerned with the "right" result as the SJA. Very few career military lawyers are courageous enough to admit that the Army view of a defense counsel's role runs counter to the best traditions of the legal profession.

In their attempt to juggle dual loyalties, some defense counsel have so diluted their partisanship that the Court of Military Appeals has seen fit to reverse convictions resulting from defense counsel's "objectivity," a problem unique to military practice. When the Court discovered that the Army was distributing a pamphlet to defense counsel advising them to discourage their clients' appeals when, in the counsel's opinion, an appeal would be a waste of the government's time and money, it strongly condemned the practice.[51] Defense counsel was criticized for following the Army's pamphlet and was admonished to be more loyal to his clients in the future. In another case defense counsel at a pretrial hearing had provided the SJA with a summary of testimony which the SJA then passed on to the trial counsel for use at the court-martial.[52] This also was a little too much cooperation.

Yet there are many instances of pressure to make the trial counsel's job easier—for instance, by not forcing him to obtain expert witnesses in certain situations or to agree to stipulate to the testimony of key lay witnesses. Pressure on defense counsel may vary with the pressure the SJA feels from his commanding general. SJAs know that some generals still personally blame the SJA when the prosecution loses a case. How many Army defense lawyers are strong enough to advance every possible theory of attack, even if the convening authority himself is the attack's object, is open to conjecture. There are times when defense counsel should urge his client to seek out a civilian lawyer to present constitutional arguments in a federal court by way of extraordinary writ—something an Army defense counsel is not authorized to do himself but which the more aggressive military defense counsel do anyway—but when a JAG captain makes such an arrangement his SJA is free to express his displeasure. The fact that many SJAs exercise self-restraint doesn't justify the preservation of their potentially corrupting powers.

It is the practice in virtually all SJA offices to rotate JAG captains to three or four different sections during the typical tour of duty. One device for manipulating results in general courts-martial that the great majority of SJAs have found effective is the premature rotation of talented defense counsel to the prosecution side of the bar. This is an old practice in the military and was documented too many times in both the 1962 and 1966 congressional hearings for the Army to deny that it is done extensively. One witness frankly admitted having done it himself:

> But as a commanding officer, I could not afford to have a winner on the defense side, so I would have him shipped over to my side, to the command side, and have him prosecute the cases.
>
> When I was a commander at Fort Riley, I did that, and so did all the other regimental commanders, and I am sure that my general would not permit some bright young attorney to defend the cases.[53]

A civilian expert explained why the practice continues:

> If the staff judge advocate has a choice between two people, he is going to take his best for prosecution. You pick your best man for the side that you feel should prevail . . . Since this is the staff judge advocate, the man who advised on the ref-

erence for court-martial, he thinks the case should be won, and he is not going to put his junior lawyer on the prosecution up against his sharpest defense counsel.[54]

No prohibition or even condemnation of this practice was included in the Military Justice Act of 1968. An SJA can still do it without violating the law.

Another problem in the defense of persons accused of military crimes is that of the civilian counsel who comes in to direct the defense. One of the many bizarre features of the 1967 trial of Dr. Howard Levy for "uttering disloyal statements" and for refusing to train Special Forces aidmen was the Army's refusal to permit civilian defense counsel Charles Morgan, Jr., Southern Director of the American Civil Liberties Union, to examine fully the 180-page dossier prepared on Dr. Levy by military intelligence agents. Even though Dr. Levy's accuser admitted that he received his information on the defendant's political beliefs from the dossier,[55] and although it is customary to release all reports upon which a military prosecution is based to the defense prior to trial, only the *military* defense counsel was allowed to see the entire document. That's because the dossier was "classified" and Morgan didn't have his security clearance then. (They take time to get.) The dossier was classified "Confidential," the lowest-level clearance, which is practically meaningless, yet Morgan had to conduct the defense without being allowed to see about 100 pages of it. The dual loyalties of the Army defense counsel were evidenced by the fact that he was permitted to view the 100 forbidden pages but was not allowed to tell either the defendant or his civilian colleague about their contents. Because the law officer would not even permit the dossier to be made a sealed part of the record, federal courts subsequently reviewing the case (on petition for habeas corpus) could not find out what was in it.

AN ARMY DEFENDERS CORPS

If Judge Ferguson is right in observing that in the Army's legal system "the dice are loaded" in favor of the lawyer who does not fight the system,[56] the problem could be eliminated by the immediate creation of a separate corps of defense lawyers that functions in a chain of command separate from that of the convening authority and the SJA. The Army claims that (1) such an arrangement would be extremely burdensome administratively, (2) devotion of full time to defense work would be both detrimental and "unattractive"[57] to lawyers, and (3) a traveling corps of defense counsel would be of less use to defendants because of a lack of knowledge of local people and conditions.

The first objection conveniently ignores the fact that since 1962 the Army has successfully operated a similar program of providing relatively independent judges through the U.S. Army Judiciary. The second objection fails to recognize that assignment to this defense corps would be only one of two or three duty assignments typically given each JAG captain during his active duty. And the third could be solved by establishing on each installation a Defense Judge Advocate's Office with an investigative staff. The lack of an investigative staff for the privileged use of Army defense counsel has been criticized by Army lawyers as a serious impediment to the proper representation of defendants.[58] This inadequacy, which effectively denies some defendants a fair trial, could be eliminated simultaneously with the abuses inherent in a system in which the defense lawyer works for and under the direction of the *de facto* prosecutor, the friendly Staff Judge Advocate.

MILITARY "BAIL"

In our country a suspect who has been arrested for committing a crime has a constitutional right to release until such time as he is convicted and a sentence has been imposed. This is the constitutional right to bail, which we have because Anglo-American jurisprudence cloaks an accused with a "presumption of innocence" until he has been found guilty beyond a reasonable doubt by a jury of his peers. Even after conviction, bail in civilian life is common pending appeal, and many convicted defendants have been given their liberty in exchange for a money bond or a promise to return to serve their sentences in case they lose their appeals.

In the American military system no right to bail exists, either before or after conviction. Before conviction a commanding officer can order into confinement a suspect in his command "as circumstances may require."[59] The *Manual for Courts-Martial* limits this vague criterion as follows:

> Confinement will not be imposed pending trial unless deemed necessary to insure the presence of the accused at the trial or because of the seriousness of the offense charged.[60]

Sometimes the charges are so trumped up and insubstantial that, upon the direction of a federal court to justify the confinement of certain suspects, the military caves in, lets them out of the stockade, and drops all charges.[61] Typically, commanders will put someone in pretrial confinement in the stockade if they feel like it and won't if they don't. It's as arbitrary as that. But recent court decisions, such as the one cited above, may persuade them to be more careful.

A respectable percentage of cases that do get reviewed by the Army's appellate courts are reversed for legal error at trial. The defendant is sometimes granted a new trial and sometimes the charges are ordered to be dismissed altogether. *Unfortunately, in such cases the accused has almost always finished serving his sentence by the time of the reversal.* What he ends up with is a prison experience dignified by a court's opinion stating he should not have had it. That is because the UCMJ, prior to the Military Justice Act of 1968, did not give the convening authority the power to release a convicted soldier pending appeal. Now he has that power under a new section of the Code,[62] but, as expected, it has been exercised with stinginess and trepidation.

THE LAW OF THE STOCKADE

It would be a bitter joke for this or any other book to pretend to advise a prisoner how to exercise his "rights" while confined in a stockade. The law of the correctional officer and his accomplices is the law of the stockade. It must be admitted that their excesses can be controlled only to the extent that responsible civilians will move themselves to care about the young men who "serve" their nation by being beaten, kicked, degraded, and tortured by their countrymen. In the Army's view, it seems, this is what stockade prisoners need to become the "men" that their tormentors consider themselves to be.

Military behind-bars brutishness has begun to receive the attention of many writers, and to exaggerate the foul treatment to which American military prisoners are subjected would be a confounding job. Therefore, since even the fullest knowledge of military prison regulations is of almost no utility to the isolated and powerless prisoner, the regulations are simply cited here and retention of civilian counsel, if humanly possible, is strongly advised. Army Regulations and the UCMJ prohibit maltreatment, torture, and arbitrary deprivation of prisoners' privileges. But they, like other notions of fundamental decency, are easily ignored by the closed military system. *Perhaps the recent recognition by the Court of Military Appeals that a stockade prisoner has the right to file an Article 138 complaint will help expose prison abuses.*[63]

It is not very likely that the military appellate courts will be able to enforce humane standards within the stockades and brigs, but the Army Court of Military Review recently decided a case that may become an important precedent. It should be explored by all defense counsel representing stockade prisoners who are placed on trial in effect for defending themselves against brutality. A prisoner named Revels was charged with disrespect and assault on a commissioned officer and with failure to obey and disrespect to a noncommissioned officer. On appeal, the conviction was reversed.

> The court held that the confinement officer [and also the first sergeant] by reason of their "gross improprieties" had divested themselves of the right to be respected. Both men had used provoking, abusive, and derogatory language toward the accused, the sergeant kicked a fence which struck the accused, and the confinement officer punched the accused in the stomach and kneed him in the groin while other custodial personnel held the accused, whose arm was in a cast. The court, condemning the use of brute force which precipitated the offenses in question, stated that the men had divested themselves of "that cloak of authority, respect, and deference which is due them."[64]

There have been many cases in which prisoners were convicted of "offenses" against those who had, in one way or another, lost the right to be respected or obeyed. The Presidio mutiny cases may be added to this category. In October 1968, when a guard shot a mentally ill prisoner, Private Richard Bunch, who was trying to escape from the ghastly, overcrowded Presidio Stockade in San Francisco, he triggered not only the death of Private Bunch but a series of events which for the first time in the Vietnam era gave the public a glimpse of what the Army's "correctional system" is like.

Bunch had threatened suicide on many occasions. The Army has a system of distinguishing between suicide "gestures" and "attempts" and no doubt felt that all Bunch had engaged in were gestures. A gesture is ignored, while an attempt will result at least in a psychiatric interview. Actually, the Army knew of Bunch's desperation because a psychiatric interview shortly before his death had revealed that he was a "manic depressive." He had talked constantly to his fellow inmates about committing suicide. A sampling of Bunch's pathetic suicide notes was turned over by guards at the stockade to Terence Hallinan, defense counsel for the Presidio "mutineers." They reveal just how far Bunch had deteriorated:

> UNITED STATES I'LL PAY
> SAVE Everyone Else
> I'LL BE THE [illegible]
> I'm Not Giving Up My CROSS
> If I Have To WORK FOR IT A
> THOUSAND YEARS
> VERY WELL, Since They Want Me,
> I'LL DO IT

> Well, IF YOUR not going to
> GIVE ME LOVE, CAN AT LEAST
> DO ME the Favor OF Complete
> Elimination. I've BUT ONE
> Click and it's OVER.

After Bunch's death wish came true, prisoners who were to be known nationally as the Presidio 27 staged a sit-down demonstration. One of them read a list of grievances and called for cleaner living conditions, psychological testing for all guards, and an end to having to work under armed guards. Although a young investigating officer had warned the military against overreacting to the demonstration, the first two soldiers were convicted of mutiny and sentenced to terms of fourteen and sixteen years. The sentences were reduced to two years only after the outraged intervention of many civilian groups and of Senators Charles Goodell of New York and Alan Cranston of California.

Conditions across the country at Fort Dix, New Jersey, were even worse. That may be the reason why in June 1969 there was no sit-down demonstration but a riot, in which 150 to 250 prisoners participated. The men threw foot lockers outside the barracks, smashed windows, and burned bedding.

In an effort to pin the blame for the uprising on a handful of prisoners with radical political views, the Army's Criminal Investigation Detachment sent dozens of agents into the stockade. They enticed a number of young, frightened prisoners with the irresistible prospect of early release from the stockade in exchange for statements incriminating the riot's "leaders." The ones the military wanted especially to get were Terry Klug, an American Servicemen's Union organizer who had voluntarily returned from Europe and had just been convicted of desertion; Bill Brakefield, an organizer for the ASU; and Jeffrey Russell, a Buddhist and pacifist who had recently become an ASU member. There were also Tom Catlow and Carlos Rodriguez, who had not been "political" before the Army convinced them to resist. Government witnesses at the trials admitted that the CID had offered help in their own cases if they would help incriminate the presumed organizers of the riot. But to a military court that in no way discredited the CID or the statements it had gathered. Russell, Brakefield, and Catlow were convicted of riot and aggravated arson.[65] Rodriguez, a Puerto Rican, was convicted of only the arson charge but received the heaviest sentence, four years' imprisonment. To the amazement of all the spectators, Klug was acquitted, but only after his civilian attorney, Henry diSuvero, had effectively exposed the lawlessness of the stockade authorities.

The riot at Fort Dix was caused as much by the new stockade commander as by anyone else. When he arrived he had tightened up on discipline and limited privileges. He required degrading trainee-type haircuts, which humiliated the men when their wives and families visited them. Prisoners had seen guards dragging other prisoners through the compound. Some prisoners had been beaten by guards. The men had been forced to stand in the hot June sun for hours for no justifiable reason. After the riot the suspects selected by the Army were thrown into disciplinary segregation (solitary confinement) and were denied the right to smoke, read, talk, exercise more than fifteen minutes a day, have visitors, keep their mattresses in their bunks during the day, or even lie down on the steel bunks during daylight hours. Some of these restrictions continued even after they were put in "administrative segregation," which is supposed to be a nonpunitive type of solitary confinement.

The Fort Dix authorities have approved the use of "the straps," by which uncooperative prisoners are bound by the ankles and wrists with their limbs lashed behind them. With the prisoner subdued, the guards can have their fun with him:

> They pick you up like a suitcase and drop you, and it's from a little higher up each time. You land on your face and chest with nothing to break your fall, and there's nothing you can do about it.[66]

Despite these practices, the Marines seem to have the edge in attracting the most creative lunatics in the American military. Not only were the guards at the Pendleton Brig permitted to have clubs to beat prisoners black and blue,[67] their engineers and carpenters had built six cells known as the Ice Box (which has since been removed). The cages comprising the Ice Box were on a concrete slab with iron bars set in, and there was only a roof to protect the prisoners from the weather. During the day, when it was hot, a canvas was draped over the box; at night, when it was cold, the canvas was taken off.[68]

Prisoners in the Pendleton Brig have been forced to eat cigarettes, which may not seem so bad to the Marine recruits who have been made to eat their own vomit.[69] Father Alban Rosen, a Franciscan priest who was a volunteer chaplain for the Marines, told a reporter:

> No matter how bad it is, you can believe just about anything the Marines tell you about the brig. I really don't doubt any of the stories, because of the

things I've seen and heard. I've seen faces beaten in. I know about the room of mirrors. The brig chaplain told me about a guard who had a detail of guys on a running pattern, constantly running —don't know how many hours. And he noticed guys just falling down from exhaustion and the guard would just come over and kick them until they got up and started trotting again. I was just talking to someone who told me that he had heard this kid screaming at the control center. The guards were working him over, and the kid came staggering out the back door bleeding and doubled over, and collapsed.[70]

To try to differentiate between the "legal" and "illegal" aspects of the various activities described would be fruitless and fraudulent. The prisoner is powerless to do anything to control his destiny or protect his person in the concentration camp called a military stockade. His only hope is to establish friendships with his fellow sufferers and contact with a civilian lawyer, who is in the best position to help him, and to bring to the public's attention the terrors their taxes support.

The blame for stockade uprisings at Fort Ord, Fort Riley, the Long Binh Jail, the Presidio, Fort Dix, and elsewhere cannot be placed on the prisoners. The great majority are not criminals in any fair sense of the word, but young men who went AWOL because they couldn't take the dehumanizing idiocy that is military life for the American draftee or enlistee. The blame truly belongs to the blossoming Eichmanns of the American military subculture, and ultimately to the civilization whose greatness diminishes with each atrocity committed in its name.

Notes

1. Major Donald W. Hansen, "Judicial Functions for the Commander," 41 *Military Law Review* 1 (1968), p. 2, quoting the great nineteenth-century authority on military law,

W. Winthrop, *Military Law and Precedents* (2nd ed., 1920), p. 54:

> [It] should be borne in mind that they are in a special sense courts of honor, whose object is the maintenance of a high standard of discipline and honor in the Army, and which, in the exercise of this jurisdiction, try many accusations based upon acts entirely unknown to the civil courts as criminal offenses.

2. *Ibid.,* p. 18.
3. Comments of General Wilkinson on the conduct of a defense lawyer at the court-martial of Cpt. W. Wilson, reported in 2 & 3 Proceedings of Courts-Martial, War Office (MSS in National Archives Record Group 153, Entry 14), cited in article by Frederick B. Weiner, "Courts-Martial and the Bill of Rights—The Original Practice I," 72 *Harvard Law Review* 1 (1958), p. 27.
4. Joint Hearings before the Subcommittee on Constitutional Rights of the Senate Committee on the Judiciary and a Special Subcommittee of the Senate Armed Services Committee, 89th Congress, 2nd Session, held on January 18, 19, 25 and March 1, 2, 3, 1966, p. 43 of transcript. (Cited hereafter as: 1966 Joint Hearings.)
5. 1966 Joint Hearings, p. 173.
6. Major Arthur A. Murphy, "The Army Defense Counsel: Unusual Ethics for an Unusual Advocate," 61 *Columbia Law Review* 233 (1961), p. 238, ftnt. 35.
7. See Chapter Four, The Military Mind.
8. *Ibid.*
9. Lt. Col. James A. Mounts, Jr., and Capt. Myron G. Sugarman, "The Military Justice Act of 1968," *American Bar Association Journal,* May 1969, p. 470. The authors state:

> The 1968 act represents a combination of various positions advocated by the services and by members of Congress.

Thus they gloss over the sections that represent a clear victory of civilian thinking over military resistance.

Senator Sam Ervin, Jr., of North Carolina, a staunch friend of the military, presents a more candid summary:

> In spite of the controversial nature of many of the reforms and concerted resistance to some or all of them by the armed services virtually until the eve of enactment, the bill passed unanimously in both the Senate and the House.

"The Military Justice Act of 1968," 45 *Military Law Review* 77 (1969), p. 78.

10. 1966 Joint Hearings, p. 186.

11. Report to Hon. Wilber M. Brucker, Secretary of the Army, by the Committee on the UCMJ and Good Order and Discipline in the Army (1960), pp. 5–8.

12. See Note 9.

13. *Levy v. Parker et al.* (Dist. Ct. M.D. Pa.), petitioner's brief, pp. 244 and 259, on file with American Civil Liberties Union, New York (prepared by Charles Morgan, Jr., and other ACLU attorneys).

14. In the Navy case of *U.S. v. Dean,* 5 USCMA 44, 48, 17 CMR 44 (1954), defense counsel was actually in a position to prove bias on the part of the president of the court, an admiral who had been heard making that statement. Without testimony to back up his accusation, no defense counsel can afford to challenge a member of the court on the ground of prejudice or lack of judicial temperament. All he can do is exhort the court to pay heed to the "presumption of innocence."

15. Maj. Ronald M. Holdaway, "Voir Dire—A Neglected Tool of Advocacy," 40 *Military Law Review* 1 (1968), p. 10.

16. Personal interview with civilian defense counsel Rowland Watts.

17. In *U.S. v. Cole,* 17 USCMA 296, 38 CMR 94 (1967), the commanding officer of a naval station posted a memorandum in which he related the story of "an old coal-burning battleship," on which a thief had been tossed into the boiler when caught by his shipmates. The implication was that the same thing might happen to his men under the procedures of the UCMJ.

18. *U.S. v. Dean* (Note 14); see Murphy, *op. cit.* (Note 6), p. 238, where the author states:

> The typical professional officer sees the military justice system as an adjunct of command, useful for promoting discipline and separating undesirable personnel from the service. He would like the system to reflect his own attitude of paternalism towards subordinates: fair but firm and unencumbered by legal technicalities.

19. Capt. Charles W. Schiesser, "Trial by Peers: Enlisted Members on Courts-Martial," 15 *Catholic University Law Review* 171 (1966).

20. The usual method of selection is for the Staff Judge Advocate or Adjutant General of a command to select a panel and to submit a list of the eligibles to the commander. Schiesser, *op. cit.* (Note 19), p. 180; *U.S. v. Crawford,* 15 USCMA 31, 35 CMR 3 (1964), p. 23. Judge Ferguson's dissenting opinion suggests that if the same standards utilized by the Supreme Court in determining exclusion of Negroes from juries were applied to the military situation the Army's exclusion of lower enlisted grades would have to be declared illegal; p. 27, and citing *Norris v. Alabama,* 294 U.S. 587 (1935).

21. *U.S. v. Crawford* (Note 20).

22. Schiesser, *op. cit.* (Note 19), p. 196.

23. In *Brown v. Louisiana,* 383 U.S. 131 (1966), five blacks entered a segregated library in Louisiana and sat down. The sheriff came in and asked them to leave. They refused and were prosecuted for "breach of peace." According to the state's witness, the visitors wanted to use the library "as a place in which to loaf or make a nuisance of themselves." The Supreme Court reversed the convictions, which had resulted from a not only selective but perverted enforcement of the breach of peace ordinance.

24. *U.S. v. Kitchens,* 12 USCMA 589, 31 CMR 175 (1961); *U.S. v. Ferguson,* 5 USCMA 68, 17 CMR 68 (1954). In *U.S. v. Hedges,* 11 USCMA 642, 29 CMR 458 (1960), the Court reversed a conviction because the convening authority had selected for his court two provost marshals, an inspector general, and an executive officer of a Marine brig!

25. "Any person who . . . (2) knowingly and intentionally fails to enforce or comply with any provision of this chapter regulating the proceedings before, during, or after trial of an accused shall be punished as a court-martial may direct." Since Article 37 prohibits the unlawful influence over courts-martial, it is a "provision of this chapter regulating . . . proceedings," and its violation could give rise to court-martial of a convening authority.

26. Article 97. During the years 1965–1968 there were only three Army general courts-martial for unlawful detention.

27. Article 107.

28. Article 93. During 1965–1968 there were only three Army general courts-martial for cruelty and maltreatment.

29. Article 134.

30. Article 117. During 1965–1968 there was only one Army

general court-martial for using provoking gestures; unfortunately, the Army's statistics do not provide a breakdown of courts-martial for each crime by rank of defendants.

31. See Chapter Five, The Soldier's First Amendment Rights.

32. See "The Law of the Stockade," later is this chapter.

33. Luther Charles West (Lt. Col. JAGC, retired) has extensively documented command influence in a Ph.D. thesis submitted to the George Washington University Law School entitled, *The Command Domination of the Military Judicial Process,* portions of which are to be published in the *UCLA Law Review.* And see *U.S. v. DuBay,* 17 USCMA 147, 37 CMR 411 (1967) and *Berry,* CM 414955 (7 June 1968).

34. When they do, it is frequently an innocent mistake caused by their basic lack of understanding of the nature of a judicial proceeding. In *U.S. v. McLaughlin,* 18 USCMA 61, 39 CMR 61 (1968), for instance, the convening authority divided up a court he appointed into three panels and allowed some members to be absent from some of the sessions so that they might pursue their other duties. This was clearly illegal under the UCMJ but was done because the convening authority obviously regarded a court-martial as his own personal agent.

35. *Williams v. Georgia,* 349 U.S. 375 (1955); *Whitus v. Georgia,* 385 U.S. 545 (1967); *Rabinowitz v. U.S.,* 366 F.2d 34 (5th Cir., 1966).

36. Article 22(b).

37. *U.S. v. Gordon,* 1 USCMA 255, 2 CMR 161, 167 (1952).

38. Joseph M. Snee, S.J., Professor of Law, Georgetown University, at 1966 Joint Hearings, p. 338.

39. Chief Judge Robert E. Quinn at 1966 Joint Hearings, p. 283.

40. John J. Finn, for The American Legion, 1966 Joint Hearings, p. 184.

41. 1966 Joint Hearings, p. 54.

42. *U.S. v. Dodge,* 13 USCMA 525, 33 CMR 57, 62 (1963).

43. *U.S. v. Gilliland,* 10 USCMA 343, 27 CMR 417 (1959). See also *U.S. v. Sachs* 39 CMR 689 (1968).

44. *U.S. v. Mallicote,* 13 USCMA 374, 32 CMR 374 (1962).

45. It is possible that the military judges will perform this function in the future.

46. Comment, "The Staff Judge Advocate and the CID,"

29 *Military Law Review* 139 (1965), p. 141.

47. West, *op. cit.* (Note 33), pp. 169–170:

> The commander concerned may note in the counsel's next efficiency report that he is an excellent officer, but of limited imagination and lacking in drive. He may state in this report that the officer concerned tries very hard to produce acceptable results but generally falls below accepted standards. He may note that the officer concerned is a neat dresser, but lacks self-confidence, and generally talks too much at social gatherings. The criticisms that a commander may level at a military lawyer in a situation of this nature are, of course, false and are designed solely to punish the officer concerned for "stepping out of line" . . . The officer concerned is "low rated" and may well fail to be promoted along with his contemporaries at his next promotion period.

48. Statement of U.S. Court of Military Appeals Judge Homer Ferguson, 1966 Joint Hearings, p. 302.

49. 1966 Joint Hearings, p. 22.

50. Murphy, *op. cit.* (Note 6), p. 234.

51. *U.S. v. Darring,* 9 USCMA 651, 26 CMR 431 (1958).

52. *U.S. v. Green,* 5 USCMA 610, 18 CMR 234 (1955).

53. Testimony of legal consultant to Veterans of Foreign Wars at 1962 Hearings of the Senate Judiciary Committee's Subcommittee on Constitutional Rights, 88th Congress, 1st Session, Report of Hearings, 1963, p. 19. See also 1966 Joint Hearings, Report of American Legion, p. 168.

54. Herbert Marks, 1966 Joint Hearings, p. 235.

55. *Levy v. Parker et al.,* petitioner's brief, p. 141 (Note 13).

56. 1966 Joint Hearings, p. 302.

57. Report of Hearings, Subcommittee on Constitutional Rights, Senate Judiciary Committee, 88th Congress, 1st Session, 1963, p. 20.

58. "The Staff Judge Advocate and the CID," *op. cit.* (Note 46), p. 159.

59. Article 10.

60. *MCM,* 1969, para. 20(c). A recent case has shown that these restrictions on confinement must be honored by commanders. See *U.S. v. Jennings,* 19 USCMA 88, 41 CMR 88 (1969).

61. *Chapparro v. Resor,* 412 F.2d 443 (4th Cir. 1969). See discussion of the Fort Jackson Eight in Chapter Five, The Soldier's First Amendment Rights.

62. Article 57(d); and see *MCM,* para. 88(f). "The discretion [of the convening authority] to defer confinement is sole and plenary." The ability to review the exercise of this discretion is therefore greatly limited. See *The Advocate,* Nov. 1969, and *U.S. v. Jennings,* 19 USCMA 88, 41 CMR 88 (1969).

63. *Dale v. U.S.,* Misc. Docket 69–55 (27 Feb. 1970); *Walker v. Commanding Officer,* Misc. Docket 69–45 (27 Feb. 1970). The main ARs governing stockades are: DOD Directive 5210.56, Use of Force of Personnel Engaged in Law Enforcement and Security Duties, May 6, 1969. AR 190–2, Installation Confinement Facilities (rev. 9 Oct. 1967); AR 190–4, Uniform Treatment of Military Prisoners (rev. 15 July 1969); AR 633–10, Military Sentences to Confinement (rev. 6 Nov. 1964). Attorneys or soldiers who want copies of these ARs may obtain them free by writing:

AG Publications Center, USA
2800 Eastern Blvd.
Baltimore, Md., 21220

64. *The Advocate,* Nov. 1969, p. 11, discussing CM 419746, *Revels* (22 Sept. 1969). For an excellent article on the "law" of the stockade, see Peter Barnes, "The Presidio Mutiny," *New Republic,* July 5, 1969, p. 21.

65. The Workers Defense League, which provided defense counsel for Russell and Brakefield, is preparing an appeal.

66. Carlos Rodriguez, quoted in *WIN* Magazine, Sept. 1969, p. 14.

67. Robert Sherrill, "The Pendleton Brig: Andersonville-by-the-Sea," *The Nation,* Sept. 15, 1969, p. 239.

68. *Ibid.,* p. 240.

69. Robert Sherrill, "We Ain't No Dogs," *Pageant* Magazine, Sept. 1969, pp. 29–30.

70. *Ibid.,* p. 33. And see Sherrill's article, "Justice, Military Style," *Playboy,* Feb. 1970.

11

Military Interrogations and Self-Incrimination

There can be no doubt that behind all the actions of this court of justice, that is to say in my case, behind my arrest and today's interrogation, there is a great organization at work. An organization which not only employs corrupt warders, oafish Inspectors, and Examining Magistrates of whom the best that can be said is that they recognize their own limitations, but also has at its disposal a judicial hierarchy of high, indeed of the highest rank, with an indispensable and numerous retinue of servants, clerks, police, and other assistants, perhaps even hangmen, I do not shrink from that word.

—FRANZ KAFKA, *The Trial*

Once upon a time police interrogators could do whatever they wanted with a suspect. But one of the things American civilization has prided itself on is the belief that, no matter how nasty the crime or corrupt the criminal, the knave is entitled to be treated humanely by the people whose station houses, squad cars, guns, and power our taxes sustain.

After years of frustration at being unable to persuade law enforcement officials that they too should obey the law, the courts began to take the fruits of forced confessions away from the police. Not long ago the Supreme Court excluded from all state trials evidence obtained in violation of a suspect's Fifth Amendment rights.[1] That more or less did it. Fitfully, and not really believing they should have to, the police started to obey the law when interrogating people suspected of crimes.

American value judgments have penetrated the military as well, and in the 1951 UCMJ Congress enacted some protections for soldiers which were not made available to civilians by court decisions until some years later. In some details the Fifth Amendment rights of soldiers are still more sweepingly protected (in law) than are those of civilians.

On the other hand, until recently military courts-martial have been almost ignored by the American press. Their proceedings are still not reported in official post-level newspapers. Semiofficial military newspapers like the *Army Times* report important decisions by the higher federal and military courts but never with the motive of exposing abuses. Where the military could prevent the circulation of one serviceman-oriented newspaper that covered court-martial trials, it did not hesitate to do so. The *Overseas Weekly,* a very popular muckraking newspaper circulated freely among American soldiers in Europe, is banned from PXs in Korea. Only recently was it given permission to commence limited circulation in Vietnam, and then only after it brought a lawsuit against the government.[2]

Because of this absence of public scrutiny and the atmosphere of fear intentionally generated in the lives of low-ranking soldiers, criminal investigation agencies in the Army can be expected to break the rules with less reluctance than their civilian counterparts. It is much easier to intimidate a soldier stationed far away from his family, friends, and advisers than a civilian suspect who can obtain some psychological reassurance by simply making a telephone call.

Congress has passed laws, the President has made

rules, and the courts have set guidelines by which the military police and Criminal Investigation Detachment are supposed to conduct themselves. But the fact is that less than one per cent of all cases tried by the armed services are reviewed by the Court of Military Appeals, the only civilian-manned court in the system. Also, before August 1, 1969, if a case was referred to any court lower than a general court-martial, legally qualified counsel was not made available to ask the pertinent questions about what methods were used to obtain statements and confessions. And as we've seen, the counsel who were appointed didn't know what to do.[3] *Consequently, in countless cases failure to give constitutionally required warnings to suspects was never recorded in any way and could never be reviewed by higher authorities.* The fact that lawyers will now be made available to defendants at special courts-martial should cause many more confessions to be thrown out and, in time, should convince the investigating authorities to rely on evidence other than confessions to obtain valid convictions. This has been one goal of Supreme Court decisions in civilian cases.

ARTICLE 31 AND THE FIFTH AMENDMENT

The Fifth Amendment to the Constitution requires that no person "shall be compelled in any criminal case to be a witness against himself." Thousands of judicial opinions and hundreds of books have been written about the right against self-incrimination, the values it is supposed to foster, the best methods for preserving it— and, on occasion, ways to get around it. The amendment grew out of a historical need to discourage torture and other uncivilized interrogation tactics by the state's law enforcement authorities. Former Associate Justice of the Supreme Court Arthur Goldberg has written that the Fifth Amendment reflects many of our fundamental values and most noble aspirations . . . our fear that self-incriminating statements will be elicited by inhumane treatment and abuses; our sense of fair play . . . our respect for the inviolability of the human personality . . . our distrust of self-deprecatory statements.[4]

What it means to you, the soldier, is that at any time you feel you might say something that could have the slightest chance of incriminating you, *the right to keep silent may be exercised, anywhere and any time.*[5] *And you do not have to tell anyone why you think that responding to a particular question might tend to incriminate you.*

The Fifth Amendment is not the only source of your right to keep silent. Article 31 of the UCMJ restates the principle, and under the interpretation of military courts provides some safeguards even broader than the Fifth Amendment. Article 31 is so vital to the interests of a soldier that it is quoted here in full:

(a) No person subject to this chapter may compel any person to incriminate himself or to answer any question the answer to which may tend to incriminate him.

(b) No person subject to this chapter may interrogate, or request any statement from, an accused or a person suspected of an offense without first informing him of the nature of the accusation and advising him that he does not have to make any statement regarding the offense of which he is accused or suspected and that any statement made by him may be used as evidence against him in a trial by court-martial.

(c) No person subject to this chapter may compel any person to make a statement or produce evidence before any military tribunal if the statement or evidence is not material to the issue and may tend to degrade him.

(d) No statement obtained from any person in violation of this article, or through the use of coercion, unlawful influence, or unlawful inducement may be received in evidence against him in a trial by court-martial.

The reasons why a special article was passed by Congress to back up a soldier's Fifth Amendment rights have been described by the Court of Military Appeals:

> . . . its purpose is to avoid impairment of the constitutional guarantee against compulsory self-incrimination. Because of the effect of superior rank or official position upon one subject to military law, the mere asking of a question under certain circumstances is the equivalent of a command. A person subjected to these pressures may rightly be regarded as deprived of his freedom to answer or to remain silent.[6]

Notice that the *affirmative obligation* is placed on the authorities to warn a suspect of his rights. If they fail to give the warning embodying all the information in section (b) of Article 31, no statement which may have been received may legally be used against the individual. The warning must be given as soon as someone is a "suspect," even though he is not in custody.[7] It must be given even if the person knows his rights beforehand, through a legal education, a layman's guide, or any other source.[8] A person's failure to deny an accusation of wrongdoing while he is "under official investigation" or in custody cannot be used against him at trial.[9] *But when an interrogator says that anything you say can be used against you, believe him. Many people feel they can talk their way out of a situation and end up making statements which, although intended to exculpate, have an incriminating effect.* On the other hand, some have a deep desire to confess to wrongdoing even if they are given the required warnings, and you should be aware that experienced interrogators know how to exploit this tendency.[10]

WHEN ARE THE WARNINGS REQUIRED?

When does a person become a "suspect," thus requiring that the warnings be given? The answer is not yet clear, but there are some guidelines indicating that warnings need not always be given. In 1966, in the case of *Miranda v. Arizona,* the Supreme Court made a ruling of great importance.

> There is no requirement that police stop a person who enters a police station and states that he wishes to confess to a crime, or a person who calls the police to offer a confession or any other statement he desires to make. Volunteered statements of any kind are not barred by the Fifth Amendment . . .[11]

When an inquiry by military police is strictly routine, and a soldier makes statements before the police consider him a suspect, those statements are *not* protected by Article 31 and will be admitted into evidence against him.[12] But the Supreme Court has indicated that any questioning which "frequently leads" to a criminal prosecution must begin with the appropriate warnings about rights, including the right to counsel,[13] and the military appellate courts may have to reassess their notions of the point in time at which a soldier becomes a suspect.

In a recent Court of Military Appeals case, the FBI, after breaking in upon and awakening a suspected deserter, asked him his name. Since his response was not what they expected to hear, he was asked, "What is your true name?" The soldier gave his true name. Because no warning had been given to him, the Court held that his response should have been excluded at trial (despite the government's argument that he was not in "custody" and that the question was solely to determine identity).[14] *If you have blurted out incriminating infor-*

mation to government agents before hearing your rights under Article 31, make sure your lawyer knows about it so that he will be prepared to try to exclude it from trial.[15]

Also keep in mind that *not all conversations with MPs need be preceded by the Article 31 warning for their contents to be admissible.* When the conversation is with a friend who happens, as an MP, to be escorting the accused from one jail to another, what the accused tells that "friend" will be admissible against him if the court deems it to be an "ordinary" private conversation and not an official custodial interrogation.[16]

Article 31 protects the soldier from more disclosures than would appear from a literal reading. A soldier may not legally be ordered to produce a sample of his handwriting,[17] although a civilian's handwriting sample may be obtained without violating the Fifth Amendment.[18] However, when civilian law enforcement agents have a legitimate independent interest in an investigation of a soldier, they don't have to tell the suspect that he need not provide them with a handwriting sample, and if they get one it will be admitted in a military court.[19] *Remember your rights, because the authorities will not remember them for you.*

Nor may the military police order you to speak for voice identification,[20] even though a voice identification obtained from a civilian in the absence of a warning does not violate the Fifth Amendment. An order to provide a urine specimen for use in a criminal prosecution also violates Article 31.[21]

Physical evidence obtained in a shocking or brutal manner will be excluded from evidence by the courts. In one famous case the Supreme Court reversed a conviction because the state of California had used a stomach pump to obtain morphine from a defendant to be used against him in a narcotics prosecution.[22] The Court expressed deep antipathy to such brutal methods and held that they amounted to a denial of due process of law. On the other hand, the involuntary extraction of blood to be used in a sobriety test, done by a doctor at a hospital to which the accused had been brought after an automobile collision, did not shock the consciences of the judges enough to be declared unconstitutional.[23]

THE RIGHT TO CONSULT A LAWYER

The Sixth Amendment to the Constitution states that "in all criminal prosecutions the accused shall enjoy the right . . . to have the Assistance of Counsel for his defense." Although the Supreme Court has never ruled on whether this section of the amendment requires that qualified lawyers be made available at military trials, it is today unquestioned that in the investigative stage a suspect, civilian or military, must be informed of his right to consult with a lawyer and of his right to keep silent. If he elects to waive his right to consult with a lawyer before making any statement, this must be done knowingly, voluntarily, and intelligently, or the courts will refuse to consider the statement.[24]

The Army has long provided lawyers at general courts-martial, but only in five per cent of special courts-martial before Congress forced it to provide them in the Military Justice Act of 1968, which became effective on August 1, 1969. The right to have an appointed lawyer *at the outset of an interrogation* is a relatively recent requirement in American law. In 1963, in the important *Gideon v. Wainwright* case, the Supreme Court held that the Sixth Amendment guaranteed the right to counsel to all defendants in serious cases.[25] In a series of subsequent cases the Supreme Court began to push forward the point at which counsel had to be supplied, until, in the *Miranda* case, it held that not only does a suspect have the right to be represented by counsel as soon as an investigation "has begun to focus on a particular suspect" but *at that strategic moment the authorities must inform the suspect of both his Sixth Amendment right to be provided with counsel and his Fifth Amendment right to keep silent. Since the Consti-*

tution applies to the military—despite the Navy's attempt to convince the Court of Military Appeals to the contrary—the warning requirements of Miranda *apply to military as well as civilian police.*[26]

It appears fairly certain that *whenever a soldier requests counsel and refuses to say anything else until a lawyer arrives, that request will have to be respected. The problem is to resist being tricked into losing the resolve to remain silent.* If you do speak, then upon trial it becomes your lawyer's function to bring that matter up to the military judge, the court, and the appellate courts—insuring that the methods of interrogation are fully explored at trial and fully recorded in the transcript.

TRICKS OF GOVERNMENT AGENTS

The Undercover Agent

One device for circumventing the *Miranda* and Article 31 rules that has worked for the military involves the use of an undercover agent to prod admissions out of a suspect. A Marine suspected of black-marketing was called to the waiting room of the investigator's office. Soon thereafter a government informer came out of the office and said to the investigator (with the suspect taking it all in), "You ain't getting nothing out of me," suggesting that the suspect and he were both in the same boat. Later, when the two got chummy, the defendant made damaging admissions to which the informer subsequently testified. The objection was made that the defendant had not been given the Article 31 and *Miranda* warnings. Even though the suspect was in custody, the Court of Military Appeals held that since there was "no coercion or unlawful influence" the admissions should not be barred.[27] It is possible that the Supreme Court would reject such an approach; but decisions on this, as on other frontiers of the law, will be made on a case-by-case basis. In the meantime, watch what you say to that friendly guy in the next cell.

Preliminary Gratuitous Advice

Another device used by Army interrogators to persuade suspects to forgo their Fifth Amendment and Article 31 rights is called the Preliminary Gratuitous Advice. Army defense counsel have been cautioned to look for its use when they discover that a client failed to demand a lawyer at the time of interrogation. An illustration of such misleading advice is the following:

> In a minute I'm going to advise you of your rights to counsel, but first you must understand that you can be counseled by anyone you desire—your first sergeant, your platoon leader, your company or battalion commander, the chaplain, the IG, an officer in the JAG Office, or even a relative.[28]

Having said that, the agent read the warnings he was required by law to read. The ruse often works, and the unsuspecting victim consults with a chaplain or a battalion commander instead of a lawyer. *Don't be fooled. Ask for a lawyer and keep quiet until you have consulted with him.*

Bluff on a Split Pair

A favorite of experienced interrogators, not necessarily military, is the Bluff on a Split Pair.[29] In this ploy the suspects are separated, and one is left waiting in the vicinity of the secretary's desk. The interrogator comes out of the room where the second suspect is being held and calls in the secretary. A little while later she exits and begins to type furiously. Every few minutes the agent comes out and angrily asks if she has "it" ready. Finally she takes "it" into the room—all with the first suspect looking on. He is then brought into a separate room, where the agent, now relaxed, sits down, leans back, and says, "Well, we've got all we need on you from your buddy; you don't have to say a thing." *In fact, the interrogator has no statement and no information.* If the bluff works, the suspect gets angry with his apparently faithless friend and makes a statement incriminating himself and the friend. If a court wanted to find a "waiver," such a statement could be found admissible.

The Promise of Immunity

Sometimes interrogators promise a suspect a light sentence or immunity from prosecution if he will make a statement implicating another party. *These tactics are illegal,* and if proven in court any statement so obtained will be deemed involuntary and not admitted into evidence against the person who made it. The best way to resist this tactic is to remember that if the prosecution considers a particular individual important enough as a potential witness it can always go through the formal procedures necessary to grant him immunity from prosecution, and thereby obtain his testimony. *No investigator can grant immunity to anyone.* A suspect would do well to believe nothing an investigator tells him except that he is entitled to ask for counsel and to keep quiet.

The Mutt-and-Jeff Routine

One of the most effective techniques of experienced investigators in the Mutt-and-Jeff routine. It's very simple. One interrogator browbeats the suspect and threatens him with unconventional but intriguing atrocities. When he leaves the room the other one speaks softly and sympathetically. He sincerely laments the miserable plight in which the suspect now finds himself and suggests how good it would feel to get it all off his chest. He might even go so far as to say that the victim got what was coming to him. This works so well that at this point the agent may walk right up to the door to let in his stenographer, who is waiting there for that moment to arrive.

These games are probably illegal, even when played one against one. In a case where the military investigator engaged in a loud-voiced "solo tirade" against the suspect, to push him "toward an emotional state," the Court of Military Appeals condemned the practice and reversed the conviction.[30] It seems plain that from now on all psychological coercion, if established, will raise serious questions of illegality.

DON'T WAIVE YOUR RIGHTS

There is no reason to waive your rights, at least not until you have discussed the matter with your lawyer and have decided it would be the best thing to do. In practice the courts are making it very difficult for the government to prove that an individual did "knowingly and intelligently" waive, especially if the defendant is of low intelligence or immature and impressionable. The Court of Military Appeals has required the government to prove beyond a reasonable doubt that the defendant waived his rights both to counsel and to silence before admitting a defendant's statement.[31]

The unknown factor is whether the courts will accept the facile argument of prosecutors and public officials that the national "crime wave" will be cured by admitting a greater number of lawlessly extracted confessions. Attorney General John Mitchell let it be known in the summer of 1969 that he would authorize the Justice Department to use confessions in federal criminal trials, whether or not the *Miranda* warnings were given, so long as the confessions were otherwise "voluntarily" made.[32] Article 31 would still prevent the use of such confessions in military trials unless the suspect had at least been warned of his right to keep silent. Of course, in the interests of "law and order" Congress could repeal Article 31. But that is not likely to happen right away, nor are the courts likely to cooperate with the Attorney General in rolling back the citizen's constitutional protections against arbitrary police authority.

Notes

1. *Malloy v. Hogan,* 378 U.S. 1 (1964).

2. And only after a federal court ordered a hearing on the question of whether the *Overseas Weekly* was being discriminated against by the Defense Department. *Overseas Media Corporation v. McNamara,* 385 F.2d 308 (D.C. Cir., 1967).

3. See discussion of special courts-martial in Chapter Nine, The Framework of Military Law.

4. *Murphy v. Waterfront Commission,* 378 U.S. 52, 55 (1964). The great American legal scholar, Wigmore, wrote of the policy behind the Fifth Amendment (8 Wigmore, *Evidence,* sec. 2251, p. 309):

> The real objection is that *any system of administration which permits the prosecution to trust habitually to compulsory self-disclosure as a source of proof must itself suffer morally thereby.* The inclination develops to rely mainly upon such evidence, and to be satisfied with an incomplete investigation of the other sources. The exercise of the power to extract answers begets a forgetfulness of the just limitations of that power. The simple and peaceful process of questioning breeds a readiness to resort to bullying and to physical force and torture . . . Ultimately the innocent are jeopardized by the encroachments of a bad system.

5. Unless you are granted immunity by a judicial authority, which in the military is the general court-martial convening authority. Immunity may be granted only for general courts-martial.

6. *U.S. v. Gibson,* 3 USCMA 746, 14 CMR 164, 170 (1954).

7. *U.S. v. Souder,* 11 USCMA 59, 28 CMR 283 (1959).

8. *MCM,* 1969, para. 140(a)2.

9. *Ibid.,* para. 140(a)4.

10. See "The Mutt-and-Jeff Routine," later in this chapter.

11. 384 U.S. 436, 478 (1966). See also *U.S. v. Tempia,* 16 USCMA 629, 37 CMR 249 (1967), discussed later in this chapter.

12. *U.S. v. Ballard,* 17 USCMA 96, 37 CMR 360 (1967).

13. *Mathis v. U.S.,* 36 U.S.L.W. 4379 (6 May 1968).

14. *U.S. v. Phifer,* 18 USCMA 508, 40 CMR 220 (1969).

15. You also have to be informed of your right to consult with a lawyer immediately. *Miranda v. Arizona,* 384 U.S. 436 (1966).

16. *U.S. v. Beck,* 15 USCMA 333, 35 CMR 305 (1965). See also *U.S. v. Vogel,* 18 USCMA 160, 39 CMR 160 (1969).

17. *U.S. v. White,* 17 USCMA 211, 38 CMR 9 (1967); *U.S. v. Rosato,* 3 USCMA 143, 11 CMR 143 (1953).

18. *Gilbert v. California,* 388 U.S. 263 (1967).

19. *U.S. v. Penn,* 18 USCMA 194, 39 CMR 194 (1969).

20. *U.S. v. Mewborn,* 17 USCMA 431, 38 CMR 229 (1968).

21. *U.S. v. Jordan,* 7 USCMA 452, 22 CMR 242 (1957).

22. *Rochin v. California,* 342 U.S. 165 (1952).

23. *Schmerber v. California,* 389 U.S. 757 (1966); *Breithaupt v. Abram,* 352 U.S. 432 (1957).

24. *U.S. v. Stanley,* 17 USCMA 384, 38 CMR 182 (1968).

25. 372 U.S. 335 (1963).

26. *U.S. v. Tempia,* 16 USCMA 629, 37 CMR 249 (1967).

27. *U.S. v. Hinkson,* 17 USCMA 126, 37 CMR 390 (1967).

28. *The Advocate,* Defense Appellate Division, U.S. Army Judiciary, July 1969, vol. 1, no. 5, p. 7.

29. Fred Inbau and John Reid, *Criminal Interrogation and Confessions* (Baltimore: Williams & Wilkins Co., 1962), p. 81.

30. *U.S. v. Planter,* 18 USCMA 469, 40 CMR 181 (1969). See also *Spano v. New York,* 360 U.S. 315 (1959).

31. *U.S. v. Westmore,* 17 USCMA 406, 38 CMR 204 (1968).

32. "Mitchell Wants Looser Rules in Confessions," News of the Week in Review, *New York Times,* August 3, 1969, p. 12.

12

Conscientious Objectors in the Army

Since tomorrow is Good Friday, I hope God will look
kindly on our attack.
　　　　　—THE CLERGYMAN, *Oh! What a Lovely War*

I am no longer a soldier. Soldiering, my dear madam,
is the coward's art of attacking mercilessly when you
are strong, and keeping out of harm's way when you
are weak. That is the whole secret of successful fighting. Get your enemy at a disadvantage; and never,
on any account, fight him on equal terms.
　　　　　—GEORGE BERNARD SHAW, *Arms and the Man*

Not every attempt to exercise a right in the Army ends
in frustration. But applying for discharge on the ground
of conscientious objection to war not only isolates the
individual from his comrades but escalates his frustration to a level that most people would find intolerable.
This is partly because approval of the discharge is a
sometime thing, and the whole effort, in the words of
one CO, is nothing but an attempt to "reason with a
system whose ultimate answer to problems is to beat
heads or kill people." For those COs with the strength
to try to deal with the system on its own terms, this

chapter seeks to describe the kind of treatment to expect and the best means of protecting oneself.

Though he likes it no better than anyone else, the sincere CO is fully prepared to go to jail for disobedience of orders that violate his conscience. If he has not struggled far in advance with his decision whether to stand firm if his discharge application is turned down, he may not have the patience and stamina to withstand the absurdities, intimidations, and illegalities to which he may be subjected. The soldier who follows the Army's procedure for securing recognition of his conscientious views is almost certain to be bombarded by everyone in the authority structure to change his mind or compromise his conscience. He is also liable to suffer arbitrary refusals to accept his application, deliberate attempts to entrap him into performing work inconsistent with his stated beliefs, mysterious disappearances of his paper work, discrimination, and actual threats against his person. *The sincere CO who is prepared to work within the system must be ready to endure these reminders of the contempt in which the conscientiously free man is held by the Military Mind.*

Many in the military do not accept the policy behind congressional recognition of COs. Some officers feel that if a person is so caught up in religion he should be a member of the cloth. Otherwise he should be treated like everyone else. One CO was informed by a high-ranking officer that there are four kinds of COs: (1) those few who are sincere and who by some fluke ended up in the Army; (2) guardhouse lawyers, who enjoy reading ARs and advising other COs of their rights; (3) cowards; and (4) subversives or "SDS members," deliberately planted there by pinkos.[1] Once someone is pigeonholed, the Military Mind doesn't have to exert much effort to understand or deal with him. (Each person must fit in one of the four categories and no overlapping is allowed.) This is the way the Military Mind deals with almost all problems, not excluding the bureaucratization of the content of a man's soul.

THE CCCO AND THE AFSC

The first and probably best advice for the soldier who thinks he may be a CO is to get in touch with an office of the Central Committee for Conscientious Objectors or the American Friends Service Committee as soon as possible. As the most established and experienced organizations for COs, they offer the most informed and comprehensive counseling service available. The CCCO publishes the best materials relating to CO applications, and these materials are either very reasonably priced or completely free. In working out the expression of his beliefs in such a way as to avoid the multitude of traps the system has created for the unwary, the sincere CO will find he needs all the help he can get. The CCCO's *Handbook for Conscientious Objectors* is an essential aid, and a new edition especially for in-service COs, *Advice for Conscientious Objectors in the Armed Forces,* has just been completed by Mike Wittels. (Consult Appendix B for a list of CCCO and AFSC offices.)

WHICH COs ARE ELIGIBLE FOR DISCHARGE

An applicant for discharge from the Army on CO grounds must be someone "who, by reason of religious training and belief, claim[s] conscientious objection to participation in war in any form."[2]

He need not be a member of an organized church and need not believe in a Supreme Being. He can be conscientiously opposed to war in any form even if the church he belongs to does not officially take that position. The claim that his conscientious objection is religiously motivated cannot be rejected if there is no proof incompatible with the claim.[3] He doesn't have to be a churchgoer. He can, if he wants to, be opposed to the Vietnam war, conscription, and all governmental authority. He can be in favor of personal self-defense,

defense of relatives, or civil disobedience. There is even an outside possibility, urged by some courts, that his conscientious objection need not be based on religious belief,[4] but it is likely that, in most areas of the United States, *any objection to war which is based on "essentially political, sociological, or philosophical views, or on a merely personal moral code"*[5] *will not be considered* a basis for discharge from the Army. In an important case in which the Supreme Court upheld the CO position of a draft resister, *United States v. Seeger,*[6] the Court defined the phrase "religious training and belief":

> Within that phrase would come all sincere religious beliefs which are based upon a power or being, or upon a faith, to which all else is subordinate or upon which all else is ultimately dependent. The test might be stated in these words: A sincere and meaningful belief which occupies in the life of its possessor a place parallel to that filled by the God of those admittedly qualifying for the exemption comes within the statutory definition.

A federal court has indicated recently that the *Seeger* test is still viable, despite congressional changes in the definition of conscientious objection. It appears that it is permissible to turn down a CO discharge application only if the "personal moral code" is the *sole* basis for the applicant's objection to war.[7]

AR 635–20 lays down the requirements that must be met before an application for CO discharge can even be considered by the Department of the Army, which makes the decision. *It is most important to remember that conscientious objection that existed prior to service and was not claimed prior to induction cannot be the basis for discharge.* The belief upon which the application is being filed must have developed, crystallized, or matured only *after* one's entry into the Army, although one can have had conscientious feelings leading up to the present CO position. Moreover, if the Selective

Service System turned down a man's application for CO status, he can file another application from within the Army if his beliefs have changed in any substantial degree since his first application was made. If a registrant was granted 1-A-O status as a noncombatant prior to entry upon active duty, and he has since discovered that his conscience cannot condone being any part of a system that wages war, he can apply for a CO discharge.[8]

The DOD directive under which all services operate states that "no vested right exists for any person to be discharged from military service . . ." and that "bona fide conscientious objection as set forth in this Directive . . . will be recognized to the extent practicable and equitable."[9] This gives the impression that the military's decision is final. That's far from the truth. After exhausting all military remedies, a rejected applicant can file a petition for a writ of habeas corpus in a federal court, which will review the military's denial and will order the soldier's release from the Army if there was "no basis in fact" for rejecting the CO discharge application. An increasing number of federal courts have been granting the writs. The factors which must exist for a reasonable chance of success are discussed later in this chapter.

PREPARING THE APPLICATION

A considerable amount of documentation is required for the CO's request to be seriously considered. The basic application, on the all-purpose DF Form, must contain a great deal of personal history, such as membership in organizations, a chronological list of all occupations ever held, and all addresses where the applicant has ever lived, together with dates. If the applicant has served less than 180 days in the military he must state his willingness to work under the Selective Service civilian work program for COs, but it is a good idea for all applicants to indicate their willingness as an act of good faith.

A number of difficult questions must be answered in depth. Like other administrative discharges, the CO discharge requires voluminous paper work. It also requires a great deal of soul searching. If the soldier who thinks he's a CO has never before probed the depths of his feelings about organized violence, or the paths of his moral and intellectual development, he will have to do it in the preparation of his CO application. This obviously cannot be done in a day or a week. *He must also be prepared, in the face of intimidation, to behave consistently with his beliefs.*

The CO will usually want to write and talk to his family, his chaplain, his lawyer, his girl friend or wife, his close friends, and, perhaps most important, his counselor from the CCCO or another organization. He should file the application only after he knows what he wants to do.

Documents or supporting letters that tend to bolster the CO's sincerity should be included in the application. (But nobody who is supplying a supporting letter should exaggerate by saying, "X has been a CO *all his life* . . . ;" because a claim based solely on conscientious conviction that existed prior to Army service will not be considered.) For most COs whose position has crystallized after entrance into the Army, there may not be anyone to whom they have expressed their sentiments. *This does not preclude the granting of a CO discharge,* so long as there are convincing character references from people who have known the applicant in the past and who can cite indications of the person's conscientious leanings or good moral character. It takes time to locate people who can attest to these things. Many soldiers have lost touch with some of those who could give helpful references, and contact has to be reestablished.

Since the CO's position has to be based on "religious training and belief," the AR requests certain information that all applicants must provide:

a. A description of the nature of belief which is the basis of claim.

b. Explain how, when, and from whom or from what source the applicant received the training and acquired the belief which is the basis of claim.

c. The name and present address of the individual upon whom the applicant relies most for religious guidance in matters of conviction relating to claim.

d. A statement as to circumstances, if any, under which the applicant believes in the use of force.

e. A description of the actions and behavior in the applicant's life which, in his opinion, most conspicuously demonstrates [sic] the consistency and depth of religious convictions which gave rise to claim.

f. A statement as to whether applicant has ever given public expression, written or oral, to the views expressed in his application as the basis for claim. If so, specify when and where.[10]

It is easy to see why counseling would be helpful, and time to think extremely important.

One of the commanding officer's obligations is to read to the applicant a provision of a federal statute that deprives those who receive CO discharges of their veterans' benefits. This is sometimes used as a basis for a tirade along the lines of "I don't know why the rest of us are willing to fight for the likes of you . . ."

STATUS AFTER APPLICATION IS SUBMITTED

One of the most important provisions in AR 635–20 concerns the disposition of applicants pending final decision. Paragraph 6(a) states:

An individual who applies for discharge based on conscientious objection will be retained in his unit and assigned duties providing the minimum practicable conflict with his asserted beliefs pending a final decision on his application. In the case of trainees, this means that they will not be required to train in the study, use, or handling of arms or weapons.

As soon as the CO submits his application, he is legally entitled to a provisional noncombatant status so that he will not be placed in the position of having to disobey an order or compromise his religious beliefs any further than he may have done already. This provision is very frequently violated, sometimes through inadvertence and sometimes with the intention of entrapping the CO into doing something that can later be thrown up to him during the interview, or that can be surreptitiously placed in his file before it is forwarded to the Department of the Army for decision. One such tactic is to place CO applicants in a training unit where they are ordered to grade the targets at the rifle range. *This is illegal since it is hardly in "minimal practicable conflict" with their asserted beliefs.* Some COs have done this, feeling they've compromised themselves. One soldier wrote:

> Then I was told to staple targets on cardboard backings for the rifle training. I did this but felt no peace within myself about it . . .[11]

In another situation, more than twenty CO applicants at Fort Ord, California, threatened to bring legal action in federal court unless an order to grade targets at the firing range was rescinded. It was. The officer in charge stated that the original order had been a "mistake," and no one could find out who had actually given it and with what ultimate purpose.[12]

INTERVIEWS

Interviews with a chaplain and a psychiatrist are required. The psychiatrist fills out a report stating whether or not he thinks the applicant is crazy enough to warrant treatment. (In the AR's language, he decides whether "the presence or absence of any psychiatric disorder . . . would warrant treatment or disposition through medical channels.") The chaplain decides whether the applicant is sincere, and submits his report.

The applicant is then given the opportunity to have an interview with an officer of the grade of O-3 (captain) or higher, "who is knowledgeable in policies and procedures relating to conscientious objector matters." *This extremely important interview gives the applicant his last contact with anyone who can personally judge his sincerity.* The soldier should exercise his right to have a lawyer present, as well as a court reporter to make a verbatim transcript (at the soldier's expense). If the officer is asked to state his opinion of the applicant's sincerity, and the opinion is positive, there will be a permanent record of the officer's finding that the CO is sincere. Try to check the examining officer's background beforehand, to prepare yourself for the interview. If the officer says for the record that he believes the CO is insincere, the attorney can ask him to state his reasons. At least one important federal court has indicated that there must be reasons for denying a CO's sincerity.[13] The decision made in Washington is based, somehow, on the file. According to the Army, it is grounded on a recommendation by an advisory board of officers from the Chief of Chaplains' Office, the Judge Advocate General's Office, and the Chief of Personnel Operations' Office.

Since *applications are sometimes "lost" on the way up,* it is advisable to have an extra copy or two in the hands of people who can be reached quickly and who can reproduce the papers should that become necessary.

Sometimes a CO's views change after he has submitted a first application which has been turned down. In such a case, a second application may be submitted, and it must be forwarded by the lower authorities unless it is "substantially the same."

FILING AFTER RECEIVING
OVERSEAS ORDERS

After this chapter was written, the Army changed its policy of permitting soldiers in transit from their home stations to an overseas assignment to file for CO discharge at overseas replacement stations. Although the revised regulation is not available at the time of this writing, it does appear that the soldier who has received overseas orders will have to file for CO discharge either before he signs out of his home station or after he arrives at his overseas station. Advance information indicates that the revised AR will state:

> An individual who has departed his unit of assignment in compliance with reassignment orders may not make application for discharge as a conscientious objector until he arrives at his new permanent duty station.[14]

GIs can no longer afford to wait until they are home on leave to receive advice, but will have to file their applications at the home station, sometimes before completing their advanced individual training. This places a great burden on the CO in receipt of overseas orders, since all he is entitled to is a seven-day delay in processing out from his home station:

> An individual on orders for reassignment who desires to apply for discharge, but does not have the required evidence (para. 4) to support an application is authorized one delay of 7 days. If at the end of 7 days the individual does not have evidence to support a written request for discharge, he will be required to comply with reassignment orders.[15]

This latest revision appears to be an attempt by the Army to reduce the number of apparent last-minute decisions by soldiers on orders for Vietnam. Whether this effort will be upheld by the courts is at least questionable. *But the CO should file as early as possible at his home station and begin immediately to gather the documentation necessary to provide support for his claim.*

This critically important change in the AR seems designed to accomplish two ends: (1) It will effectively remove jurisdiction of the West Coast federal courts over a great many CO discharge applications. Since these federal courts were fairly liberal in ordering the Army to release COs whose applications had been turned down, the reduction in CO habeas corpus applications will be welcomed by military commanders at Fort Lewis and at the California bases. (2) Lawyers willing to help COs and other GIs for no fee or minimal fees are probably more abundant on the West Coast than anywhere else in the country. The revised AR will cut off this supply of effective legal assistance for a great many CO applicants. And those who file their CO discharge applications in Vietnam will not have lawyers available to assist at the interview with an 0–3 officer, a very important stage in the process. (A lawyer can be of great value in preparing the CO for the hearing and in getting information on the record.)

It is important not to be dissuaded or tricked into foregoing the fight to file at the home station. When filing at overseas replacement stations was permitted, soldiers with applications in hand were told to file them "later," or when they "completed processing," or "tomorrow," even when tomorrow was the shipping date.

If after some weeks a CO's application is disapproved, it does not mean that there is no legal alternative left. If he is in contact with an attorney, certain measures can be taken which may result in federal court review. In the past GIs were forcibly taken from overseas replacement stations to the planes. Sometimes they were dragged by MPs and occasionally they were bound hand and foot. One soldier at Oakland was wheeled in a laundry cart. These measures were taken as the "minimum reasonable force to obtain compliance with orders."[16]

Whether these measures will still be used to ship soldiers to Vietnam remains to be seen. It is possible that courts-martial with very stiff sentences will be resorted to as a more realistic means of deterring Vietnamphobia in the future.

HABEAS CORPUS AND INJUNCTIONS

If the denial of CO status is arbitrary and has "no basis in fact," or if the Army fails to follow the procedure set down in its own regulation, then there remains the possibility of obtaining a federal court order directing the Army to release the soldier from its custody. However, since shipping orders frequently arrive simultaneously with the denial of CO discharge, it is important for a GI's attorney to apply to a federal district court for an order temporarily restraining the Army from shipping the applicant to Vietnam until the courts have had a chance to rule on the legality of the Army's action. The courts have indicated that such an order may be forthcoming if the soldier can show that (1) he has a good chance of prevailing on an appeal from the Army's decision to the court, (2) he would suffer irreparable damage if the order were not granted, (3) no irreparable damage would be suffered by the Army or the public if the order were granted.[17]

Until late in 1969 some courts were requiring soldiers whose CO discharge applications had been turned down to apply to the Army Board for Correction of Military Records (thereby "exhausting" their administrative remedies completely) before hearings would be granted on habeas corpus petitions.[18] What that did was to forestall a decision on the legality of the Army's refusal to recognize an alleged CO's status, keeping the soldier in the Army for quite a few more months, at least. It was argued by lawyers representing COs that the Board for Correction of Military Records had no particular expertise in CO matters; some federal courts agreed, and took jurisdiction of CO habeas corpus petitions without first requiring a review by the Board.[19]

Finally the Justice Department reversed its position; a soldier no longer needs to apply to the Board before filing his habeas corpus petition in federal court when he feels his CO discharge has been illegally turned down.[20] However, if a CO at that stage is given an order to engage in activities that conflict with his conscience and he disobeys it, the military can still court-martial him.[21] In such a case the CO should try to obtain an injunction from a federal district court forbidding the Army to continue with the court-martial.[22] *But such cooperation from the federal courts cannot be counted on.* Perhaps to forestall civilian intervention, the Court of Military Appeals has indicated that it will consider an argument of illegal denial of CO status as a *defense to prosecutions* for disobeying orders flowing from the illegal denial.[23]

The sincere CO who has no civilian lawyer and whose application has been turned down is in a very difficult position. The latest revision of AR 635–20 authorizes an appeal to the Army Board for Correction of Military Records but provides no further stay on orders in conflict with his beliefs. He must either obey the orders (to handle weapons or to go to a war zone) or be court-martialed for disobedience and raise the illegality of the CO discharge denial as a defense. If he is convicted and sentenced to more than thirty days, he is likely to be shipped to a stockade at a different post.[24]

NONCOMBATANT STATUS

It is easier to gain recognition as a CO with noncombatant status than to get a CO discharge. In 1968, 27.8 per cent of discharge applications were approved while 76.7 per cent of noncombatant status requests were granted.[25]

Noncombatant status has been defined by the Defense Department as:

1. service in any unit of the Armed Forces which is unarmed at all times;
2. service in the medical department of any of the Armed Forces, wherever performed; or
3. any other assignment the primary function of which does not require the use of arms in combat provided that such other assignment is acceptable to the individual concerned and does not require him to bear arms or to be trained in their use.[26]

Additionally, noncombatant training is defined as "any training which is not concerned with the study, use, or handling of arms or weapons."

The procedure for filing an application for noncombatant status as a CO is exactly the same as that described above for the CO discharge. Usually those who receive recognition as noncombatants are assigned to the Army medical service. However, they are reminded by their unit commanders that they are soldiers first and medics second. It is possible for someone who has applied for and received noncombatant status, either while in the Army or before induction, to come to the realization that he cannot be any part of the military machine.[27] In such a case the noncombatant can file for CO discharge, explaining in his application how his present beliefs have evolved. It will be recalled that a request for discharge based solely on conscientious objection that existed at the time of induction but was not claimed, or which was claimed and turned down by Selective Service, will not be granted. The Army has argued further that in the case of a CO who was granted a 1-A-O noncombatant status by Selective Service, his beliefs must have changed substantially before he can receive a discharge. One court at least has rejected this argument and ordered the discharge of a medic who had entered the Army as a noncombatant.[28]

If a soldier simply wishes to perform noncombatant

duties, informal arrangements can sometimes be made with the company commander, even if noncombatant status has been turned down. But this places the CO in a potentially perilous situation, since either he or his commanding officer could be transferred to another unit, and the CO could once again be exposed to orders to train with arms and be subject to court-martial for refusal.

Anyone who is in doubt as to whether he is a CO would be wise to file an application for noncombatant status anyway. Then, if his conscience should compel him to refuse orders in the future, the denial of CO status could possibly be raised as a defense at a court-martial.

ONE MAN'S STRUGGLE: CONSCIENCE VS. THE SYSTEM

The almost incredible experience of Edward Stringham at the Presidio Army Base in San Francisco provides an illuminating lesson for COs who trust in the rationality of the system. After he had (1) filed his CO discharge application twice, (2) been subject to court-martial charges which were dropped, (3) been detained at Oakland, Fort Ord, and the Presidio for more than a year, and (4) litigated his right to the CO discharge in the federal courts all the way up to the Supreme Court —where Justice Douglas ordered a stay in his overseas orders—it became apparent in the summer of 1969 that the Army was going to stall a final decision on the case until his discharge date, more than a year away.

> This knowledge totally destroyed the fragile rationalization I had held on to for the preceding six months, namely that temporal, personal prostitution was necessary if one was to use his own case to attempt to somehow change the legal structure in some small way. If the Army was successful in stalling, and in that at least they seem competent,

until after my normal discharge then there was no possibility that my case would have any effect on the system . . .[29]

After having impressed his Army colleagues as well as his advisers and counselors with the strength of his convictions, Stringham decided to go on a fast, a quiet, determined fast. He decided to fast until he literally dropped. In his words, he could "no longer sustain, nor be sustained by the system."

There was one attempt after about fifteen days where it was casually mentioned by a warrant officer that one could be prosecuted by court-martial for refusing to eat since not to eat was willful destruction of government property. I admitted to him that anything was possible under the UCMJ but I believed there was considerable weight to the fact that this fast was conducted for religious reasons.[30]

Stringham fasted a total of twenty-three days and received an amazingly rapid discharge from the Army. But not as a CO. It was a general discharge for "unsuitability."[31] So far as the Army was concerned, Stringham never really was a conscientious objector.

Notes

1. Interview with Edward Stringham. His case is discussed later in this chapter.
2. AR 635–20, para. 1. (Selective Service uses same rule.)
3. *Dickinson v. U.S.,* 346 U.S. 389, 396 (1953).
4. *U.S. v. Sisson,* 297 F. Supp. 907 (D. Mass. 1969); *Koster v. Sharp,* 2 SSLR 3210 (E.D. Pa. 1969); *Goguen v. Clifford,* 2 SSLR 3410 (D.C. N.J. 1969); Noyd v. MacNamara, 296 F. Supp. 136 (O. Colo. Mar. 29, 1967).
5. AR 635–20, para. 3(b)3 (rev. 21 Jan. 1970).
6. 380 U.S. 163 (1965).
7. *U.S. v. Levy,* No. 19507 (8th Cir., decided 8 Dec. 1969). See *Counterdraft,* Jan.–Feb. 1970. vol. 2, no. 7, p. 10.
8. Army manuals on medic training clearly indicate that the

medic is primarily a soldier. See also articles in military medical journals, e.g., "In the War To Win Men's Minds Medicine Can Be Considered To Be a Weapon," *U.S. Medicine,* July 14, 1967, vol. 3, p. 14.

9. DOD Directive No. 1300.6 (10 May 1968), sec. IV,B.

10. AR 635–20, para. 4(a)2.

11. Pvt. James M. Taylor, at Fort Ord, California. Alice Lynd, *We Won't Go—Personal Accounts of War Objectors* (Boston: Beacon Press, 1968), p. 133.

12. Interview with Edward Stringham.

13. *U.S. v. James,* 2 SSLR 3231 (4th Cir., 1969).

14. AR 635–20, para. 6(a) (rev.——1970); para 6(b) has been rescinded.

15. AR 635–20, para. 6(a) (rev.——1970).

16. Col. H. H. Arnold, *New York Times,* April 20, 1969.

17. *Kalmen v. Laird,* 2 SSLR 3142 (N.D. Calif. 1969).

18. *Craycroft v. Ferrall,* 408 F.2d (9th Cir., 1969); *Krieger v. Terry,* 2 SSLR 3216 (9th Cir., 1969). Some courts even added the inappropriate requirement that Article 138 should be resorted to first.

19. *Brooks v. Clifford,* petition for rehearing denied, 2 SSLR 3139 (4th Cir., 1969).

20. *Negre v. Larsen,* 2 SSLR 32, No. 24,067 (9th Cir., 1969). Acting on their own, the courts can insist that the Board for Correction of Military Records rule first, despite the Justice Department's concession, but this is not very likely.

21. *Lee v. Pearson,* 18 USCMA 545, 40 CMR 257 (1969).

22. *Cooper v. Barker,* 291 F. Supp. 952 (D. Md. 1968). And see *Johnson v. Caple,* 2 SSLR 3144 (D. Hawaii 1969).

23. *U.S. v. Noyd,* 2 SSLR 3218 (1969).

24. AR 635–20, paras. 6(c) and (d).

25. *News Notes,* compiled by Mike Wittels, CCCO, May–Aug. 1969, p. 1.

26. DOD Directive No. 1300.6, sec. III.

27. See Note 8.

28. *Healy v. Beatty,* 2 SSLR 3141 (S.D. Ga. 1969).

29. Letter from Edward Stringham, Oct. 27, 1969.

30. *Ibid.*

31. Most COs aren't as fortunate as Stringham, who didn't have to wait out legal maneuverings while in the stockade. For a detailed account of another CO's ultimately successful struggle to gain release from the Army, see Brian Donovan, "The Man Who Beat the Army," *New Republic,* Jan. 31, 1970, p. 17.

13

Administrative Discharges: Getting Out for Good

You'll never amount to anything, blockhead! Your heart's not in it. Your senior officer sees it in little things. Yesterday, when I made the fat gal, I admit you grabbed her husband as I commanded, and you *did* kick him in the stomach, but did you enjoy doing it like a loyal Private? Or were you just doing your duty? I've kept my eyes on you, blockhead. You're a hollow reed and a tinkling cymbal. You won't get promoted.
—BERTOLT BRECHT, *The Caucasian Chalk Circle*

The soldier who prefers to be something else should realize that the ARs don't really tell him how to get out of the Army. For that kind of advice it is necessary to consult with those who have had successful experiences in convincing the system that it would be better off without certain soldiers. Organizations that can help you do this are listed in Appendix B.

The administrative discharge from the Army comprises no part of military justice and is not governed by the Uniform Code of Military Justice. It is based instead on the commander's traditional power to separate from the service anyone who in his opinion does not belong in the Army. Some of the safeguards provided for soldiers in the UCMJ against arbitrary criminal prosecution have been applied as well to reduce the commander's power to discharge a soldier administratively, but the power is still fundamentally arbitrary. This chapter presents the grounds for administrative discharges from two points of view: (1) that of the soldier who wants to get out, who will normally waive a hearing; and (2) that of the soldier who wants to stay in (or to secure a better type of discharge than has been awarded by the commander with discharge authority).

Although the administrative discharge machinery exists entirely apart from the court-martial apparatus, so far as the law and governing regulations are concerned, the soldier must not forget that both systems are used by the commander to foster what he understands to be efficiency within his command. It should also be understood that the grounds for obtaining or granting administrative discharges are vague and, even more important, overlapping. As a result, it frequently becomes impossible to predict how a particular case will be handled by any one commander, the "discharge authority." A homosexual incident could, for example, result in a soldier's court-martial or an administrative discharge on the grounds of unfitness, national security, unsuitability, or psychiatric disability, or for "the convenience of the government," depending on the circumstances and the attitudes and policies of his particular commander.

There are five kinds of discharge from the Army. The two punitive discharges, the Dishonorable Discharge (DD) and the Bad Conduct Discharge (BCD), can be given only after court-martial conviction. The administrative discharges are: (1) the Undesirable Discharge (UD), which for practical purposes is as at least as damaging as a bad conduct discharge to the soldier returning to civilian life; (2) the General Discharge under honorable conditions, which carries with it a stigma but no penalties from the point of view of veterans' benefits; and (3) the Honorable Discharge, which is still treated as something special, as a "reward" for meritorious service, even though more than ninety per cent of discharges are honorable.

GROUNDS FOR GETTING OUT

One reason for the confusion in this area is that, in addition to the three administrative discharges, Army Regulations provide numerous grounds for awarding them, and for the most part no particular ground *requires* that a particular kind of discharge be given. For instance, if a soldier is discharged for unsuitability, he will almost always be given the general discharge, but the discharge authority could award him an honorable discharge. And although the UD is given when the ground is unfitness, the discharge authority is free, in some circumstances, to award a general discharge certificate.

Unfitness and Unsuitability

Discharges from the Army for "unfitness" are rarely obtained without a long series of painful incidents that have resulted in courts-martial. The regulation lists the following categories of unfitness:

1) Frequent incidents of a discreditable nature with civil or military authorities.
2) Sexual perversion including but not limited to—
    a) Lewd and lascivious acts.
    b) Indecent exposure.
    c) Indecent acts with, or assault upon, a child.
    d) Other indecent acts or offenses.
3) a) Drug addiction, habituation, or the unauthorized use, sale, possession, or transfer of any narcotics, hypnotics, sedatives, depres-

sants, stimulants, hallucinogens, or other known or habit-forming drugs and/or chemicals or the introduction of such drugs and/or chemicals onto any Army installation or other Government property under Army jurisdiction.

b) The unauthorized sale or transfer of marijuana.

c) The unauthorized use or possession of marijuana.

4) An established pattern for shirking.

5) An established pattern showing dishonorable failure to pay just debts.

6) An established pattern showing dishonorable failure to contribute adequate support to dependents, or failure to comply with orders, decrees, or judgments of a civil court concerning support of dependents.

7) Homosexual acts . . .[1]

Just about all the grounds for discharge because of unfitness could be used to initiate court-martial proceedings against the offender. The discharge authority decides which alternative is appropriate in each case. Sometimes the soldier is court-martialed and discharge proceedings are begun immediately after his conviction. In many of these cases the soldier receives his discharge while confined in a stockade. If the commander decides on a discharge (whether before or after court-martial), it is likely to be the UD. When the convening authority lacks sufficient evidence to refer a case to court-martial and attempts to discharge a soldier administratively instead, the soldier has a right to demand a hearing before a board of officers convened by the discharge authority to investigate the case. The soldier can be represented by counsel and can cross-examine government witnesses. The rights available to soldiers who contest their elimination from the service are discussed later in this chapter.

The grounds for discharge for "unsuitability" are general inadequacy and certain medical and psychiatric conditions—not acts which would lend themselves to correction by court-martial. Since they usually result in a general discharge rather than a UD, the soldier is better off being eliminated from the service for unsuitability than for unfitness. These are the official categories of unsuitability:

1) Inaptitude;
2) Character and behavior disorders;
3) Apathy;
4) Alcoholism;
5) Enuresis (bed wetting);
6) Homosexuality—homosexual tendencies, desires, or interest, without overt homosexual acts.[2]

The Army is stingy with discharges on the ground of unsuitability, possibly because it would rather brand someone who can't conform as an undesirable and because it cannot be absolutely certain that someone is not faking inaptitude or a behavior disorder. "Apathy" doesn't mean simply that the person lacks enthusiasm about the Army. It encompasses a lack of concern about one's life and welfare that borders on mental illness.

Misconduct: Fraudulent Entry, Civilian Crimes, AWOL, or Desertion

AR 635–206 authorizes the administrative discharge of soldiers who have engaged in particular forms of misconduct involving fraudulent entry into the service, conviction of a crime by a civilian jurisdiction, and going AWOL or deserting. The discharge will be a UD unless the soldier has been decorated in battle or there are other extenuating circumstances.

1) *Fraudulent Entry into the Army.* A variety of common misrepresentations permit the Army to discharge a soldier for fraudulent entry into the service:

a) Concealment by the soldier of his prior service;

b) Concealment by aliens of their true citizenship status;

c) Concealment of the soldier's conviction by a civil court of a crime for which he was sentenced to more than a year in jail;

d) Concealment of any other criminal record;

e) Concealment of the fact that the soldier was a juvenile offender;

f) Concealment of medical defects;

g) Concealment of absence without leave or desertion from prior service;

h) Concealment of other disqualifications.

It is emphasized that none of the above grounds for discharge is mandatory upon a commander. In all administrative discharges the commander is given the broadest possible discretion to retain soldiers in the Army, even after a board of officers has recommended discharge. Moreover, fraudulent enlistment can be punished under Article 83 of the UCMJ.

2) *Conviction by Civil Court.* If an individual has been convicted by a civil court, state or federal, of a crime for which the penalty under the UCMJ would be confinement for more than one year, the Army *may* discharge him. If the crime is one of "moral turpitude," which usually means a sex offense, the Army may discharge him even if the penalty imposable would be less than a year in jail.[3] The soldier may be retained in the service if he has received a decoration, or for any other reason the discharge authority considers sufficient.

3) *AWOL and Desertion.* Desertion and absence without leave for more than one year are grounds for an administrative discharge for misconduct. So many thousands of men have been AWOL for such long periods of time that this section is rarely, if ever, used.[4] If the soldier is confined in a mental institution, or if he has suffered a crippling disability during his AWOL, he is more likely to be given a discharge *in absentia.* If charges are not filed within three years from the date a

soldier deserts, the statute of limitations precludes prosecution thereafter *during peacetime*. However, the Court of Military Appeals has held that during the Vietnam era we have been at war, at least for the purposes of the statute of limitations. Thus, since the military knows it can prosecute returning deserters at any time in the future, it will not be discharging many AWOL soldiers *in absentia*.

Homosexuality

A homosexual act is defined by the Army as "bodily contact between persons of the same sex, actively undertaken or passively permitted by either or both with the intent of obtaining or giving sexual gratification, or any proposal, solicitation, or attempt to perform such act."[5] Although the AR covering homosexuality, 635–89, has recently been rescinded, and the subject is now treated as just another ground for an unfitness or unsuitability discharge, commanders still think in terms of the old categories; thus it will be useful to review them. Although the official categories seem to have been eliminated, Army policy will probably be much the same.

The Class I homosexual act involved assault, coercion, fraud, or children under sixteen. The most serious offenses fell into this category and were usually referred to court-martial. Class II encompassed consensual homosexual activity between adults and some Class I cases that had not been tried by court-martial. Class III consisted of servicemen who had not engaged in a homosexual act during military service but who had a verified record of preservice homosexual acts. *Class III homosexuality, involving no acts during service, could not and still cannot result in court-martial*. But all the acts which fell into categories I and II could, and still can.

Most discharges for homosexuality are for consensual activity between adults, and the discharge is typically the UD. When a single homosexual episode "stemming solely from immaturity, curiosity, or intoxication" took place, the soldier could not be eliminated from the service for homosexuality.[6] Those who were separated for Class III homosexuality typically got a general discharge under honorable conditions; since this said, in effect, that there must be something wrong with the individual, it was a kind of punishment without due process of law. Many people have been thus stigmatized for a condition that existed prior to service and despite the fact that their service records were excellent. There has been no indication that this practice is going to change.

Someone who wishes to get out of the Army as the type of homosexual formerly under Class III regulations can trigger the process by reporting his *preservice* homosexual activity to his company commander or the chaplain and admitting to present tendencies, fears, or temptations. Evidence of his homosexual leanings may be provided by those on the outside with whom he has committed homosexual acts or who send him intimate letters or homosexual publications. There are risks in doing this, since a confession may still have to be signed in the course of waiving board action and the confession becomes part of the GI's permanent file. As a result, it might be difficult for him to obtain a job with a government or state agency, or with some private industries.

Dependency or Hardship

The Secretary of the Army may, in his discretion, discharge a soldier on the grounds of:

a. Dependency, when by reason of death or disability of a member of his family occurring after his enlistment, induction, or order to active duty, members of the enlisted person's family become principally dependent upon him for care or support.

or

b. Hardship, when in circumstances not involving death or disability of a member of his family, his separation from the service will materially affect the care or support of his family by alleviating undue and genuine hardship.[7]

The key to understanding these grounds for administrative discharge is to remember that the Secretary of the Army is granted almost absolute discretion in determining what degree of hardship must exist before an application is granted. (On the other hand, federal courts are just beginning to order discharges on grounds other than conscientious objection.) The Army assumes that some hardship results in every family when one of its men is called to military service. Thus it has set up several general guidelines by which a soldier's application is to be judged: the hardship or dependency must not be of a temporary nature; it must have been greatly aggravated by the soldier's entering the Army; every reasonable effort must have been made by the soldier to alleviate the condition of hardship or dependency; his release from the Army must be the only readily available means for alleviating the problem.[8]

Although a situation has to be extremely severe for a soldier to hope for a discharge, it may be to his advantage to file an application (on a DF) even if he has been discouraged from doing so. *Nobody can legally stop him from trying.* Besides, temporary advantages can be obtained by filing. Someone who is home on emergency or ordinary leave from an overseas assignment can apply for hardship discharge at the installation nearest his home[9] (or perhaps directly at the Pentagon). This will result in the soldier's being held at the local installation pending decision on the discharge application.[10] For someone on overseas orders who has not yet left his home installation, the filing of a hardship discharge application will delay his shipment. *The regulation states that he must be held at the home station pending final decision.*[11]

A CO discharge application may no longer be filed at an overseas replacement station, and a soldier en route overseas cannot expect the replacement station personnel to accept his hardship discharge application. But, in his discretion, the replacement station commander may hold someone for thirty days after he has filed for hardship discharge to allow time to gather the necessary supporting evidence, such as letters and affidavits. Then, when the application and evidence are submitted, the commander can hold on to the soldier pending final decision by the Department of the Army. However, it is rare for an overseas replacement station commander to accept a hardship discharge application. Without a special request from an important civilian official or higher officer, the soldier seeking to submit a hardship discharge application while en route overseas has virtually no chance of being taken seriously.

Medical Reasons

Not infrequently someone is inducted into the Army who, because of a disqualifying medical condition, should not have been inducted. When this happens the soldier may obtain release if he files an application within four months after his induction and is able to convince a board of Army doctors that he was not medically qualified for induction.[12]

A statement from a civilian doctor that in his opinion the soldier has a disqualifying condition under the Army's induction standards, and that the condition existed prior to induction, would be very helpful in getting the bureaucratic ball rolling. The soldier should somehow manage to get his medical records photocopied and attach them to a request in his company, on the standard DF, that a medical board be convened for the purpose of examining him for a particular condition listed in AR 40–501, Chapter 2, where the Army's standards of medical fitness for induction are listed. A copy of the request for release and supporting evidence should be sent to: Chief, Physical Standards Division, Department of the Army, Office of the Surgeon General, Washington, D.C., 20315, with an appeal that the application be expedited.[13]

When a soldier develops a physical disability during his service that renders him unfit to remain in the Army[14] (these standards are somewhat lower than those for induction), he should consult AR 635–40 for the procedures to follow.

National Security

When dealing with persons who have committed homosexual acts, the Army frequently chooses to separate them from the service by administrative means, whether or not it has a strong case for court-martial. It takes the opposite view in security or political cases. If there is any pretext available for court-martialing a political dissenter for security-related offenses, such as mutiny, soliciting sedition, or making disloyal statements with design to create disaffection, the Army will court-martial him. In those instances where the Army could not build a case, or could not silence a dissenter even after putting him in the stockade, it has been driven to discharge the organizer administratively. In some cases the dissenters have protested being discharged as "undesirables" and have brought lawsuits to obtain honorable discharges instead of the UDs they were awarded. Since there are so many GI organizers in the service today, it is highly unlikely that more than a handful will receive administrative discharges as "threats to national security." The Army doesn't want to reward antisystem activities by making it easy for the protesters to get out. But when, in the *Army*'s opinion, "the retention of an individual is not clearly consistent with the interests of national security, he will be discharged." Criteria for determining when an individual's retention is not justified are given in AR 604–10:

> a. Willful violation or disregard of security regulations;
>
> b. Intentional unauthorized disclosure to any person of classified information, or of other information the disclosure of which is prohibited by law;

c. Any deliberate misrepresentation, falsification, or omission of material fact;

d. Any criminal, infamous, dishonest, immoral, or notoriously disgraceful conduct, habitual use of intoxicants to excess, drug addiction, or sexual perversion;

e. All other behavior, activities, or associations which tend to show that the member is not reliable or trustworthy.[15]

The last subparagraph is a way of saying the authorities can discharge anybody they want to any time they think it's necessary. The legal question is whether an individual can, for activities which are unpopular with the brass, be branded an undesirable and deprived of valuable veterans' benefits or, in the case of career soldiers, of pensions, pay, and allowances.

A soldier who has carefully considered the step may attempt to initiate a security investigation on himself as a means of securing a discharge on security grounds. He should realize that the discharge is discretionary and that at least while the application is pending he will suffer a number of inconveniences, such as (1) being frozen in his present rank, (2) being refused a security clearance or getting kicked out of his military job if a clearance is a prerequisite, (3) being followed by agents of the government.

Of course, the soldier should be cautious about the kinds of activity he claims to be currently engaged in, since there are a number of articles of the UCMJ that have been used to stifle dissent and he might unwittingly expose himself to a prosecution for mutiny or soliciting sedition. However, mere expression of sympathy for the cause of someone the Army considers to be subversive is not a court-martial offense. (See Chapter Five, The Soldier's First Amendment Rights.)

One way of starting the process is to request that one's DD 98 (Armed Forces Security Questionnaire) be returned for the purpose of providing information believed to justify a security discharge. (Remember: Any false statement on an official form is punishable as a federal crime.) An anonymous letter to the soldier's commanding officer alleging that the person is "subversive" is another certain method for initiating an investigation. The letter may also be sent to: Assistant Chief of Staff for Intelligence, Department of the Army, ATTENTION: Chief, U.S. Army Personnel Security Group, Fort Holabird, Maryland, 21219.

After an investigation is completed, recommendations are forwarded to Washington. If the Assistant Chief of Staff for Intelligence believes that a security discharge is warranted, the Judge Advocate General's Office will prepare a "Letter of Allegations" which will be forwarded to the soldier involved. He will then have to decide whether to contest the nature of the discharge (which will be a UD) before a Field Board of Inquiry or to waive the board hearing. If he does not waive, it is entirely conceivable, under Army Regulations, that he will be put in the position of having to refute secret testimony which has been summarized for him by the board. But if a soldier himself has initiated the security discharge, there would seem to be no reason for his demanding the board hearing. In the case of a soldier who has received a security discharge involuntarily, there is an automatic review by the Army Security Review Board.[16]

Minority

Some young men who desire to enlist in the Army manage to obtain false identifications or phony birth certificates and enlist when they are fifteen or sixteen years old. Others, over seventeen, manage to get into the Army without the legal requirement of their parents' or guardian's consent. Many of these boys become convinced that they made a mistake. A few can get out.[17]

1) If a young man enlisted or was *voluntarily* inducted before he attained the age of seventeen, *is still not seventeen years old,* and provides "satisfactory evidence of his date of birth," his enlistment is considered

to be void. To get out of the Army, he doesn't even have to file a discharge application. The discharge authority *must* issue an order releasing the boy from the service.[18]

2) If a young man was *involuntarily* inducted (drafted) before he had attained the age of eighteen years and six months, is still under that age, and provides satisfactory evidence of his birth date, his induction is considered to be void. As in the case above, the discharge authority must issue an order releasing him from the Army. There is no need to file a discharge application.[19]

3) If a young man *enlisted before he was seventeen* and has not reached the age of eighteen, he must be discharged unless (*a*) he is under charges or in confinement for a serious offense committed after he became seventeen or (*b*) his immediate commanding officer recommends that he be retained and the Secretary of the Army goes along with the recommendation. In that event, the parents or guardian can apply for the young man's discharge and probably obtain his release.[20] But if he has reached the age of eighteen, he won't be discharged.[21]

4) If a young man volunteered for the draft and was "voluntarily inducted" when he was under seventeen but has not yet reached the age of eighteen years and six months, he can apply for discharge, and this will probably be granted unless he is under charges or in confinement or unless the commanding officer recommends that he be retained (as in category 3, above). On the other hand, if he is eighteen years and six months, he won't be discharged.[22]

5) If a young man was *over seventeen when he enlisted* but did not have the written consent of his parents or guardian, *and he is not yet eighteen years old,* he must be discharged upon the application of his parents and proof of age. If he had the written consent of his parents or guardian when he enlisted at seventeen, he cannot be released on the ground of minority.[23]

6) If a young man was over seventeen years of age

when he was *voluntarily inducted* but did not have the written consent of his parents or guardian, and *he has not yet reached eighteen years and six months,* he must be discharged upon the application of his parents and proof of age. If he had the written consent of his parents or guardian when he was voluntarily inducted at seventeen, he cannot be released on the ground of minority.[24]

In all the cases catalogued above the proof of age must consist of (1) an authenticated copy of a birth certificate or (2) an affidavit of the parents or guardian explaining why no birth certificate is available, together with other proof listed in the AR.

Miscellaneous Reasons

There are a number of additional grounds for discharge, some of them obviously applicable to certain limited categories of personnel. An example is the discharge for marriage, pregnancy, or parenthood of female members of the Army.[25] Some grounds are so broad that the commander can release anyone he wants to for any reason that commends itself to him. A commander may approve a request for discharge "for the good of the service" when the soldier has engaged in conduct that could be made the subject of a court-martial.[26] The UD is usually given for this kind of discharge. Other sections permit "separation for the convenience of the government"—which includes the grounds of erroneous induction, discharge of aliens unlawfully in the United States, and release of those who at induction did not meet the medical fitness standards—and separation for the "national health, safety, or interest."[27] The latter ground allows for a soldier's release to work in a defense-related activity that is in critical need of his skills. (Political connections help in securing this one.) Also included in the "convenience of the government" section are those who become sole surviving sons of families who have lost someone in the Vietnam war.

There is also the "resignation," a device through

which officers have the opportunity to be released from the service for acts that normally result in court-martial for enlisted men.[28] Other reasons for discharge are retirement and completion of one's enlistment contract or statutory tour of active duty.

FIGHTING A DISCHARGE: BOARDS, HEARINGS, AND PROCEDURAL RIGHTS

Imagine if you will a system of justice with the burden of proving innocence imposed on the defendant, secret informants, no right to trial, no right to see the evidence, no right of cross-examination, no rule against double jeopardy, no protection against punishment even when found innocent, no right to legally qualified counsel, no independent judge, no independent judicial review, and no clearly defined rules of what is and is not against the law.

This, in harsh terms, and with very little exaggeration, is the system which can brand a man as "undesirable," "unfit," or "unsuitable," deprive him of his serviceman's rights, his accruing pension and retirement, his employability, and his honor.[29]

These remarks by Senator Sam Ervin, who is no foe of military power, aptly describe the military administrative discharge system. For at least a decade the Senator from North Carolina has sought to inject the prerequisites for fundamental fairness into the despotic mechanism by which thousands of men each year are labeled undesirables. By the time this guide is distributed, his latest congressional bill[30] may well have become law. Presently, the armed services operate under the authority of a Department of Defense directive which was promulgated immediately before the 1966 congressional hearings in Senator Ervin's committees.[31] This directive was a great improvement over earlier ones. Some of the witnesses at the hearings expressed the belief that the directive was sprung at the end of 1965 to forestall reform of the administrative discharge system. (A directive can be rescinded or modified at any time, while a statute removes any such discretion from the Defense Department.) The gesture succeeded and the existing system remains a halfway house between complete arbitrariness and administrative due process.

It is a fact that only with the assistance of qualified counsel can a soldier be expected to exercise his procedural rights at a court-martial. This observation is equally true for administrative discharge boards. Unfortunately, a lawyer is provided to someone facing board action only if the convening authority feels one is "reasonably available." Otherwise the counsel requirement can be fulfilled by the selection of a nonlegally trained officer to represent the "respondent" (the soldier facing board action). Most officers are as unqualified to assist in these proceedings as they were to defend special court-martial cases.[32] Senator Ervin's bill would make a lawyer mandatory in every situation where the respondent soldier could be given a UD, but it would not require a lawyer for board actions that could result merely in a general discharge. *The soldier facing board action now should insist on being provided with legally trained counsel, regardless of the fact that the regulations do not require the convening authority to assign a lawyer to each respondent.* He should indicate that if he receives a UD he will contest it as unconstitutionally granted by retaining civilian counsel to bring an action in federal court. He might point out that it is partly because of the fear of a court's declaring the present system unconstitutional that Congress is in the process of making the appointment of a lawyer mandatory in cases when a UD can be given.

Under the existing ARs the respondent has a right to appear in person and either remain silent or testify in his own behalf. He may cross-examine the witnesses who appear for the government but has no right to compel the attendance of, or to cross-examine, the people who submit the investigative reports and affidavits that are commonly used as evidence. A respondent may present the testimony of witnesses he is able to obtain, but if he wants an unwilling or unavailable military witness to appear and testify he must first ask the board to request the witness' presence. If the board of officers feels the witness' testimony will add materially to the respondent's case, it can then ask the person who convened the board to obtain the witness. However, if the board declines to request the attendance of the witness, the soldier is out of luck, unless his counsel can convince the convening authority to call the person who is sought.

The Ervin bill would limit the use of hearsay testimony; it would give the respondent the right in each instance to confront his accuser or any witness against him. It would also give the respondent and his counsel power to summon witnesses equal to that of the government. And to insure an accurate record of the proceedings, it would require a verbatim transcript of the testimony in cases where a UD could be granted. No such requirement exists now.

Under the current directive the convening authority is not permitted to award a discharge lower than the one recommended by the board that has heard a soldier's case. If a board recommends that a soldier be separated from the service and awards him a general discharge, the discharge authority cannot convert it into a UD. Nor can the convening authority discharge the soldier administratively if the board recommends retention (unless he gets special permission from Washington to do so).[33] The Ervin bill would make this policy ironclad. When a board recommends retention, the discharge authority would be prevented from ever discharging a soldier for the same acts that the board considered, or from setting up a second board to consider the same acts. On the other hand, under the Ervin bill the convening authority would retain his authority to suspend a discharge recommended by a board and to retain the soldier in the Army.

In national security discharge cases, it is still lawful for boards to consider secret evidence. When information or sources of information have not been disclosed to the respondent for "security" reasons (usually to protect the identity of a government informer), the board is supposed to "summarize" the substance of the damaging information and the respondent is expected to rebut or respond to such evidence thus presented in summary form. The Ervin bill would abolish the use of secret evidence.

After a discharge has been recommended by a board, the discharge authority is supposed to review the findings and recommendations and determine whether the discharge is warranted by the evidence. This provides an added opportunity for a soldier or his counsel to present arguments to the person who makes the ultimate decision. In security discharge cases, there is an additional review by the Army Security Review Board before final action is taken.

Board for Correction of Military Records

The Army Board for Correction of Military Records is composed of civilians who work for the Army in Washington, D.C., and who serve as board members on a part-time basis. The board has the broad power to "correct any military record" for the purpose of removing an error or correcting an injustice.[34] This includes the power to review an anticipated discharge. A soldier's application may be sent directly to the board on a DF. If he is no longer in the Army, a letter will suffice. However, hearings are not automatically granted, and the assistance of a civilian lawyer is very useful. After a soldier has been discharged, he must first apply to the Discharge Review Board to correct any error that may have occurred on the lower levels—unless he requests back pay also. When back pay is demanded the former soldier may apply directly to the Board for Correction of Military Records before filing an action in a federal court.

Discharge Review Board

The Discharge Review Board is a permanent body of officers in Washington, D.C., with the power to review, upon request, a discharge from the Army.[35] Anticipated discharges are not reviewed. The board cannot review the conviction of a general or BCD special court-martial, nor can it award back pay. A request for a hearing will always be granted, but the board has no subpoena power to compel the testimony of witnesses, and it must rely on the military records and the petition for review.

Federal District Courts and
the United States Court of Claims

The federal district courts will occasionally issue restraining orders to prevent threatened illegalities from being put into effect by the Army—but only when the petitioner can show he would suffer irreparable harm as a result. It is difficult but possible to obtain a federal court order restraining the Army from issuing a less than honorable administrative discharge, pending review by the Board for Correction of Military Records. The soldier has to show he would have a good chance of ultimately prevailing in his arguments before the board.[36] Even after a soldier is out of the Army, it is possible to seek a declaratory judgment in a federal district court that the administrative discharge he received is illegal and to obtain a court order restoring him to duty. The court can then pave the way for subsequent administrative correction of records. This is a specialized area of administrative practice, and a civilian lawyer is essential. If all the ex-soldier is seeking is back pay and allowances that have been illegally forfeited, they too may be recovered in a federal court.

An alternative forum is the U.S. Court of Claims. It doesn't have the power to order the Army to restore someone to duty, but it can award a money judgment for back pay and allowances when it determines a discharge has been illegally granted; if the ex-soldier wants the nature of the discharge to be changed in his Army records, he must go to one of the boards discussed above and request that changes be made in accordance with the court's decision. *When the discharge is part of a court-martial sentence, the Court of Claims cannot overturn the conviction,* although there is still the possibility that if the court-martial conviction was obtained in violation of the soldier's *constitutional* rights the Court of Claims might have jurisdiction to review it.[37]

If your lawyer lives a great distance from the Court of Claims in Washington, D.C., a commissioner can be appointed by the court to hear the case in his locality.

The Ervin bill provides for review of some administrative discharges by the Court of Military Appeals, which at present has nothing to do with them. If that provision becomes law, consult your lawyer to determine whether you can obtain legal relief through that court.

Notes

1. AR 635–212, para. 6(a) (rev. 28 Nov. 1969 and 21 Jan. 1970). Officers are covered by AR 635–100.
2. AR 635–212, para. 6(b) (rev. 21 Jan 1970).
3. AR 635–206, para. 33(b) (rev. 15 July 1966).
4. AR 635–206, sec. VII. As a result of congressional pressure to crack down on Vietnam war deserters, a companion section authorizing the separation of certain wartime and peacetime deserters was rescinded (Change 5, 4 Oct. 1969).
5. AR 635–212, para. 6(a) (rev. 21 Jan. 1970).
6. AR 635–89, para. 2(b), rescinded.
7. AR 635–200, ch. 6, para. 6–4 (rev. 9 April 1968).
8. AR 635–200, ch. 6, para. 6–5.

9. AR 635–200, ch. 6, para. 6–6(a)2.

10. AR 635–200, ch. 6, para. 6–6(c).

11. AR 635–200, ch. 6, para. 6–6(a)4.

12. AR 635–200, ch. 5, para. 5–9 (rev. 25 April 1969).

13. *Counterdraft,* 1969, vol. 2, no. 1. Practical advice on the filing of administrative discharge applications may be obtained from time to time in this informative guide for draft and military counselors. See address in Appendix B, under California.

14. See AR 40–501, ch. 3.

15. AR 604–10, para. 2–4 (rev. 18 Sept. 1969).

16. AR 604–10, ch. 7.

17. AR 635–200, ch. 7.

18. AR 635–200, ch. 7, para. 7–5(a)3.

19. *Ibid.*

20. AR 635–200, ch. 7, para. 7–5(a)4.

21. AR 635–200, ch. 7, para. 7–5(a)1(a).

22. AR 635–200, ch. 7, para. 7–5(a)5.

23. AR 635–200, ch. 7, para. 7–5(a)7.

24. *Ibid.*

25. AR 635–200, ch. 8.

26. AR 635–200, ch. 10.

27. AR 635–200, ch. 5.

28. AR 635–200, ch. 9.

29. Remarks of Senator Ervin at Judge Advocate General's Conference, Charlottesville, Virginia, July 16, 1969; *Congressional Record,* 91st Congress, 1st Session, Aug. 11, 1969, vol. 115, no. 136.

30. S. 1266, 91st Congress, 1st Session, March 4, 1969.

31. DOD Directive 1332.14, Dec. 20, 1965.

32. See Chapter Nine, The Framework of Military Law, for a discussion of the inadequacies of nonlawyers as defense counsel at special courts.

33. AR 635–200, para. 1–13(a)2.

34. 10 USC 1552.

35. 10 USC 1553.

36. *Schwartz v. Covington,* 341 F.2d 537 (9th Cir., 1965).

37. *U.S. v. Augenblick,* 393 U.S. 348 (1969).

14

An Army of the People

. . . and I am waiting
for a rebirth of wonder
and I am waiting for someone
to really discover America
and wail
and I am waiting
for the discovery
of a new symbolic western frontier
and I am waiting
for the American Eagle
to really spread its wings
and straighten up and fly right . . .
                    —LAWRENCE FERLINGHETTI, *I Am Waiting*

If here, reborn more in horror than in wonder, we have
really discovered America, then the myths that sustain
our Army will not easily be shattered, especially since
our national policy makers cling to the myths with the
same tenacity they exhibit in refusing to discuss them.
If, therefore, the citizen-soldier or veteran can hope to
convince his congressman that only radical reform of

the Army can save it, he must know what the typical hawk congressman is really thinking, and an X ray of those thoughts could look something like this:

Crap! *All* armies are lawless, and they'd be crazy to be anything else. If those ivory-tower eggheads got their way, we'd give it all up and the Chinese and Russians would be here tomorrow. First, you can't train people to kill by being nice to them. Second, if the recruit didn't know beforehand that the court-martial system was stacked against him he'd never obey an order and you'd have a mob, not an Army. So when we talk to the voters we tell them their sons have "rights," and when we have to we send letters to the military demanding that so-and-so's rights be respected. But the generals understand, and rightly so, that they may— no—they *must* run *their* Army as *they* see fit. It's always been that way and it always will be.

Maybe so. But for this, the oldest dilemma of any free society, it is the people who must decide where the balance will be struck. Abraham Lincoln posed the question:

Must a government of necessity be too *strong* for the liberties of its people, or too *weak* to maintain its own existence?

A nation's existence. We can destroy the world in a couple of megaseconds, but somehow a lot of people feel America would cease to exist if we modernized the military and made it law-abiding. They feel this way because cherished and time-honored falsehoods are not easily forsaken. In the meantime, equally cherished and time-honored values must, like the raw recruit, hurry up and wait. But they have waited long enough, and it is time to bury the myths that crush the citizen-soldier.

THE MYTH THAT DISCIPLINE WILL CRUMBLE IN COMBAT IN THE ABSENCE OF TERROR IN TRAINING

It must be admitted that in a totalitarian environment which is not just total but uninterrupted many men can be converted into cold-blooded killers and taught to find their "joy in the lust of killing."[1] But since such a goal is disclaimed by the American military establishment, and since there do exist some civilian controls over the military's methods, we may now assess the effectiveness of and necessity for the psychological and physical brutalities that have been described in earlier chapters.

For hundreds of years, at least, army manuals have exhorted officers to recognize the intimate relationship between discipline and morale. Even Baron von Steuben, the Prussian military theorist whose codes were adopted wholesale by the American revolutionary army two centuries ago, realized the importance of morale in armies that reflected the caste systems of eighteenth-century Europe. These, for example, are some of von Steuben's "Instructions for the Captain":

> His first object should be, to gain the love of his men, by treating them with every possible kindness and humanity, inquiring into their complaints, and when well founded, seeing them redressed. He should know every man of his company by name and character. He should often visit those who are sick, speak tenderly to them, see that the public provision, whether of medicine or diet, is duly administered, and procure them besides such comforts and conveniences as are in his power.[2]

His "Instructions for the Sergeants and Corporals" convey the same message:

> In teaching the recruits, they must exercise all their
> patience, by no means abusing them, but treating
> them with mildness . . .[3]

What has the American Army done with this ancient
advice from an authority who was not exactly noted for
mollycoddling the troops? Even as we enter a new
decade in the electronic age, our Army has adopted the
caste system's paternalistic, authoritarian shell and discarded its attendant wisdom. Its officers believe that
instant obedience in combat will be assured through
dehumanization, humiliation, and, particularly in the
Marines, physically brutalizing its men. Yet in the
studies that are available to the Army on "why men
fight," no data has been developed to support or justify
the continuation of these practices on the ground of
either combat effectiveness or military necessity.

During World War II a team of social psychologists
conducted for the War Department an extensive study,
consisting of numerous opinion surveys, on the attitudes
of American fighting men. In an attempt to discover the
motivations that made men fight, they interviewed a
veteran division of two Mediterranean campaigns, as
well as company-grade officers who had served in the
European and Pacific theaters. The enlisted men were
asked the question:

> Generally, in your combat experience, what was
> most important to you in making you want to keep
> going and do as well as you could?

Seventy-eight per cent of the responses included these
motivations: (1) to get the war over with; (2) not to let
their buddies down; (3) to get home to their loved ones;
(4) a sense of doing one's duty; and (5) self-preservation.

A small percentage mentioned patriotism or hatred
for the Nazis. *Only one per cent of the men said they
fought because of "leadership and discipline," in which
was included the fear of court-martial.*[4] Of course, as
the authors point out, the men might not have wanted

to admit the extent to which these factors were important to them. But by the same token the officers probably exaggerated (as they tended to do in the other surveys) the importance of their own leadership in getting the men to fight. The question asked the officers was worded this way:

When the going is tough for young men, what do you think are the incentives which keep them fighting?

Only nineteen per cent of their comments expressed the belief that the men fought because of motivations of leadership or fear of discipline.[5] One thing that supports these findings is the fact that if a soldier wanted to go AWOL, desert, or misbehave in the face of the enemy he did not need to fear the death penalty. Except in cases of murder it was virtually never used. So he was not faced with the dilemma of possible death on the battlefield versus certain death if convicted of a crime. He fought, the authors concluded, for other reasons, largely determined by what he expected of himself and what he knew his buddies and his family expected of him.[6]

The implications are apparent to everyone but the people who run the military establishment. *Americans do not fight primarily because they are afraid of criminal punishment if they should refuse.* These findings were confirmed by studies made during the Korean war:

Positive status legends [exaggerated stories about a commander's combat performance] often referred to the commander's democratic eccentricities, his concern for human life, or his tolerance of deviations from the policies of the larger organization. Such positive legends assured the commander of warm, affectionate responses and willing cooperation from his subordinates.[7]

No new survey is required to "prove" that such findings and conclusions apply to combat morale in Vietnam. As a matter of fact, it is almost the universal feeling of combat veterans that combat conditions automatically "equalize" privates, NCOs, and officers to the point where all social distinctions temporarily disappear, and the fear of court-martial is played down. (Most officers in combat learn very quickly to become "one of the boys," and there are stories of terrible accidents that have befallen officers who failed to appreciate that fact of life in time.) Combat conditions *require* a spirit of cooperation between leaders and led that might well be instilled in training in an enlightened Army.

When the combat performance of the low-ranking officer is compared with that of the low-ranking enlisted man additional proof is provided that deprivation and terror are not necessary to make good soldiers. It is known that through friendships, class protectiveness, and dismissal procedures officers escape court-martial for crimes that enlisted men go to jail for. It is also apparent that officers enjoy a great many more physical comforts, considerably more privacy, and the sense of well-being that accompanies displays of respect. Yet no military authority has ever suggested that because of these luxuries officers are less reliable than corporals in combat. And of course they are not.

THE MYTH THAT THE GLORIFICATION OF TRIVIA INCREASES COMBAT PROFICIENCY

From generals to noncoms, the military services are consumed with the notion that constant repetition of useless tasks, combined with a curious glorification of their significance, somehow imparts skills and encourages habits that bear on the soldier's ability to fight. In the World War II research project seventy-four per cent of enlisted men surveyed agreed with the statement that "the Army places too much importance on 'spit and polish.'" (The figure seems low, but it presumably included NCOs, who tend to *favor* "spit and polish.")

Even forty per cent of the officers agreed with the statement![8] Of course the opinions of the soldiers who must put up with "Mickey Mouse" still do not count for very much. Thus the senseless polishing of buckles, buttons, boots, and barracks, the psychopathological "just so" arranging of things on bunks, floors, and company areas for periodic or impromptu inspections, the compulsory gestures of patriotism and deference, the marching and drilling and tin-soldiering are justified mainly on the ground of inculcating the *habit* of obedience. The average soldier doesn't need an expert to tell him that these activities are not only uninspiring but also counterproductive. The English psychologist C. W. Valentine has observed:

> There seems to be a frequent assumption, underlying the enforcing of some minor regulation or the constant repetition of routine drill, that the repeated performance of boring and obnoxious things, in response to orders, will make a man more submissive to orders to do more important things . . . But this is very questionable psychology. Indeed there are reasons for thinking that the enforcing of regulations which men feel to be unnecessary may actually have the opposite effect.[9]

> I do not suggest that it can be *proved* that the prolonging of intensive routine, given for the mere sake of discipline, cannot influence obedience on the field of battle. All we can say is that it seems unlikely, or at least uncertain, and that no satisfactory evidence for it can be found, so that it is hardly worth while spending much time on it when there are other clearly important things to be done.[10]

The author adds that even if an attitude of obedience can be transferred from a training sergeant to a sergeant on the battlefield, then there is every reason to assume that attitudes of resentment, annoyance, and disgust are just as likely to be transferred.[11] Another psychologist,

Norman Copeland, agrees that the net result is to lower the soldier's morale and make him less effective:

> Psychologists have exploded the asinine idea that if a man's nose is not kept to the grindstone during the whole of his waking hours he will inevitably come to a bad end. Men who work hard for a reasonable number of hours, and are then allowed a generous measure of liberty, will prove keener, happier, more efficient and better disciplined than those who are kept hard at it continually.[12]

THE MYTH THAT THE THOUGHTFUL SOLDIER IS A DETRIMENT IN COMBAT

A dominant school of thought holds that, since it is unnatural to ask human beings to kill others, drastic measures must be taken to get the recruit in the frame of mind where he can overcome his normal revulsion to killing. To do this you must brutalize him to the point where he becomes a Thing, a robot which will do its master's bidding. This is the traditional portrait of the professional soldier, a hired gun who asks no questions. In World War II most soldiers responded to their training as might have been expected. *Ninety per cent* of the officers agreed with the statement, "A noncom should teach his men to obey all rules and regulations without questioning them." Eighty-one per cent of the NCOs and sixty-three per cent of the privates also agreed.

It may well be that the soldier who hesitates could be a threat to discipline *as it is understood by his superiors*. To that extent it is no myth that the conscientious, thinking soldier might be a detrimental factor, or at least not a helpful factor in combat. On the other hand, one of the lessons that all civilized nations were supposed to have brought home with them from World War II was that a soldier, no matter what his rank may be, has a *duty to disobey certain kinds of orders,* such as those to kill all noncombatants in an occupied village. In the Song My massacre in Vietnam, a number of American soldiers appear to have received and obeyed orders from a superior authority to kill hundreds of nonresisting civilians, including babies. Unless such a gruesome incident can be considered a "victory" for the American military psychologists who direct the Army's training programs, the thoughtful soldier should not be deemed a threat to discipline or a detriment in combat.[13] In fact it is the other way around. The mindless slaying of innocent people is the real threat to the civilization we are supposed to be upholding. Yet when so much emphasis in Army training is put on blind obedience and dehumanization and so little on the limits of lawful authority and meaningful matters of conscience,[14] atrocities are a logical result.

The realization that "superior orders" is no defense for war crimes should provide one more argument for the establishment of a truly representative jury system in the military. If a soldier in combat is to have the courage to refuse to obey an illegal order to kill an obviously innocent noncombatant civilian or a subdued prisoner, he must have the confidence that in any court-martial for disobedience of the order his refusal will be upheld. Knowledge that the court would consist of a cross section of his peers would increase that confidence.

THE MYTH THAT ENLISTED MEN SUPPORT THE ARMY'S CASTE SYSTEM

Right up to the first shot in all social upheavals and revolutions, there are those who, behind their mental Kremlins of self-delusion, insist that the oppressed are content with their oppression. The militarists of modern America may well earn their niche in history's hall of delusion. If they cling to the fantasy that the burgeoning GI movement and the GI underground press are merely a result of the Vietnam war and will disappear when the war is over, they are missing a central truth. The underground press has struck a responsive chord in GIs not just because it attacks the war and the establishment but because it gives courageous voice to the complaints American citizen-soldiers have always had about the military caste system. They are the same complaints the protesters' fathers once had and wished they could do something about. Because of that, the GI underground press will not (in the absence of fascism) either be crushed or fade into oblivion.

There are, of course, reasons why all this is happening right now, reasons rooted in social and technological developments that cannot be reversed. One of the most important is the increasingly high educational level of the citizens who are called to be soldiers, with the inevitably higher levels of expectation that spill over into bitterness at being treated like "dying cockroaches" by cretins. Just as important is the fact that, for the first time, soldiers can count on civilian support. Nor does the military establishment have any right to be surprised at the feedback of verbal violence it is being forced to endure at the hands of privates with portable printing presses. It has all the data it needs to find solutions to its problems. But it has chosen to ignore (in practice if not in official literature) the warnings it received from its own research teams of World War II, that officers who *believed* they knew what their men thought of them and of the Army's caste system were pitifully wrong.

One measure of the gap was the response to a question on feelings about military courtesy. Seventy-four per cent of the enlisted men surveyed felt that the Army placed too much importance upon saluting and "sir-ring"—military courtesy—and even twenty-three per cent of the officers thought so[15]:

Officers could be easily misled by the rituals of deference exacted from all enlisted men. They were "sirred" and saluted and rarely answered back. It is easy to understand how during the course of time they could come to mistake these compulsory outward symbols of deference for voluntary respect and fail to perceive underlying hostilities and resentments. Officers were practically entrapped into assuming that they were symbols of respected authority.[16]

Thus officers had no idea of the depth of the resentment and hostility of the men within their command.[17] When one caste system's attitudes were reinforced by those of another, the level of unreality seems almost amusing today. White southern officers actually believed that Negroes (who were kept in segregated outfits) would rather be commanded by a white than a Negro, and by a white southerner rather than a white northerner![18] (The white southerner reasoned that he would better "understand" the Negro.) Meanwhile, white officers from the North also believed (but not in the same overwhelming percentages) that Negroes would rather be commanded by whites than by Negroes.

The forced symbolic expressions of respect failed in World War II, as they fail today, to create favorable inner attitudes. In fact no draftee needs a psychologist to tell him that they have precisely the opposite effect.

Although the social scientists put forth their conclusions tentatively, they had little hesitation in evaluating the Army's social system from the point of view of the ends it was supposed to serve:

> . . . it must be recognized that the basic social system of the Army impeded rather than facilitated a meeting of the minds. Not only were the experiences of officers and men different, but also the barriers of power and social distance were almost insurmountable.[19]

THE MYTH THAT MILITARY JUSTICE IS FAIR AND IMPARTIAL

Despite the fact that no fundamental changes have been made in the Army's caste system during the past century, it is seriously maintained that the court-martial system, whose machinery remains in the hands of military commanders, functions fairly and impartially and even "better" than most civilian courts.

We have seen throughout this guide that the GI who believes in equal enforcement of the law can expect to be disappointed. Court-martial reforms have been turned into sham by manipulation of commanders. Officers who commit crimes are given the opportunity to resign while the enlisted man is court-martialed. On no evidence privates can be convicted of making disloyal statements, while on plenty of evidence the top law enforcement officer and the Sergeant Major of the Army can be let off the hook.

By the subtlest methods, commanders have carried their message to their courts. The Staff Judge Advocate's power has enabled him to give the prosecution every advantage. Conflicting loyalties of defense counsel dissuade some of them from taking every legal and ethical step within their power to assist a client, and even so the present system is infinitely better than the lawyerless special court that the Army kept as long as it could.

Things are done to prisoners in military stockades that we thought happened only in totalitarian countries. Pretrial confinement is used to punish people for exercising their constitutional right to free speech—to stifle lawful political dissent. The constitutional right of privacy is mocked by Gestapo-like shakedown inspections. Although it is not a crime to be a conscientious objector, a CO may be entrapped into violating his principles, arbitrarily denied recognition, and treated as a criminal.

The recruit is terrorized into believing that he is a Thing with no rights, in spite of Army information programs whose apparent purpose is the opposite. Officers turn their backs on physical and psychological abuses because they believe that is what makes tough soldiers. In an Army where actual training is subordinate to enforcing the trappings of militarism, the crime of disrespect is more serious than physical abuse of a trainee or prisoner. The Army will simply transfer a guard who shoots a prisoner in the back, while court-martialing the prisoners who peacefully protest the guard's crime and sentencing them to many years in jail.

Most disheartening is the extent to which the truth has been concealed from the people who count in Congress, the parade of "expert" witnesses whose criticisms have failed to confront the reality of America's militarization. Perhaps the most disappointing expert is the Chief Judge of the Court of Military Appeals, Robert E. Quinn, who wrote nine years ago:

> . . . pronouncements by the highest court of legal doctrine are sterile exercises in semantics, if there is only grudging compliance with the letter, and little regard for the spirit, of the law.[20]

The judge seemed to hint that there might still be a special problem with the military. However, he assessed the system once again in 1968:

> Indeed, there are defects, but these are defects of inefficiency and inconvenience, not vices that tend to destroy or diminish the fundamentals of a fair trial.[21]

The judge's later statement is completely misleading because it suggests the Court presides over a fundamentally fair and lawful system of justice. With the exception of a few areas, such as the Article 31 pre-interrogation warning, neither courts nor lawyers have had much success in securing compliance with either the letter or the spirit of the law.

THE MYTH THAT THE
EXISTING SYSTEM WORKS

After World War II a number of commissions, committees, and boards were appointed to study the Army's social and legal systems. The UCMJ emerged from several years' struggle between civilian and military forces. As has become apparent, the military lost a few battles but won the war against social progress. But this does not mean that the defects that persist today were not discerned by conscientious members of the military establishment. They were studied in depth by a joint enlisted-officer board appointed by the Secretary of War. Named after the general who headed the group, it became known as the Doolittle Board, which held hearings and issued a report. This is how it viewed the problem, twenty-four years ago:

> The causes of poor relationships between commissioned and enlisted personnel are traceable, in general, to two main factors:
> a) Undeniably poor leadership on the part of a small percentage of those in positions of responsibility.
> b) A system that permits and encourages a wide official and social gap between commissioned and enlisted personnel.
> There is need for a new philosophy in the military order, a policy of treatment of men, especially in the "ranks," in terms of advanced concepts in social thinking. The present system does not permit full recognition of the dignities of man. More definite protection from the arbitrary acts of superiors is essential.[22]

The Doolittle Board recommended, among other things:

> . . . That there be definite equality of treatment of both enlisted and commissioned personnel

in the administration of military justice, making all equally liable under military law for errors and faults; that the higher the rank the more severe be the punishment . . .

. . . That all regulations and instructions be so written that they not only stipulate the limited "privileges" which are essential to the performance of duties in positions of responsibility but also . . . will prohibit or minimize possible abuses of authority . . .

The abolishment of all statutes, regulations, customs and traditions which discourage or forbid social association of soldiers of similar likes and tastes, because of military rank.

That necessary steps be taken to eliminate the terms and concepts, "enlisted men" and "officers," that suitable substitutes be employed (e.g., members of noncommissioned corps, members of commissioned corps, etc.) and that all military personnel be referred to as "soldiers."[23]

Some of the changes in Army Regulations were doubtless made to pacify public opinion, which was crying out for more fundamental reforms. A year after VE Day, a poll was taken by the American Institute of Public Opinion on the question, "Do you think it would be a good idea or a poor idea if Army officers and enlisted men had the same food, clubs, and social privileges?" *Seventy-two per cent of the American public said it would be a good idea.*[24] Eighty-six per cent of former enlisted men thought it would be a good idea, and the ex-officers split fifty-fifty in their views. Even with such strong sentiment for an Army that would reflect the values of an egalitarian and democratic society, the military and its friends in Congress managed to channel the reformers' energies into the drafting and adoption of the Uniform Code of Military Justice, which, as many commentators have pointed out, has proven to be neither uniform nor just.

The existing system is in more trouble now than it

was at the end of World War II. It not only has to deal with antiwar dissenters who are being supported by civilians in the first alliance of its kind in American history; it must cope with the anger of a great many people at having been lulled into supporting the Vietnam war in the first place. Now that freedom of speech for GIs has been "discovered," there is no way to make them "forget" it. The levels of expectation of buck privates have risen in direct proportion with their educational level and their electronic-age sophistication. The crisis of legitimacy of all our national institutions[25] cannot be put off limits in the Army, which each day bombards the soldier with reminders that it, not he, is out of step with the times; that it, not he, is disloyal to American values; and that it, not he, had better shape up if it knows what's good for it.

THE MYTH THAT OUR ARMY IS AMERICAN

Of course, a simple way of avoiding the problem is to eliminate the draft. If the military services were manned by volunteers, presumably they would not share, at least not to the same extent, the draftee's complaint at the loss of his human dignity. Faced with the resistance of its military leaders to changing a system which has nurtured their rise to power, the United States may sometime be forced to return to an all-volunteer Army. But that would only shelve the issues being raised today if a general mobilization once again became necessary. Besides, we should surely consider whether it would be best to end once and for all a military caste system which destroys individual dignity and undermines military justice.

If we assume that the Army will have a continuing need to draw on the nation's reluctant youth for its manpower, the existing system must be imbued with a new philosophy, completely restructured, greatly reduced in size, and Americanized. Since it won't Americanize itself, the pressure to do this must come from the GIs themselves, from the people, and from the Congress. Unfortunately, in glorifying our victory in World War II the veterans' organizations have forgotten their own miseries in the Army; the GIs never get to testify at congressional hearings conducted by former officers; the people have been told it is "unpatriotic" to question how their sons are treated; and the only ones who seriously try to help them fight back are labeled "subversive."

In November of 1969 the first major conclave of national organizations working in the field of servicemen's rights in the Vietnam era came together in Washington. The National Conference on GI Rights convened to discuss "The Citizen-Soldier and the Crisis in Military Law." Participants included congressmen, lawyers, and GI assistance organizations from all over the country. At the end of the conference the panels on various aspects of GI rights made recommendations which, with some modifications, were adopted by the conference. The panel on the Uniform Code of Military Justice and Due Process made a number of general and legislative proposals which were endorsed by the conference. Reprinted in Appendix A, they provide a framework for the developing national debate over the quality of life and justice in the armed forces.

Senator Joseph Tydings of Maryland has introduced a bill in Congress which takes into account many of the problems discussed in these chapters and which mirrors some of the conference's proposals. His bill proposes that the members of a general court-martial be selected by an independent officer *at random* from among officers and enlisted men. It proposes also that a separate military trial command be set up which would free defense counsel from the control of Staff Judge Advocates and convening authorities.[26]

The bill is truly revolutionary, but even if it were passed in the near future, which is extremely unlikely, it would not stop the lower-level illegalities that are perpetrated against lower-ranking GIs by higher-ranking NCOs and officers. No reform of military justice that does not eliminate the irrational customs, controls, and inhumanities of a caste system can be expected to insure the degree of legitimacy which the Army must have to function, and which it barely has today. Discipline, defined by the Army itself as "a state of mind which leads to a willingness to obey an order no matter how unpleasant or dangerous the task to be performed,"[27] can only be enhanced by changes that will increase morale.

If the professional soldier who looks upon the movement for GI rights with utter dismay remembers that it is the defects in the system rather than the people who have tried to administer it with compassion and wisdom that are under attack, the pain of transition should not be that great. Our Army is where it is because morale can no longer be bought with movies and beer. Its court-martial system does what it does because justice can never be purchased by exhortations that commanders should behave. Men with power like to use it, and those with too much tend to abuse it. In a real sense, all the American people must unite to take back the power they have lost to the military. But it is the GI himself who must lead the struggle. As Dr. Martin Luther King wisely said, "Freedom is never voluntarily given by the oppressor; it must be demanded by the oppressed."

Notes

1. See Chapter Four, The Military Mind.
2. Baron von Steuben, *Regulations for the Order and Discipline of the Troops of the United States,* Part I (Philadelphia: Charles Cist, 1785), ch. 24, p. 135.
3. *Ibid.,* p. 146.
4. Samuel A. Stouffer *et al., The American Soldier: Combat*

and Its Aftermath, Vol. II (Princeton University Press, 1949; New York: Science Editions, 1965), pp. 107–111. This is part of a four-volume study based on data collected by the Research Branch, Information and Education Division of the War Department during World War II.

5. *Ibid.*

6. *Ibid.,* p. 113.

7. Roger W. Little, "Buddy Relations and Combat Performance," *The New Military,* Morris Janowitz, ed. (New York: Science Editions, 1967), p. 211.

8. Samuel A. Stouffer *et al., The American Soldier: Adjustment During Army Life,* Vol. I (Princeton University Press, 1949; New York: Science Editions, 1965), p. 419.

9. C. W. Valentine, *The Human Factor in the Army: Applications of Psychology to Training, Selection, Morale and Discipline* (Hampshire, England: Gale & Polden, Ltd., 1954), p. 69.

10. *Ibid.,* p. 86.

11. *Ibid.,* p. 89.

12. Norman Copeland, *Psychology and the Soldier: The Art of Leadership* (London: George Allen & Unwin, Ltd., 1944), pp. 69–70.

13. A problem is that the people who are considered by some commanders to be the best fighters may also be those who would be most likely to commit atrocities (*Newsweek,* Dec. 8, 1969, p. 35):

> "When you're in Vietnam, there is a shift in your thinking from humanitarian values to simply doing a job," says Dr. Albert Kastl, a thirty-year-old clinical psychologist in San Francisco who spent a year in Vietnam. "Our job was getting disturbed people back into combat so they could kill more people. And we did our job very well."

See also Chapter Eight, Orders To Commit War Crimes and Other Illegalities.

14. See Chapter Two, Basic and Advanced Individual Training, and Chapter Four, The Military Mind.

15. Stouffer, *op. cit.* (Note 8), p. 419.

16. *Ibid.,* p. 396.

17. *Ibid.,* pp. 392–393.

18. *Ibid.,* p. 580.

19. *Ibid.,* p. 395.

20. Robert E. Quinn, "The U.S. Court of Military Appeals

and Military Due Process," 35 *St. John's Law Review* 225, 254 (1961).

21. Robert E. Quinn, "Some Comparisons Between Courts-Martial and Civilian Practice," 15 *UCLA Law Review* 1240 (1968), p. 1258.

22. Stouffer, *op. cit.* (Note 8), p. 379. See also Report on the Secretary of War's Board on Officer–Enlisted Man Relationships, Sen. Doc. #196, 79th Congress, 2nd Session (1946).

23. *Ibid.,* p. 380.

24. *Ibid.,* p. 379.

25. Kenneth E. Boulding, "The Impact of the Draft on the Legitimacy of the National State," *The Draft,* Sol Tax, ed. (Chicago: University of Chicago Press, 1967), pp. 191–192:

> Legitimacy may be defined as general acceptance by all those concerned in a certain institution, role, or pattern of behavior that it constitutes part of the regular moral or social order within which they live. Thus legitimacy is a wider concept than the formal concept of law, even though the law is a great legitimator. At times, however, law itself may become illegitimate and when it does so its capacity to organize society is destroyed.

26. S. 3117, 91st Congress, 1st Session, introduced on Nov. 5, 1969.

27. Report to Hon. Wilber M. Brucker, Secretary of the Army, by the Committee on the UCMJ and Good Order and Discipline in the Army (13 Oct. 1960). See discussion of this, the Powell Report, in Chapter Ten, Courts-Martial in Action.

Appendixes

APPENDIX A

Resolutions of the National Conference on GI Rights

Reproduced below are the resolutions drafted by the Committee on the UCMJ and Due Process and passed by the National Conference on GI Rights, which convened in Washington, D.C., November 13–14, 1969.

1. The military court system should be abolished and in its place should be substituted a system in which a civilian jury commissioner would control the selection of military jurors.

2. All trial counsel and defense counsel should operate out of a civilian office set up by the office of the Attorney General of the United States.

3. All military judges should be civilians.

4. The role of the Staff Judge Advocate should be restricted solely to that of advising the convening authority. The Staff Judge Advocate should have no judicial functions.

5. The reviewing powers of the convening authority should be removed and juries should be made to understand and to take seriously their sentencing responsibilities. No longer should military courts be permitted to hand down severe sentences, thus passing the buck of clemency.

6. The members of the Courts of Military Review should be given tenure. They should be appointed by the Secretary of Defense to sit as interservice courts of review. Civilians should comprise a majority of the members of these courts.

7. Courts of Military Review should be given all the extraordinary writ powers now exercised by the federal courts under the All Writs Act.

8. Courts of Military Review should be assigned to geographical areas similar to those now in the jurisdiction of federal Courts of Appeal, and their members should be made easily accessible to military lawyers throughout the world.

9. Any kind of command influence by anyone should be made a federal offense and triable in a federal court.

10. Military trial courts should be selected on a random basis so that any court in which a private is tried will have a majority of lower-ranking enlisted men.

11. The Court of Military Appeals should be authorized *by statute* to use extraordinary writ power. Also the federal courts should be authorized by statute to utilize extraordinary writ power over military cases, after exhaustion of military remedies.

12. Due process guarantees in administrative discharge proceedings should be greatly extended.

13. All vestiges of the military caste system which are not absolutely necessary for the accomplishment of the military mission should be abolished. That would entail, for example, making the traditional salute voluntary and eliminating the possibility of court-martial for enlisted men who fail to salute. That would also include the elimination of the demeaning class system whereby enlisted men and officers are required to use separate mess halls, clubs, rest rooms, and entrances to buildings.

14. A crash program for the reeducation of all military personnel should be embarked upon to inculcate in them an understanding and appreciation of the values of human dignity and individual rights for which our country was brought into being.

Amendment 1: The Conference proposes that all enlisted men be allowed the right to elect their own officers.

Amendment 2: This Conference shall encourage its members and delegates to educate GIs on the provisions of the Nuremberg Code and their right to disobey orders that violate international law and decency.

APPENDIX B

GI Newspapers and Coffeehouses, Counseling Organizations and Lawyer Referral Services

Listed here are, first, GI underground newspapers and coffeehouses, through which counseling or referrals to lawyers or military counselors can sometimes be obtained. The second list gives the names of organizations that provide either counseling or lawyer referral services. It has not been possible to investigate the nature of the counseling provided by each group. Although some local groups provide excellent counseling service, it is suggested that, when possible, an office of a national organization be consulted as well, such as (1) the American Civil Liberties Union (ACLU), which generally takes only "test" cases; (2) the Central Committee for Conscientious Objectors (CCCO); and (3) the American Friends Service Committee (AFSC).

GI NEWSPAPERS AND COFFEEHOUSES

ALABAMA

Left Face
Box 1595
Anniston, Ala., 36201

CALIFORNIA

About Face
Box 54099 Terminal Annex
Los Angeles, Calif., 90054

The Ally
Box 9276
Berkeley, Calif., 94709

As You Were
Box 1062
Monterey, Calif., 93940

Bayonet
Box 31387
San Francisco, Calif., 94131

Duck Power
c/o San Diego Free Press
751 Turquoise
San Diego, Calif., 92109

Eyes Left!
Box 31387
San Francisco, Calif., 94131

Final Flight
Box 31387
San Francisco, Calif., 94131

The Looper
Box 31387
San Francisco, Calif., 94131

Marine Blues
Box 31387
San Francisco, Calif., 94131

The Oak
Box 31387
San Francisco, Calif., 94131

Task Force
Box 31268
San Francisco, Calif., 94131

Truth Instead
Box 31387
San Francisco, Calif., 94131

Up Front
Box 60329 Terminal Annex
Los Angeles, Calif., 90060

COLORADO

Aboveground
Box 2255
Colorado Springs, Colo.,
    80901
(303) 634–9225

Homefront
318 East Pikes
Peak Avenue
Colorado Springs,
    Colo., 80901
(303) 634–9225

DISTRICT OF COLUMBIA

GI Press Service
1029 Vermont Avenue,
    N.W.
No. 907
Washington, D.C., 20005

OM
c/o Link
1029 Vermont Avenue,
    N.W.
Rm. 200
Washington, D.C., 20005

GEORGIA

Patriots for Peace
Box 5437
Main Post Office
Columbus, Ga., 31092

Rap!
Box 894 Main Post Office
Columbus, Ga., 31902

ILLINOIS

Dull Brass
9 S. Clinton, Rm. 225
Chicago, Ill., 60606

A Four-Year Bummer
Box 2325 Sta. A
Champaign, Ill., 61820

Vets Stars & Stripes for
    Peace
Box 4598
Chicago, Ill., 60680

Vietnam GI
Box 9273
Chicago, Ill., 60690

INDIANA

Aerospaced
Box 1015
Kokomo, Ind., 46901

KANSAS

The AWOL Press
Box 425
Manhattan, Kans., 66502

KENTUCKY
Fun, Travel & Adventure
Box 336
Louisville, Ky., 40201

LOUISIANA
G.A.F.
525 Wichita Street
Shreveport, La., 71101

MARYLAND
Forward March
38 Maryland Avenue
Annapolis, Md., 21401

The New Salute
Box 9783 Eudowood Branch
Baltimore, Md., 21204

Open Ranks
Baltimore GIs United
Against the War in
Vietnam
Box 9783, Eudowood
Branch
Baltimore, Md., 21204

The Pawn
Box 481
Frederick, Md., 21701

MASSACHUSETTS
Top Secret
595 Mass. Ave., Rm. 205
Cambridge, Mass., 02139

MICHIGAN
Broken Arrow
Box 9571 North End Station
Detroit, Mich., 48202

NEW JERSEY
Shakedown
Box 68
Wrightstown, N.J., 08562

NEW YORK
The Bond (ASU)
156 5th Avenue
New York, N.Y., 10010

GI Voice
Box 825
New York, N.Y., 10009

The Obligore
Box 732
New York, N.Y., 10022

SPD News
156 5th Avenue
New York, N.Y., 10010

NORTH CAROLINA
Bragg Briefs
Box 437
Spring Lake, N.C., 28309

PENNSYLVANIA
The Ultimate Weapon
Box 8633
Philadelphia, Pa., 19101

SOUTH CAROLINA
The Chessman
Box 187
Frogmore, S.C., 29920

Short Times
Box 543
Columbia, S.C., 29202

TENNESSEE
Flag-in-Action
Box 2416
New Providence, Tenn.,
37040

TEXAS
Fatigue Press
101 Avenue D
Killeen, Tex., 76541

Gigline
P.O. Box 31094
Summit Heights Station
El Paso, Tex., 79931

The GI Organizer
Box 704
Killeen, Tex., 76541

Oleo Strut
101 Avenue D
Killeen, Tex., 76541
Your Military Left
Box 561
San Antonio, Tex., 78206

VIRGINIA

Rough Draft
Box 1205
Norfolk, Va., 23501

Spartacus
Box 4027
Petersburg, Va., 23803

WASHINGTON

Counterpoint
515 20th E.
Seattle, Wash., 98102

Fed Up!
Box 414
Tacoma, Wash., 98409

Shelter Half Coffeehouse
15437 South Tacoma Way
Tacoma, Wash., 98409
(206) GR 5-9875

COUNSELING SERVICES

U.S.A.

ALABAMA

Alabama Civil Liberties
Union
P.O. Box 1972
University, Ala., 35486

ALASKA

Alaska Civil Liberties
Union
Box 129
College, Alaska, 99701
(907) 479-6633

ARIZONA

Arizona ACLU
7014 N. 16th Street
Phoenix, Ariz., 85020
(602) 944-1482

Draft Counseling Service
Santa Rita Hall
1017 East Hadley
Phoenix, Ariz., 85007
(612) 258-5826

Tucson Draft Counseling
Service
45 W. Pennington, Suite 407
Tucson, Ariz., 85701
(602) 623-7951

CALIFORNIA

ACLU
503 Market Street
San Francisco, Calif., 94105
(415) 433-2750

ACLU of Southern Califor-
nia
323 West Fifth Street, Rm.
202
Los Angeles, Calif., 90013
(213) MA 6-5156

AFSC
980 N. Fair Oaks
Pasadena, Calif., 91103
(213) 282-5812

Associated Students of the
University of California
Draft Help
209 Eshelman Hall
University of California
Berkeley, Calif., 94720
(415) 642-6000

Bay Area Peace Action
Council
992 Valencia Street
San Francisco, Calif., 94110
(415) 282-8160

CCCO
437 Market Street
San Francisco, Calif., 94105
(415) 397-6917

Counterdraft
Committee of P.A.C.
P.O. Box 74881
Los Angeles, Calif., 90004

Draft Co-op
424 Lytton Avenue
Palo Alto, Calif., 94301
(415) 327-3108

Draft Counseling Service
La Mesa, Calif.
(714) 276-8866

Draft Help
1715 15th Street
Sacramento, Calif., 95814
(916) 447-9726

GI Civil Liberties Defense
Committee
P.O. Box 26972
Los Angeles, Calif., 94111

GI Help
483 Guerrero Street
San Francisco, Calif., 94110

Lawyers' Selective
Service Panel
1182 Market Street, Rm. 404
San Francisco, Calif., 94102
(415) 626-7877

National Lawyers Guild
Los Angeles Regional Office
c/o Haymarket
507 North Hoover
Los Angeles, Calif., 90004
(213) 666-8118

National Lawyers Guild
San Francisco Regional
Office
197 Steiner Street
San Francisco, Calif., 94117
(415) 863-5193

New Adult Community
1924 Island Avenue
San Diego, Calif., 92101
(714) 239-2119

Pacific Counseling
Service
288 Alvarado Street
Monterey, Calif., 93940
(408) 373-2305

Pacific Counseling
Service
1733 Jefferson Street & 18th
Oakland, Calif., 94612
(415) 836-1039

Pacific Counseling
Service
520 E Street
Room 512
San Diego, Calif., 92101
(714) 234-1305

Pacific Counseling
Service
491 Guerrero Street
San Francisco, Calif., 94110
(415) 621-7035, 836-1039

Resistance
483 Guerrero Street
San Francisco, Calif., 94110
(415) 626-1910

COLORADO

ACLU
1711 Pennsylvania Street
Denver, Colo., 80203
(303) 825-5176

AFSC
1460 Pennsylvania Street
Denver, Colo., 80203
(303) 534-6285

CONNECTICUT

AFSC
144 S. Quaker Lane
W. Hartford, Conn., 06119
(203) 232-9521, 242-8943

Connecticut Civil Liberties
Union
721 Main Street, Rm. 312
Hartford, Conn., 06103
(203) 525-1345

New England Committee for
Nonviolent Action
RFD 1, Box 197 B
Voluntown, Conn., 06384
(203) 376-9970, 376-0287

Storrs Draft Information
Committee
Community House
N. Eagleville Road
Storrs, Conn., 06268
(203) 429-5900

WASHINGTON, D.C.

American Veterans
Committee
1333 Connecticut Avenue
Washington, D.C., 20036
(202) 293-4890

LINK
The Serviceman's Link to
Peace
1029 Vermont Avenue, N.W.
Rm. 200
Washington, D.C., 20005
(202) 638-4126

National Capital Area Civil
Liberties Union
1424 Sixteenth Street, N.W.
Suite 501
Washington, D.C., 20036
(202) 483-3830

Washington Peace Center
2111 Florida Avenue, N.W.
Washington, D.C., 20008
(202) 234-2000

DELAWARE

Delaware Draft Counseling
and Educational Service
1106 N. Adams Street

Wilmington, Del., 19801
(302) 658-7602

FLORIDA

ACLU
502 Olympia Building
Miami, Fla., 33131
(305) 373-2052

AFSC
Peace Center of Miami
3356 Virginia Street, Rm.
202
Coconut Grove, Fla., 33133
(305) 443-9836

GEORGIA

ACLU
Southern Regional Office
5 Forsyth Street, N.W.
Atlanta, Ga., 30303
(404) 523-2721

AFSC
41 Exchange Place, S.E.
Atlanta, Ga., 30303
(414) 523-6628

Atlanta Workshop in Non-
violence
253 Ninth Avenue, N.E.
P.O. Box 7477
Atlanta, Ga., 30309
(404) 875-0646

Augusta Draft Information
Service
3021 Fox Spring Road
Augusta, Ga., 30904
(404) 738-5262

Revolutionary Youth
Movement
Box 5421E
Atlanta, Ga., 30307
(404) 522-2075

HAWAII

American Servicemen's
Union

1434 Makaloa Street, Rm. 9
Honolulu, Hawaii, 96814
(808) 949-1768

Draft and Military Information Center
Church of the Crossroads
1212 University Avenue
Honolulu, Hawaii, 96814
(808) 946-1113

Hawaii Resistance
27 Wilikoki Place
Kailua, Hawaii, 96734
(808) 262-9236

The Resistance
1035 University Avenue
Honolulu, Hawaii, 96822
(808) 955-1026

IDAHO

Campus Christian Ministry
822 Elm Street
Moscow, Idaho, 83843
(208) 882-2536

ILLINOIS

ACLU
6 South Clark
Chicago, Ill., 60603
(312) 236-5564

AFSC
407 S. Dearborn Avenue
Chicago, Ill., 60605
(312) 427-2533

Cadre (Chicago Area Draft Resisters)
519 West North Avenue
Chicago, Ill., 60610
(312) 664-6895

Chicago Legal Defense Committee
173 W. Madison Street
Chicago, Ill., 60602
(312) 641-0134

De Kalb Association for Draft Counseling
633 W. Locust
De Kalb, Ill., 60115
(815) 758-0005

Draft Information Center
Universalist Unitarian Church
908 Hamilton Boulevard
Peoria, Ill., 61603
(309) 673-5391

Midwest Committee for Draft Counseling
711 South Dearborn Street
Chicago, Ill., 60605
(312) 427-3350

National Conference on GI Rights
% GI Defense Organization
431 S. Dearborn Street, Suite 813
Chicago, Ill., 60605
(312) 922-0065

Peoria Draft Information Center
1005 N. University
Peoria, Ill., 61606
(309) 674-9453

INDIANA

Evansville Draft Project
1901 Lincoln Avenue
Evansville, Ind., 47711
(812) 479-0556

Indiana Civil Liberties Union
423 Board of Trade Building
Indianapolis, Ind., 46204
(317) ME 5-4056

Indianapolis Draft Project
222 E. 16th Street
Indianapolis, Ind., 46202
(317) 923-9563

IOWA

AFSC
4211 Grand Avenue
Des Moines, Iowa, 50312
(515) 274–0453

AFSC
311 North Linn
Iowa City, Iowa, 52240
(319) 338–7250

Hawkeye Area Draft
Information Center
212 Dey Bldg.
Iowa City, Iowa, 52240
(319) 337–9327

H.O.U.S.E.
1310 7th Street
Des Moines, Iowa, 50314
(515) 282–6846

Iowa Civil Liberties Union
1101 Walnut Street
Des Moines, Iowa, 50309
(515) 282–0923

United Campus Christian
Ministry
2718 University Avenue
Des Moines, Iowa, 50311
(515) 255–1216

KANSAS

Draft Help
1801 Anderson Avenue
Manhattan, Kans., 66502

Lawrence Peace Center
107 West 7th Street
Lawrence, Kans., 66044
(913) 842–7932

United Ministries in Higher
Education
Service Careers Information
Center
1021 Denison Avenue
Manhattan, Kans., 66502

KENTUCKY

Kentucky Civil Liberties
Union
205 South 4th Street
Louisville, Ky., 40202
(502) 583–8421

LOUISIANA

ACLU
606 Common Street,
Rm. 302
New Orleans, La., 70130
(504) 522–0617

Southern Legal Action
Movement
P.O. Box 50435
New Orleans, La., 70150
(504) 861–7926

Rev. Homer Singleton
501 E. Sale Road
Lake Charles, La., 70601
(318) 477–2191

MAINE

AFSC
20 Boynton Street
Bangor, Maine, 04401
(207) 945–5584

Maine Civil Liberties Union
142 High Street, Rm. 411
Portland, Maine, 04101
(207) 774–5444

MARYLAND

ACLU
1231 N. Calvert Street
Baltimore, Md., 21202
(301) 685–5195

AFSC
319 E. 25th Street
Baltimore, Md., 21218
(301) 366–7200

MASSACHUSETTS

AFSC Draft Information
Center

5 Longfellow Park
Cambridge, Mass., 02138
(617) 876–7939

Boston Draft Resistance
 Group
102 Columbia St.
Cambridge, Mass., 02139
(617) 547–8260

Civil Liberties Defense
 Fund, Inc.
2 Bow Street
Cambridge, Mass., 02138
(617) 864–8680

Civil Liberties Union of
 Massachusetts
3 Joy Street, Rm. 4
Boston, Mass., 02108
(617) CA 7–9459

Draft Information Service
134 Chandler Street
Worcester, Mass., 01602
(617) 755–8170

In-Service Legal Committee
Vietnam Moratorium
 Committee
44 Brattle Street
Cambridge, Mass., 02138
(617) 868–9133

Resist
763 Massachusetts Avenue
Rm. 4
Cambridge, Mass., 02139
(617) 491–8076

Valley Peace Center
1 Cook Place
P.O. Box 418
Amherst, Mass., 01002
(413) 253–3683

MICHIGAN

ACLU
808 Washington Blvd. Bldg
234 State Street

Detroit, Mich., 48226
(313) 961–4662

AFSC
1414 Hill
Ann Arbor, Mich., 48104
(313) 761–8283

Draft Counseling Center
502 E. Huron
Ann Arbor, Mich., 48108
(313) 769–4414

Draft Counseling Service
Central Methodist Church
23 E. Adams
Detroit, Mich., 48226
(313) 965–5422

Draft Information Center
507 E. Grand River
Suite 205
East Lansing, Mich., 48823
(517) 351–5283

Resistance
Canterbury House
330 Maynard
Ann Arbor, Mich., 48104
(313) 665–0606

Resistance
31 King Street
Detroit, Mich., 48202
(313) 874–4334

MINNESOTA

AFSC
807 Fourth Street, S.E.
Minneapolis, Minn., 55415
(612) 331–5101

Minnesota Civil Liberties
 Union
925 Upper Midwest Bldg.
Minneapolis, Minn., 55401
(612) 333–2534

Twin Cities Draft
 Information Center
529 Cedar Avenue

Minneapolis, Minn., 55404
(612) 333–8471, 333–3717

MISSISSIPPI

Mississippi Civil Liberties
Union
Community Education
Extension
203 West Capitol Street
Jackson, Miss., 39201

United Campus Ministry
P.O. Box 7
University, Miss., 38677

MISSOURI

ACLU of Western Missouri
1016 Baltimore, Rm. 322
Kansas City, Mo., 64105
(816) 842–3564

AFSC
447 De Baliviere Avenue
St. Louis, Mo., 63112
(314) 862–8070

Experimental Campus
Ministry
740 DeMun
St. Louis, Mo., 63130
(314) PA 6–1565

Legal Aid & Defender
Society
1029 Oak Street
Kansas City, Mo., 64106
(816) 221–8135

Peace Information Center
6244 Delmar Boulevard
St. Louis, Mo., 63130
(314) 474–6750

Vietnam Information Center
AFSC
4723½ Troost
Kansas City, Mo., 64110
(816) 753–1619

NEBRASKA

Omaha Draft Information
Service

1616 North 51st Street
Omaha, Nebr., 68104
(402) 553–5316

NEW JERSEY

ACLU
45 Academy Street, Rm. 203
Newark, N.J., 07102
(201) 642–2084

Draft Information Center
173 Nassau Street
Princeton, N.J., 08540
(609) 924–5487

Plainfield Area Draft
Information and
Counseling Center
Watchung and North
Avenues
P.O. Box 455
Plainfield, N.J., 07061
(201) 754–3838

NEW MEXICO

ACLU
131 LaVega, S.W.
Albuquerque, N.M., 87105
(505) 877–5286

NEW YORK

ACLU
156 Fifth Avenue
New York, N.Y., 10010
(212) 675–5990

AFSC
15 Rutherford Place
New York, N.Y., 10003
(212) 777–4600

AFSC
821 Euclid
Syracuse, N.Y., 13210
(315) 475–9469

American Servicemen's
Union
156 Fifth Avenue
New York, N.Y., 10010
(212) 675–6780

Buffalo Draft Resistance
37 E. Ferry Street
Buffalo, N.Y., 14203
(716) 882-2109

Capital Area Peace Center
727 Madison Avenue
Albany, N.Y., 12208
(518) 463-8297

Catholic Peace Fellowship
151 Columbia Heights
Brooklyn, N.Y., 11201
(212) JA 2-5162

Catholic Peace Fellowship
339 Lafayette Street
New York, N.Y., 10012
(212) 673-8990

Chelsea Draft Information
and Counseling Service
St. Peter's Episcopal Church
346 West 20th Street
New York, N.Y., 10010
(212) 929-2391

Clergy and Laymen
Concerned About Vietnam
475 Riverside Drive
New York, N.Y., 10027
(212) 749-8518

Draft Counseling Center
72 N. Parade Street
Buffalo, N.Y., 14211
(716) 897-2871

Draft Counseling Center
732 Genesee Street
Rochester, N.Y., 14611
(716) 328-9559

Episcopal Peace Fellowship
300 Ninth Avenue
New York, N.Y., 10022
(212) 675-2141

GI Civil Liberties Defense
Committee
Box 355, Old Chelsea Station
New York, N.Y., 10011
(212) 243-4775

GI Counseling Services
339 Lafayette Street
New York, N.Y., 10012
(212) 533-8920

Greenwich Village Peace
Center
133 West 4th Street
New York, N.Y., 10014
(212) 533-5121

LEMPA
105 Avenue B
New York, N.Y., 10009
(212) 533-6948

Long Island Draft
Information and
Counseling Service
East Meadow, N.Y.
(516) WE 1-5765

National Emergency
Civil Liberties Committee
25 East 26 Street, Rm. 914
New York, N.Y., 10010
(212) 683-8120

National Lawyers Guild
Military Law Project
1 Hudson Street
New York, N.Y., 10013
(212) 227-0385

New York Civil Liberties
Union
156 Fifth Avenue
New York, N.Y., 10010
(212) WA 9-6076

Religious Society of Friends
(Quakers)
41 Westminister Road
Rochester, N.Y., 14607
(716) 271-0900, 442-3506

Rochester Draft Resistance
Project
732 Genesee Street
Rochester, N.Y., 14611
(716) 464-9908

War Resisters League
339 Lafayette Street
New York, N.Y., 10012
(212) 228-0450

Workers Defense League
112 East 19th Street
New York, N.Y., 10003
(212) AL 4-4953

NORTH CAROLINA

AFSC
1818 S. Main Street
High Point, N.C., 27260
(919) 882-0109

Draft Information Service
Box 12261
Raleigh, N.C., 27605
(919) 787-6707

North Carolina Civil
   Liberties Union
P.O. Box 1872
Greensboro, N.C., 27402
(919) 273-1641

Quaker House
324 Ray Avenue
Fayetteville, N.C., 28301
(919) 483-5279

OHIO

ACLU
506 Lawyers Building
1302 Ontario Street
Cleveland, Ohio, 44113
(216) SU 1-6276

ACLU
203 East Broad Street
Suite 202
Columbus, Ohio, 43215
(614) 228-8951

AFSC
915 Salem Avenue
Dayton, Ohio, 45606
(513) 278-4225

Ohio University Draft
   Counseling Center
18 N. College Street
Athens, Ohio, 45701
(614) 594-5511

OKLAHOMA

Oklahoma Civil Liberties
   Union
P.O. Box "M"
Norman, Okla., 73069
(405) 329-6772

OREGON

ACLU
309 Senator Building
732 S.W. Third Street
Portland, Oreg., 97204
(503) 228-0979

AFSC
4312 S.E. Stark Street
Portland, Oreg., 97214
(503) 235-8954

Draft and Military
   Information Center
Rm. 1A
EMU, University of Oregon
Eugene, Oreg., 97403
(503) 342-1411, Ext 321 or
   1907

PENNSYLVANIA

ACLU
260 South Fifteenth Street
Philadelphia, Pa., 19102
(215) PE 5-7103

ACLU
508H Laurence Hall
Wood Street & Boulevard
   of the Allies
Pittsburgh, Pa., 15222
(412) 521-0170

AFSC
160 North 15th St.
Philadelphia, Pa., 19102

CCCO
2016 Walnut Street
Philadelphia, Pa., 19103
(215) 568–7971

Mennonite Central
Committee
Peace Section
21 S. 12th Street
Akron, Pa., 17501
(717) 859–1151

Philadelphia Resistance
2006 Walnut Street
Philadelphia, Pa., 19103
(215) 561–5080

Pittsburgh Peace & Freedom
Center
618 S. Millvale
Pittsburgh, Pa., 15224
(412) 362–9000

Pittsburgh Resistance Office
3601 Blvd. of the Allies
Pittsburgh, Pa., 15213
(412) 621–3337

RHODE ISLAND

Rhode Island Civil Liberties
Union
Box 4772
Rumford, R.I., 02916
(401) 434–7596

SOUTH CAROLINA

Committee of Fort Jackson
Conscientious Objectors
Box 1197
Columbia, S.C., 29202

Columbia Draft Information
Service
P.O. Box 1283
Suite 704
Columbia Building
1203 Gerrais
Columbia, S.C., 29201

TENNESSEE

ACLU
P.O. Box 91
Knoxville, Tenn., 37901
(615) 524–1787

TEXAS

AFSC
4717 Crawford Street
Houston, Tex., 77004
(713) 675–2681

AFSC
109 Durango Street
P.O. Box 1398
San Antonio, Tex., 78206
(512) 223–3371

Austin Draft Information
Center
2330 Guadalupe Street
Austin, Tex., 78705
(512) 477–3480

Draft Counseling Service
102 N. Sampson
Houston, Tex., 77003
(713) 225–4642

GIs for Peace
P.O. Box 31094
Summit Heights Station
El Paso, Tex., 79931

Texas Civil Liberties Union
1512 Guadalupe
Austin, Tex., 78701
(512) 477–3478

VERMONT

Vermont Ecumenical
Council and Bible Society
189 S. Winooski Avenue
Burlington, Vt., 05401
(802) 864–7723

Vermont Civil Liberties
Union
P.O. Box 266
Burlington, Vt., 05401
(802) 658–0196

VIRGINIA

ACLU
1205 West Main Street
Richmond, Va., 23220
(703) 355–3021

Tidewater Draft Counseling
Service
c/o Unitarian Center
903 Graydon Avenue
Norfolk, Va., 23507
(703) 627–5371, 420–9401

WASHINGTON

ACLU
2101 Smith Tower
Seattle, Wash., 98104
(206) MA 4–2180

Campus Christian Ministry
530 N. Garden Street
Bellingham, Wash., 98225
(206) 733–3400

Seattle Draft Counseling
Center
6817 Greenwood Avenue N.
Seattle, Wash., 98103
(206) SU 9–0252

Tacoma Draft and
Military Services
3019 N. 21st Street
Tacoma, Wash., 98406
(206) SK 9–2153

WISCONSIN

AFSC
317 N. Brooks
Madison, Wis., 53715
(608) 257–5131

AFSC
3529 N. 3rd Street
Milwaukee, Wis., 53212
(414) 342–3636, 425–6962

Beloit Anti-Draft Union
846 Harrison Street
Beloit, Wis., 53511
(608) 364–4808

Wisconsin Civil Liberties
Union
1840 N. Farwell Avenue
Rm. 303
Milwaukee, Wis., 53202
(414) 272–4032

Wisconsin Selective Service
Lawyers Panel
303 State Street
Madison, Wis., 53703

CANADA AND OVERSEAS

CANADA

Toronto Anti-Draft
Programme
2347 Yonge Street
Suite 14
Toronto 12, Ontario

ENGLAND

SUPPORT
5 Caledonian Road
London N.1
01–278–1976

JAPAN

AFSC
2–41, 1-chome Migashi
Gotanda
Shinogawa-Ku
Tokyo

GERMANY

Where It's At
1 Berlin 12
Post fach 65

Index

INDEX

Administrative Discharges: defined, 311–12; for conscientious objection, 61–62, 296–98; for dependency or hardship, 62–63, 318–20; for homosexuality, 166, 317–18, 321; for medical reasons, 33, 320–21; for minority, 323–25; for miscellaneous reasons, 325–26; for misconduct: fraudulent entry, civilian crimes, AWOL or desertion, 315–17; procedure for fighting, 326–31; for security reasons, 321–23, 329; types of, 312–13; for unfitness and unsuitability, 40, 313–15

Advanced Individual Training, 45, 36, 196; assignments, 38; classwork, 39; leave, 38–39; pockets of sanity, 40–41; special training companies, 39–40

Advice for Conscientious Objectors in the Armed Forces, 296

American Bar Association Journal, 245

American Civil Liberties Union, 99, 116, 120, 130, 265

American Friends Service Committee, 296, 303

American Servicemen's Union, 124, 126, 135, 271

Amick, Daniel, 114–15, 116

Army Board for Correction of Military Records, 305–6, 329–30

Army Language Aptitude Test, 13–14

Army Regulations, 72, 123, 216, 220–21, 347; on activities of Inspector General, 187–88; on administrative discharges, 311, 313, 315, 321; on appearance, 9; on change of status, 60; on clothing, 10; on conscientious objection, 297, 299–301, 302, 303, 304, 306; on contacting your congressman, 189–90, 201; on degrading or depersonalizing actions,

19–20, 22; on early release from active duty, 63–64; on exercise of authority, 182, 183, 204–5; on homosexuality, 317–18; on interference with or inspection of mail, 159; on KP, 11; on marriage, 163–64; on medical discharges, 33; on medical fitness for induction, 320; need to study, 41; on occupational specialties, 48–49; on overseas duty, 58–59; on political activity, 131–32; on private debts and obligations, 170; on processing, 12; on racial discrimination, 193–95; on rare and unusual qualifications, 13; on right of assembly, 128–29, 130; on security discharges, 321–22; on treatment of prisoners, 268

Army Security Review Board, 329

Army Times, 281

Attorney General's list, 138

Authority and the Soldier, 71

Basic Training, 45, 147; civilian clothing, 11; first formation, 17–18; grass drill, 18–19; Legal Assistance Office, 34, 36–38; medical rights, 29–34; Military Mind and, 19, 21; physical brutality, 26–29; pockets of sanity, 40–41; psychological brutality, 19–26, 70; seeing the chaplain, 34–36; special training companies, 39–40; *see also* Advanced Individual Training

Bennett, Charles E., 113–14

Bill of Rights, 97, 106

Board for Correction of Military Records, 305–6, 329–30

Bond, Julian, 101–2

Bond v. Floyd, 101–2

Brakefield, Bill, 271

Brown, Rap, 82

Brutality, *see* Basic Training; Military Mind

Bunch, Richard, 269

Caste System, 67, 70, 72, 78, 80, 83, 115, 147–48, 168, 170–71, 245–53, 341–43, 346–47

Catch-22, 41, 79

Catlow, Tom, 271

Central Committee for Conscientious Objectors, 296, 299, 303

Central Intelligence Agency, 201–2

Chafee, Zechariah, 94
Chain of Command, 181–83
Chaplains, 34–36, 37, 124, 301, 302
Charges, see Complaints
Civil Rights Acts, 191, 195
Coffeehouses, 40–41, 136
Coles, Dr. Robert, 91
Companies: always volunteer, 51–52; changing assignments (DA form 2469), 46–47, 52–53; company duties, 50–51, 171; double-check all advice, 55; KP duty, 49–50, 171; occupational specialties, regulations concerning, 48–49; paper work, following up on, 53–54; processing into, 45–47; promotions, 55–57; special training, 38–39; volunteering for overseas duty, 54–55; your bosses, 47; see also Overseas Shipment
Complaints, how to file, 148, 150–51, 180–81; Article 138 and, 183–87, 189, 196–97, 207; be polite, 9–10; chain of command, 181–83; civil actions in local courts, 197–98; federal courts and habeas corpus, 235–37; the Inspector General, 48, 184, 187–89, 191, 195, 207; racial discrimination, 191–95; suing the Army, 198; "suing" your sergeant (Art. 139), 194–97; writing your congressman, 184, 186, 189–91
Connor, Lieutenant General A. O., 73–74
Conscientious Objection, 208–9, 221; Edward Stringham's struggle, 308–9; eligibility for discharge, 61–62, 296–98, 306; filing after receiving overseas orders, 303–5; injunctions, 306; interviews, 301–2; habeas corpus petitions, 305–6; Military Mind and, 294–95; noncombatant status, 306–8; preparing the application, 298–300; status after submission of application, 300–1; whom to contact, 296
Courts / Courts-Martial, 313–14, 321, 327, 331; American press and, 281; attempted reforms of, 241–42; bail, military, 266–68; civilian counsel and, 265; convening authority, 226, 228, 229, 247, 253–59; Court of Military Appeals and, 233–34, 235; defense counsel, prob-

lems of, 261–65, 282; enlisted men on, 249–51; federal courts and habeas corpus, 235–37; general, 229, 231–32, 234, 235, 245, 264, 282, 287, 349; the Judge Advocate General, 234–35, 255–56; the military judge, 226–27, 229, 253; Military Mind and, 242–48; of Military Review, 232, 234, 235; need for Army Defenders Corps 266; nonjudicial punishment (Art. 15), 225–26; president of, 227, 229; punitive discharges and, 227; selection of court members, 253–59; selective enforcement of the law in, 251–53; special, 228–31, 282, 287; the Staff Judge Advocate, 259–66, 344, 349; stockade, law of, 268–73; summary, 227–28; Supreme Court and, 233–34, 235; *voir dire*, 246–47; *see also* Interrogations

Court of Inquiry, 186
Cranston, Alan, 270
Criminal Investigation Detachment, 156, 271, 282

Daniels, George, 120
Debs v. United States, 95

Defense Language Institute, 13–14, 53
Department of the Army, 297, 301, 304
Department of Defense, 131, 221, 298, 306–7, 326–27; directive on dissent, 112–13, 114, 135
Discharge Review Board, 329, 330
Discharges, punitive, 312; bad conduct, 227, 228, 312; dishonorable, 227; *see also* Administrative Discharges; Early Releases
Dissent, *see* Freedom of Speech; Vietnam
Doolittle Board, 346–47
Douglas, William O., 308
Drugs, 7, 40–41, 134, 138, 162–63, 217, 223, 313–14

Early Releases: overseas returnees, 63; police work, 65; seasonal employment, 64–65; students and teachers, 63–64
Ervin, Sam, 326, 327, 328–29, 331
Espionage Act (1917), 94, 118

Federal Bureau of Investigation, 134, 137, 260, 285

Federal Tort Claims Act, 198

Ferguson, Homer, 104, 259–60

Fifth Amendment Rights, *see* Interrogations

First Amendment Rights, *see* Freedom of Speech

Flood, Daniel, 73–74

Freedom of Speech, 76; appellate military courts and, 99–103, 104, 105, 110, 112, 122; background in the military, 92–97; congressional statutes to aid, 103; criticism of American society, the military, and the war, 112–17, 106–7, 253, 321; First Amendment and, 97–98, 127–28; Fourteenth Amendment and, 108; free association rights, 133–39; importance of, 97–98; inciting others to break the law, 117–21; Military Mind and, 90–93; national security and, 122–23, 137–39; political activities and, 131–32, 134–35; pornography and obscenity, 125–27; protest demonstrations and, 127–31; right to complain, 103–6; threats, insults, and disrespectful language, 106–12; threat to pursue rights concerning, 103–5; underground publications and, 123–25, 127

Gideon v. Wainwright, 287

GIs United Against the War, 135, 136

Goldberg, Arthur, 282–83

Goodell, Charles, 270

Gray, Young Claude, 115–16

Greenley, David I., 129–30

Griswold v. Connecticut, 165

Habeas Corpus, *see* Writs

Hallinan, Terence, 270

Handbook for Conscientious Objectors, 296

Harvey, William L., 120

Hodson, Kenneth J., 243, 258–59, 262

Homosexuality, 134, 166, 312, 314, 315, 317–18, 321

House Armed Services Committee, 113

Howe, Henry Jr., 99–100, 101, 111

Huffman, Private, 136

Induction and Processing, 3–4, 150, 320; Army policy concerning, 11–12; clothing issue, 10;

DA Form 20, importance of, 12; dehumanization techniques during, 6–9; haircut, illegality of, 8–10; illegal induction, 4–6; keep a diary, 7–8; KP during, 11; personnel interview, choosing your MOS, 12–13; personal possessions and civilian clothing, 7, 10–11; reenlistment interview, 15; testing and tests, 13–14

Infantry Journal, 80–81

Inspector General, 103, 183, 184, 187–89, 191, 195, 207; and illegal search cases, 153–54

Interrogations: don't waive your rights, 291; forced confessions, 281–82; required warnings, 285–87; right to consult a lawyer, 37–38, 287–88, 289; self-incrimination, the Fifth Amendment and Article 31, 282–84, 287, 289; tricks of government agents, 288–91

Johnson, Lyndon B., 99

Joint Chiefs of Staff, 110

Jones, Danny R., 197–98

Judge Advocate General, *see* Courts / Courts-Martial

Justice Department, 215–16, 305–6

King, Martin Luther, 350

Klug, Terry, 271

Korea/Korean War, 63, 122, 123, 164, 167–68, 281, 337

KP Duty, 11, 46, 49–51, 171, 205

Laird, Melvin, 215–16

Lawyers, military, *see* Legal Assistance Office; Interrogations

Leave, 38–39, 161–62

Legal Assistance Office, 29, 34, 36–38, 62, 125, 170, 182, 183, 197

Levy, Dr. Howard, 202, 246, 265

Lincoln, Abraham, 334

MacArthur, Douglas, 122

Mailer, Norman, 72

Manss, R. W., 243

Manual for Courts-Martial, 27, 108, 109, 116–17, 156, 159, 208, 219, 222–23, 230, 267

Medical Rights, *see* Basic Training

Meningitis, symptoms of, 30

Met, Thomas, 115–16

Military Justice Act (1968), 222, 226–27, 254–55, 265, 267, 287

Military Law, sources of: Army Regulations, 220–22; Congress, 214–15; the Constitution, 213–14; court cases and published opinions, 223–24; DOD directives, 221; *Manual for Courts-Martial*, 219, 220, 222–23; standing operating procedures, 223; Supreme Court and military jurisdiction question, 215–18; Uniform Code of Military Justice, 214–15, 219–20, 221; *see also* Courts / Courts-Martial

Military Mind, 19, 21, 30, 33, 67–68, 116, 124; authoritarian personality, 68–70; black career soldier and, 82–84; communism and, 84–86; and conscientious objection, 295; cover your ass psychology, 75–76; criticism and, 77–78; fear, humiliation, and obedience, 70–75; glorification of killing, 80–82; glorification of trivia, 78–80; and individuality, 147; and military court system, 242–48; *see also* Basic Training, physical and psychological brutality; Military Myths

Military Myths: that our Army is American, 348–50; that enlisted men support Army caste system, 341–43; that the existing system works, 346–48; unfairness of military justice, 344–45; that glorification of trivia increases combat proficiency, 338–40; that terror equals discipline, 335–38; that thoughtful soldier is detriment in combat 340–41

Military Occupational Specialty, 12–13, 48

Miranda v. Arizona, 285, 288, 291

Mitchell, John, 291

Moratorium for Peace (1969), 129

Morgan, Charles Jr., 265

My Lai Massacre, *see* Vietnam

Naked and the Dead, The, 72

National Agency Check, 137

National Conference on GI Rights, 349

National Lawyers Guild, 138

Nixon, Richard M., 216

Nuremberg Code, 202, 203

O'Callahan v. Parker, 148, 162, 165, 166, 215–18, 219–20, 222

Officers Candidate School, 14, 20

Officer's Guide, 77, 81–82

Orders, illegal: 200–1; to commit war crimes, 201–4; concerning situations beyond one's control, 210; Fifth Amendment and, 201; illegal administrative action and, 208–9; to observe nonpenal regulations, 209–10; as punishment, 204–8

Orwell, George, 85

Overseas Shipment, delaying of: 58–60; change of status, 59–60; compassionate reassignment, 62–63; conscientious objector claim, 61–62; going AWOL, 60–61; hardship to family, 60; inadequate training, 58–59; selecting departure date, 58; Vietnam orders and, 61

Overseas Weekly, 281

Passes, 41, 160–61

Permanent Party, life as, *see* Companies

Peterson, Bruce, 138

Phifer, John Walter, 5

Powell Report, 244–45

Priest, Roger, 110, 111, 120–21, 134–35

Privacy, right to: automobiles, 169–70; drugs and, 162–63; employment and exploitation, 171–73; family life and obligations, 168–69; Fourth Amendment and, 151, 152, 153, 157, 158, 159, 163; Fifth Amendment and, 157–58; inspections and searches, 151–59; leave and, 161–62; legal question, 146–48; living quarters, 147–48, 149–50; mail, 159–60; marriage and sex, 163–68; military appellate courts and, 154, 155, 161, 163–64; passes and, 160–61, 162; private debts and obligations, 170–71; probable cause requirements, 151; religious practices, 173–74

Promotion, 55–57

Public Information Office, 19

Quinn, Robert E., 149, 345

Recycling, threat of, 30–31

Rein, David, 110, 121
Reinecke, Edwin, 59
Resor, Stanley R., 114
Rivers, L. Mendel, 111, 114, 136
Rodriguez, Carlos, 271
Rosen, Alban, 272–73
Russell, Jeffrey, 271

Schenck v. United States, 95
Seale, Bobby, 111
Secretary of the Army, 186, 318–19
Selective Service System, 297–98, 307
Sherrill, Robert, 77
Smith Act (1940), 118–19
Special Services, 46–47
Spock, Dr. Benjamin, 93
Staff Judge Advocate, see Courts/Courts-Martial
Stapp, Andy, 124
Steuben, Baron von, 335–36
Stockades, 268–73, 344
Stolte, Kenneth Jr., 114–15, 116
Stringham, Edward, 308–9
Student Nonviolent Coordinating Committee, 101–2
Supreme Court, 101, 116, 130, 135, 137, 139, 198, 222–24, 235, 287, 288, 308; on First Amendment rights, 7, 94, 96, 97, 98, 100–2, 106, 117, 118, 119, 121, 125–26, 127, 128, 133, 173, 297; on Fourth Amendment rights, 152, 155, 157, 162, 165; on Fifth Amendment rights, 281, 282, 285, 286, 287; on Sixth Amendment rights, 287; military courts and, 233–34; on military jurisdiction question, 148, 215–18, 219–20

Taylor, Telford, 204
Tydings, Joseph, 349

Uniform Code of Military Justice, 71, 96–97, 214–15, 216, 219–20, 221, 241, 244–45, 249, 251, 254, 255, 262, 267–68, 316, 322, 346, 349; and administrative discharges, 312; on breaking arrest (Art. 95), 209; on conduct unbecoming an officer (Art. 133), 99, 222; on conspiracy (Art. 81), 137; on contemptuous language (Art. 88), 99, 110–11; on convening Court of Inquiry (Art. 135), 186; on damage or taking of property by member of armed forces (Art. 139), 195–96, 197; on disorders to the prejudice of good order and discipline in the service (Art. 134), 25, 96, 108–9, 110–11, 112, 119, 161, 166, 222–23, 253; on disrespectful language and contempt (Art. 91), 108; on disrespect to officers (Art. 89), 109–10; on fraudulent enlistment (Art. 83), 316; on freedom of speech during combat (Arts. 100, 101, 104, 106), 123; on illegal orders, 200–1, 209; on investigative hearings prior to trial (Art. 32), 231–32; on looting and pillaging (Art. 103), 25; on nonjudicial punishment (Art. 15), 104, 225–26, 227–28; on disobeying orders (Art. 92), 223; on physical brutality (Art. 128), 27; on provoking and reproachful words or gestures (Art. 117), 107, 108–9; on right to file a complaint (Art. 138), 41, 48, 64, 103, 160–61, 183–87, 189, 195, 196–97, 207, 268; on selection of courts-martial members (Art. 25), 256–57; on self-incrimination (Art. 31), 157–58, 201, 281, 283–84, 285–86, 288, 289, 291, 345; on soliciting others to mutiny, desert, or commit sedition (Art. 82); 120; as tool to punish command influence in courts-martial (Arts. 37, 98), 252, 258; on treatment of prisoners, 268; on UCMJ violations (Art. 98), 186

U.S. Court of Claims, 331

U.S. Court of Military Appeals, 99–101, 103, 104, 105, 106, 110, 120, 122, 149, 154, 155, 159, 167, 170, 209, 222, 233–34, 244, 249, 250, 252, 254, 256, 257, 258, 259–60, 262, 263, 268–69, 282, 284, 285, 288, 290, 306, 317, 331

United States v. Adams, 149

United States v. Seeger, 297

United States v. Voorhees, 122

Valentine, C. W., 339

Vietnam/Vietnam War, 33, 35–36, 39, 57, 59, 62, 82, 85, 86, 102,

158–59, 164, 167, 208, 216, 244, 246, 281, 296, 303, 317, 325, 337–38; conscientious objectors and, 304, 305; deferments from, 61; GI dissenters and, 114–16, 120–21, 130–31, 253, 342, 348; My Lai massacre, 202–3, 204, 341; and the reenlistment counselor, 15; return from and early release, 63; volunteering for overseas duty and, 54–55

War Crimes, 201–4
Watts, Rowland, 5
West, Luther Charles, 74–75
Westmoreland, General, 76, 105
Wittels, Mike, 296
Workers Defense League, 5
Writs: extraordinary, 233, 236, 264; habeas corpus, 5, 102, 113, 162, 215, 218, 230–31, 233, 234, 236, 298, 305–6; mandamus, 236
Wulf, Melvin L., 130